Political Campaigning and Communication

Series Editor
Darren G. Lilleker
Bournemouth University
Bournemouth, UK

The series explores themes relating to how political organisations promote themselves and how citizens interpret and respond to their tactics. Politics is here defined broadly as any activities designed to have an impact on public policy. The scope of the series thus covers election campaigns, as well as pressure group campaigns, lobbying, and campaigns instigated by social and citizen movements.

Research included in the series might focus on the latest strategies and tactics within political marketing and campaigning, covering topics such as the strategic use of legacy, digital and social media, the use of big data and analytics for targeting citizens, and the use of manipulative tactics and disinformation.

Furthermore, as campaigns are an important interface between the institutions of power and citizens, they present opportunities to examine their impact in engaging, involving and mobilizing citizens. Areas of focus might include attitudes and voting behavior, political polarization and the campaign environment, public discourse around campaigns, and the psychologies underpinning civil society and protest movements.

Works may take a narrow or broad perspective. Single-nation case studies of one specific campaign and comparative cross-national or temporal studies are equally welcome. The series also welcomes themed edited collections which explore a central set of research questions.

For an informal discussion for a book in the series, please contact the series editor Darren Lilleker (dlilleker@bournemouth.ac.uk), or Ambra Finotello (ambra.finotello@palgrave.com).

This book series is indexed by Scopus.

More information about this series at
http://www.palgrave.com/gp/series/14546

Miloš Gregor · Petra Mlejnková
Editors

Challenging Online Propaganda and Disinformation in the 21st Century

palgrave
macmillan

Editors
Miloš Gregor
Department of Political Science
Masaryk University
Brno, Czech Republic

Petra Mlejnková
Department of Political Science
Masaryk University
Brno, Czech Republic

ISSN 2662-589X ISSN 2662-5903 (electronic)
Political Campaigning and Communication
ISBN 978-3-030-58623-2 ISBN 978-3-030-58624-9 (eBook)
https://doi.org/10.1007/978-3-030-58624-9

Cover illustration: Colin Anderson Productions pty ltd/Getty Images

This Palgrave Macmillan imprint is published by the registered company Springer Nature Switzerland AG
The registered company address is: Gewerbestrasse 11, 6330 Cham, Switzerland

Preface

We have been teaching a course on propaganda at Masaryk University for about ten years. When we started teaching the course, it was conceived primarily as a historical exercise—a presentation of what propaganda looked like during World War I, World War II, and the Cold War. Alternatively, we presented students interesting examples from undemocratic countries, such as China or North Korea. For us, it was a hobby which allowed us to connect our primary fields of interest: political marketing and security studies. The course served as a reminder to us of just how dangerous a path politics can take when political communication and marketing tools get out of control and fall into the wrong hands or should they be misused for the wrong purposes—the dark side of political marketing, as Nicholas O'Shaughnessy would say. It never occurred to us to design a course beyond that of a historical overview.

The situation changed in 2014 because of events associated with the Russian annexation of Crimea. Social media and even established mainstream media began to be overwhelmed by wondrous stories which often contradicted each other. The absurd propagandistic narrative had been there for months before the serious media became oriented and purged them. At that time, we realised that propaganda and disinformation were not just a historical relic and privilege of old political structures far beyond the democratic world; current examples from Europe had begun to penetrate not only our teaching but our research and other activities as well.

In the beginning, there was an analysis of manipulative propaganda techniques which appeared on the most widely read so-called alternative websites in the Czech Republic. This step fully revealed to us the diversity and wildness of the information world in which objectivity, facts, and knowledge play second fiddle. A world in which strong opinion is more than analysis, and the louder one is right, where a lie repeated a hundred times becomes true. At this point, we began to address the issue of modern propaganda and disinformation fully. Since 2016, we have carried out several analyses of how these phenomena work on both the Czech national level and internationally. We have participated in dozens of public debates and delivered hundreds of lectures, both for the general public and academic audiences in the Czech Republic as well as abroad. In addition to other ventures, we have helped to establish the student projects 'Zvol si info' (Choose your info) and 'Fakescape' dedicated to media literacy and critical thinking primarily among high schools students. All of these activities culminated in a three-year research project, the output of which is the edited volume you are holding in your hands.

The project brought together research institutes and academics from Masaryk University examining the issue of modern online propaganda and disinformation from various perspectives. Our aim was to focus on aspects which have been neglected in recent research and to put the whole phenomenon into the context of the developing online information environment and the post-truth era—as we have done in this edited volume. In the twenty-first century, there has been a significant shift in how propaganda and disinformation work, what tools they use, and how they affect society. In this respect, the post-truth era is not just a catchy phrase but an umbrella term encompassing transformations in society as well as technological progress.

* * *

The phenomena of online propaganda and disinformation are multidisciplinary and related to many issues and aspects. To ensure the integrity of the edited volume, we decided to focus on two main areas connected with changes related to media manipulation; this book, therefore, consists of two parts: the first is focused on the changing nature of propaganda and disinformation, and the second deals with measures individual actors (may) consider. Whereas the first part describes changes more on a theoretical level, the second reflects experience from Europe and European countries since measures are always closely related to the information, social, and political environments. Each of the parts consists of four chapters focused on individual aspects.

The first chapter establishes the whole context of the edited volume and sets up the framework in which the other chapters operate. It is meant as a kind of opening chapter or introduction to the edited volume explaining the theoretical concepts of propaganda and disinformation and the related terms we use throughout the book. We explain how propaganda and disinformation are defined and what the most commonly used manipulative techniques are. Emphasis is put on their development, especially in the past decade when they experienced a revival in the online environment. The authors introduce the concept of the post-truth era and the associated psychological aspects and principles, such as selective exposure, cognitive dissonance, or confirmation bias. The role of social media and related echo chambers and how they enhance these effects on an audience are also discussed. The very new term 'infodemic', which was widespread in the context of COVID-19 pandemic, is introduced. **The second chapter** deals with the main technological developments impacting how online propaganda and disinformation may be delivered and increasing its effectivity, contextualised by the changing features of the information environment and the value of the information itself. Deepfakes, trolling, and robotrolling—highly personalised, precisely targeted, and emotionally adaptive artificial intelligence—are discussed. **The third chapter** is dedicated to security threats related to the spread of propaganda and disinformation in the online environment. It reflects the changes propaganda and disinformation have undergone recently and reacts to the development described in the previous chapters. Authors discuss threats on a personal, societal, and political level, which provides structural support for the chapters devoted to specific measures. **The fourth chapter** completes the first part of the edited volume with a discussion of propaganda and disinformation through the prism of fundamental human rights—specifically, freedom of speech. The provided legal perspective confronts the issue of disinformation with existing components of the fundamental freedom. The understanding of the limits of the freedom to hold opinions is further developed through the freedom to impart information as well as the corresponding freedom to receive information and ideas. The resulting typology of protected speech provides a suitable framework for the following discussion on permissible limits applicable to 'the freedom'.

These chapters are written with an emphasis on the changing information environment in the twenty-first century, which is connected with our evolution into an information-centric society. Authors describe the most significant changes as regards the technological development and evolution of social media, which have affected the information environment in terms of types of actors and the tools at their disposal. The shift has had an impact on the activities and strategies propagandists implement, all of which are underscored by the exploitation of existing cognitive (not only) vulnerabilities of addressees. The chapters bring a clear picture of what we are currently witnessing all around the world and what kind of societal, political, and security challenges we face.

The second part moves from defining the challenges to possible reactions to the current state of the art or that of the near future. The chapters are dedicated to the diverse ways of countering propaganda and disinformation—the possibilities of detection, prevention, and counteraction. The section starts with **the fifth chapter** dedicated to computer-supported approaches of detecting disinformation and manipulative techniques based on several criteria presented in the chapter. The authors focus on the technical aspects of automatic methods which support fact-checking, topic identification, text style analysis, and message filtering on social media channels. **The sixth chapter** follows up on the technological approaches to detecting disinformation and manipulation but from a legal perspective. It deals with the legal aspects of using autonomous algorithmic tools, the requirements for the forensic analysis of digital evidence, and a relevant legal framework for collecting and evaluating available evidence in order to tackle these issues. The last two chapters are dedicated to approaches and examples of how state and non-state actors currently face propaganda and disinformation as well as what kind of measures and countermeasures they establish based upon their domestic political situation. **The seventh chapter** introduces an analytical framework for the analysis of institutional countermeasures against propaganda and disinformation and presents case studies from the European Union, NATO, and national actors. **The eighth chapter** is dedicated to the role of civil society in tackling the problem, with a focus on the Visegrad Group—countries of central Europe (Czech Republic, Hungary, Poland, and Slovakia) with a similar political context upon first sight but with different approaches once given a closer look.

The second part of the volume covers burning areas of technological, legal, institutional, and non-governmental (counter)measures. Authors provide readers with case studies from the European region, all targeting societal, political, or security challenges. The only exception is a chapter focused on technological methods inasmuch as it does not make sense to limit the topic geographically since technological knowledge and methodological approaches are not affected by state borders. In other words, the chapters introduce how different state and non-state actors sharing democratic principles and with more or less similar geopolitical contexts might react to the issue of propaganda and disinformation. These case studies of measures and countermeasures are meant as an example of potential approaches and their discussion. It is also a reminder of the necessity to reflect upon regional contexts.

The edited volume ends with a concluding chapter which provides readers with a summary of the main points delivered in the volume together with an outline of further possible developments in the field. We suggest a society-centric approach as a way for democratic regimes to adapt, with emphasis on human and societal resilience (including the protection of networks) composed from the areas covered in this edited volume.

Many publications dealing with this topic have been produced recently (several of which are referred to in the individual chapters). However, we hope that the edited volume you are holding right now will be a useful guide to the world of online propaganda and disinformation in the twenty-first century and will give you original insight into the issue. Dear readers, we wish you an inspirational reading, and should the book help you to understand some of the aspects described or it provokes you to conduct your own research on the topic, we will be more than satisfied.

Brno, Czech Republic

Miloš Gregor
Petra Mlejnková

Acknowledgements

Firstly, we would like to thank Darren Lilleker, the editor of the series, who demonstrated a lot of enthusiasm about this project and who encouraged us to realise it. Thank you so much, Darren!

Next, to all good people at Palgrave Macmillan who gave us the opportunity to publish this piece of work. We are glad Palgrave Macmillan is open to supporting projects such as ours and thus help scholars and readers all around the world understand how propaganda and disinformation evolved to their present-day form as well as how the post-truth era affects political systems all around the globe. Without their support, most of the information and knowledge we were able to gather over the last few years would be useless. Thank you for your trust and belief in publications focusing on this topic. In particular, we are grateful to Anne-Kathrin Birchley-Brun and Ambra Finotello, our editors, for their advice, patience, and assistance.

A big thank you goes naturally to all the contributors to this book. Thank you for being courageous enough to work with us, and thank you for your energy and hard work; the result is more than worth it! We hope you enjoyed the work on this exciting project as much as we did.

The edited volume has been written as an output of the research project 'Manipulative techniques of propaganda in times of the Internet' funded by the Grant Agency of Masaryk University (MUNI/G/0872/2016).

Many thanks to our colleagues at the Department of Political Science and the International Institute of Political Science of Masaryk University. In particular, special credit for their endless support of our research on propaganda and disinformation goes to Stanislav Balík, Vít Hloušek, Lubomír Kopeček, and Otto Eibl, who patiently supported us throughout this whole project.

Thanks to all our friends, colleagues, security experts, and NGO fellows who inspire us over and over again: Nicholas J. O'Shaughnessy, Paul Baines, Tom Nichols, Karel Řehka, and František Vrábel. There are many of you, and we are probably not able to name you all; however, we do appreciate your support and feedback.

We must not forget to say a big thank you to Brad McGregor for his excellent proofreading and copyediting services.

And last but not least, we want to express a huge thanks to our immediate and extended families, especially for their continuous support, patience, understanding, and encouragement.

Once again, thank you all. We could not have done this without you.

Contents

Notes on Contributors

Vít Baisa was a research assis tant at the Natural Language Processing Centre, Faculty of Informatics, Masaryk University. In his research, he focuses on language modelling, large language data processing, and multilingual data. He has been involved in projects related mainly to corpus linguistics and lexicography.

Jakub Drmola is an assistant professor at the Department of Political Science, Faculty of Social Studies, Masaryk University. In his research, he primarily focuses on terrorism, cybersecurity, space security, artificial intelligence, and emergent threats.

Miloš Gregor is an assistant professor at Masaryk University teaching courses on political communication and marketing, propaganda, disinformation, and fake news. As a researcher, he has been involved in the projects 'Analysis of Manipulation Techniques on Selected Czech Websites, Manipulative Techniques of Propaganda' (funded by Masaryk University) and 'Strategic Communication and Information Operations in the Context of Cyber Security' (funded by the National Cyber and Information Security Agency), as well as several research projects dedicated to electoral campaigns (e.g. together with Otto Eibl, he co-edited the volume *Thirty Years of Political Campaigning in Central and Eastern Europe*, Palgrave Macmillan, 2019). Together with Darren Lilleker, Ioana A. Coman and Edoardo Novelli, Gregor co-edited the volume *Political Communication and COVID-19: Governance and Rhetoric in Times of*

Crisis, Routledge 2021. Together with Petra Mlejnková, he is a mentor on the projects 'Zvol si info' (Choose your info) and 'Fakescape', both dedicated to media literacy awareness; both projects were awarded in the international Peer to Peer: Global Digital Challenge competition initiated by Facebook. He is a co-author of *The Best Book on Fake News, Disinformation and Manipulation*!!! (CPress, 2018) Gregor is intimately involved in the popularisation of the problem of disinformation and the ways in which it can be recognised; to that end, he has delivered over two hundred lectures and public speeches since 2018.

Jan Hanzelka is a Ph.D. candidate and a specialist researcher at the Department of Political Science, Faculty of Social Science, Masaryk University. His research interest focuses on issues of new technology and political extremism. He is currently researching new media in connection with radicalisation and hate speech as well as the securitisation of the social media space.

Ondřej Herman is a Ph.D. candidate and researcher at the Department of Information Technologies, Faculty of Informatics, Masaryk University. In his research, he focuses on language modelling and large language data processing. He has been involved in projects dealing with lexicography.

Aleš Horák is an associate professor of Informatics at Masaryk University. His research concentrates on natural language processing, knowledge representation and reasoning, tylometry, authorship attribution, and corpus linguistics. His work has been published in, among others, Oxford University Press and Routledge.

František Kasl is a Ph.D. student at the Institute of Law and Technology, Law Faculty, Masaryk University. His main research topics are related to the protection of personal data, privacy, electronic communications, and the regulation of emerging technologies.

Miroslav Mareš is a professor at the Department of Political Science, Faculty of Social Studies, Masaryk University (FSS MU). He is the guarantor of the study programme Security and Strategic Studies and a researcher at the International Institute of Political Science, FSS MU. He focuses on the research of political violence, extremism, and security policy, namely in the central European context. He co-authored (with Astrid Bötticher) *Extremismus— Theorien—Konzepte—Formen* (Oldenbourg Verlag, 2012) and *Militant Right-Wing Extremism in Putin's*

Russia. Legacies, Forms and Threats (with Jan Holzer and Martin Laryš; Routledge, 2019) and has authored or co-authored more than two hundred other scientific academic articles, chapters, and books.

Petra Mlejnková (Vejvodová) is head of the Department of Political Science, Faculty of Social Studies, Masaryk University (FSS MU) and is a researcher at the International Institute of Political Science, FSS MU. She focuses on research of extremism and radicalism in Europe, propaganda, and information warfare. She is a member of the expert networks the Radicalisation Awareness Network, the European Expert Network on Terrorism Issues, and the Czech RAN CZ expert network coordinated by the Ministry of the Interior of the Czech Republic. She has published several texts on disinformation and propaganda and the European Far-Right. She is also a co-developer of a semi-automatic analytical tool to detect manipulative techniques. Besides academia, she has also mentored the media literacy projects 'Zvol si info' (Choose Your Info) and 'Fakescape'. Together with Miloš Gregor, she co-published *The Best Book on Fake News, Disinformation and Manipulation!!!* (CPress, 2018), a popular literature book empowering the general public.

Miroslava Pavlíková is a Ph.D. student of political science at Masaryk University. Her dissertation thesis deals with information warfare and its position in Russian strategic thinking. She is also a senior research fellow at the Centre for Security and Military Strategic Studies, University of Defence. She graduated from Security and Strategic Studies at Masaryk University and attended courses on history, politics, and international relations at Loughborough University in the United Kingdom.

Radim Polčák is the head of the Institute of Law and Technology at the Law Faculty at Masaryk University. He is the general chair of the Cyberspace conference; editor-in-chief of Masaryk University's *Journal of Law and Technology*, and the head of the editorial board of *Revue pro právo a technologie* (Review of law and technology). He is a founding fellow of the European Law Institute and the European Academy of Law and ICT, a panellist at the .eu ADR arbitration court, and a member of various expert and advisory governmental and scientific bodies and project consortia around the European Union. He has also served as a special adviser on the Robotics and Data Protection Policy to the European Commission. Polcak has authored or co-authored over 150 scientific papers, books, and articles, namely on topics related to cyberlaw and legal philosophy.

Barbora Šenkýřová is a Ph.D. student at the Department of Political Science, Faculty of Social Science, Masaryk University. Her main research areas are related to local politics, political participation, and direct democracy. She has worked on the research of manipulative techniques in the media since 2016.

Jonáš Syrovátka is a Ph.D. student of political science at Masaryk University. His main area of expertise is the development of the Russian political system and its history. He also works as programme manager at the think-tank, the Prague Security Studies Institute, where he focuses on projects concerning disinformation and strategic communications.

List of Figures

List of Tables

Part I

CHAPTER 1

Explaining the Challenge: From Persuasion to Relativisation

Miloš Gregor and Petra Mlejnková

1.1 Introduction

A chapter describing the history of phenomena such as propaganda and disinformation could begin with the obligatory statement 'even the ancient Greeks' or 'the problem is as old as mankind itself'. Moreover, it would be correct. The truth is that information has always been crucial in politics and warfare, and those who possessed it and could manipulate it were able to confuse the enemy, the adversary, or the public. As O'Shaughnessy states, there was no golden age of truth (O'Shaughnessy 2020, 55). Information and its manipulation, therefore, have always been present in our lives.

M. Gregor · P. Mlejnková (✉)
Department of Political Science, Faculty of Social Studies,
Masaryk University, Brno, Czechia
e-mail: mlejnkova@fss.muni.cz

M. Gregor
e-mail: mgregor@fss.muni.cz

M. Gregor and P. Mlejnková (eds.), *Challenging Online Propaganda and Disinformation in the 21st Century*, Political Campaigning and Communication,
https://doi.org/10.1007/978-3-030-58624-9_1

Propaganda and disinformation have changed along with every new technology used for information and intelligence. With the development of the media and information environment, the possibilities of propaganda and disinformation have also changed (see Chapter 2). Rarely—or slowly—however do the goals of propaganda change; they are by and large an effort to influence, manipulate, and persuade a target audience. The tools that propaganda deploys have undergone much more dynamic development—from word of mouth, through leaflets and posters, to modern communication technologies. The latest significant shift has been the advent of the Internet and social media in particular. While it may have seemed that propaganda was in hibernation after two world wars and the ensuing Cold War, the events of recent years have refuted this.

At the beginning of the twenty-first century, propaganda was mainly associated with nondemocratic regimes geographically far from the Western (democratic) world, as North Korea or China are. Democratic regimes felt far from attempts at manipulation, far from threats of exposure to external political influence through disinformation campaigns, and far from attempts at meddling in the internal affairs of sovereign regimes and their societies. Exceptions and controversial cases can be spotted, and various conflicts can serve as a good example; however, these strategies and techniques were far removed from the values represented by Western liberal democracies. Yet, no later than 2014, exactly ten years after Facebook came into being, the Western world began to struggle with massive propaganda and disinformation campaigns targeting societies across the world. Since that time, we have been able to trace with extreme precision the connection between propaganda and disinformation campaigns and the conflict in Ukraine. Nevertheless, it is not only state or state-sponsored actors actively running such campaigns, but it is also extremist and terrorist organisations building, in a very professional way, propaganda so as to threaten or radicalise and recruit individuals, as Daesh has.

Since then, the whole issue of propaganda and disinformation has been faced with a fate similar to many other scholarly terms and concepts which have become more widely used by politicians, the media, and the general public, thus misleading understanding and the use of individual terms in the wrong way or the wrong context. The clear example is the modern and catchy phrase *fake news*, which is now used by some politicians as a label for media asking unpleasant questions or drawing attention to the past scandals of politicians.

The purpose of this chapter, therefore, is to describe the concepts of propaganda and disinformation, their development, and how they relate to each other. Other related concepts, such as fake news, misinformation, disinformation campaigns, psychological and information operations, and influence operations will be introduced and put into the context of the aim of this edited volume. In the last part of the chapter, changes in society, media, and the information environment will be introduced: what the Internet and social media especially have brought to propaganda and disinformation, and how both the understanding and functional level of propaganda and disinformation have changed in the so-called post-truth era. Last but not least, the dynamic development connected to the COVID-19 pandemic will be mentioned. It is no surprise that this emotionally tense period has brought about a new level of disinformation and public distrust.

1.2 Propaganda

One of the most problematic aspects of propaganda is its definition of anchoring. A century ago, Lasswell defined propaganda as the management of collective attitudes through the manipulation of significant symbols (Lasswell 1927, 627). According to Ellul, propaganda is a process aiming to provoke action, to make the individual cling irrationally to a process of action. It does not lead to a choice, but to a loosening of the reflexes—to an arousal of an active and mythical belief (Ellul 1973, 25). The minimalistic definition says that propaganda is a deliberate attempt to persuade people to think and behave in a desired way (Taylor 2003, 6). It encompasses conscious, methodological, and planned decisions to employ techniques of persuasion designed to achieve specific goals intended to benefit those organising the process. The methods employed vary according to the communications channels available—speeches, songs, art, radio, television, or the Internet. Propaganda uses communication to convey a message, an idea, or an ideology which is designed primarily to serve the self-interests of the person or people doing the communicating. An essential component of propaganda is information in the form of a lie or at least not the whole truth. This information is designed to serve the primary interests of the propagandist, invoking a common pattern of one-way, manipulative communication that solicits the action—or inaction—of the masses (Baines et al. 2020, xxv). Concealment of inconvenient facts and censorship are inseparable counterparts to propaganda (Taylor 2003, 14).

The understanding of propaganda differs across many historical, cultural, ideological, and political contexts. The first use of the notion of propaganda dates back to 1622 and the establishment of the Sacred Congregation for the Propagation of the Faith (originally Congregatio de Propaganda Fide in Latin), through which Roman Catholic cardinals managed their missionary activities (Guilday 1921). In the twentieth century, political regimes began to use the term more actively. Dictatorial regimes have never fought shy of the word 'propaganda' when self-labelling. During World War II—and even before—Nazi Germany had its Ministry of Popular Enlightenment and Propaganda, and the Soviet Union had its Propaganda Committee of the Communist Party. Marxism-Leninism referred to propaganda as the rational use of historical and scientific arguments to indoctrinate the educated and enlightened people. In both countries, propaganda was perceived positively and as an inevitable element leading to political victory (Smith 2019). Similar examples could be found in China (Central Propaganda Department) or Vietnam (Central Propaganda Department of the Communist Party of Vietnam). In contrast, democratic countries used the word 'propaganda' to label the communication activities of their opponent. Their departments avoided self-labelling themselves as propagandistic; the United Kingdom established the Ministry of Information and the United States had the Office of War Information.

The aim of propaganda is to shape the people's worldview, creating desired group, class, and society-wide role models as well as consciousness. It presents the institutionalised dissemination of essentially systematically arranged ideas, theories, opinions, doctrines, or whole ideologies. Propaganda may or may not ask for belief; it usually does not employ a rational appeal. As Baines, O'Shaughnessy, and Snow remind, 'It does not seek credibility based on the provision of accurate information … the genre is almost exclusively defined by its emotive content and rejection of non-emotive forms of persuasion' (Baines et al. 2020, xxv). Propaganda is distinguished from other forms of communication by intention and by emphasis on manipulation of the recipient. The deliberate selectivity of information and manipulation of propaganda also distinguishes itself from the educational process (Smith 2019). However, the boundaries between education and propaganda can be perceived differently, both from an information and ideas perspective and from the point of view of the recipient—as was shown in the Soviet Union's understanding of the term.

All propaganda is inherently built on a trinity of concepts: mythology, symbolism, and rhetoric (O'Shaughnessy 2004). Effective use of these foundational elements differentiates between successful persuasion and unsuccessful efforts to influence masses. Mythology represents the core of any piece of propaganda. Propagandists usually exploit history and tradition as well as national characteristics as a source. A myth is a story, a narrative rather than an ideology, an idea or principle. These myths usually tell a story which clearly identifies the heroes and villains, good and bad behaviour patterns illustrated via publicly known cases. They are not told in sophisticated language; contrariwise, they use easy to recognise and easy to identify symbols—or at least their essence or meaning can be transmitted through a mere sign (O'Shaughnessy 2016, 140). Myth can often be accompanied by fiction, which is to the propagandist something other than a mere lie—it represents a profounder form of reality, an alternative narrative which embodies the sought after ideal state of affairs (O'Shaughnessy 2020, 66). Symbols are essential not solely to mythology but to effective communication and persuasion in general, including propaganda. It springs from the fact that successful mass communication has an inherently emotive nature, and symbols are crucial connections to emotions. Therefore, the presentation of symbols can stand in place of argument. Anything can become politically symbolic if the right context is found (O'Shaughnessy 2016, 216). The last part of the triad is rhetoric. In a classic example, George Orwell represents the strength of language in his masterpiece, *1984*. In his novel, the author illustrates—besides other tools in the total totalitarian absorption of power and control of an individual's life—that control of the people's mind lies in the control of language (Orwell 1949). Understanding the motives and mechanisms of the group mind is the key to controlling and managing the crowds, and the tool of rhetoric is the correct use of language (Bernays 1947). Rhetoric is built on explicit or implicit framing which provides the recipient with simplistic clues and a clear path to understanding the matter correctly (O'Shaughnessy 2016, 256).

Whereas propaganda in the twentieth century could afford an explicit lie because there were only limited ways to verify information, the situation changed with the advent of the Internet. In general, a big task of the propagandist is to gain trust, create credibility, and persuade the audience to trust the source. Today, explicit lies can often be easily verified; our access to many information sources radically reduced the effectiveness of lies and their impact on society—in cases where we are willing to find the correct information (which is discussed later on in this chapter). Upon learning that part of a message was wrong, credibility suffers. And vice versa, if a fact-checked part of a message is correct, the effect is the opposite: The audience is more likely to believe the whole message and believe the source in the future again. The propagandists' strategy today is therefore usually not telling lies but rather selecting the truth and mixing it with manipulative content. The final mixture also contains lies, but in that case, who cares about lies all around when it is based on a real story. A different way of processing the truth is also to create an atmosphere of uncertainty in terms of feeding feelings of 'everybody lies' and 'the truth is not relevant anymore' because 'nothing is as it seems'. This means propagandists do not convince the audience about one particular 'truth'. Instead, they use selected manipulative techniques and even lies to raise doubts about the credibility of a target audience's information sources or induce apathy in them with overwhelming conflictual information. This is a strategy applied by authoritarian regimes. With the development of modern technologies, however, it has become more difficult for these regimes to control the flow of information. Instead, they produce an incredible volume of information, making the information overwhelming to navigate. It produces 'data smog', where useful information becomes hard to find (Shenk 1997).

The strategy of creating 'data smog' or 'information noise'—flooding the information environment with plenty of alternative and conflicting stories and information, some truthful, some not; some verifiable, some not; relevant or irrelevant—creates the illusion that nothing is as it seems, and it is difficult to search for the truth. In that case, nobody really cares about being caught telling lies, because the propagandist's primary aim is not to build one's own credibility or a coherent ideology as much as it is to persuade that the enemies lie. The information is, after all, weakened by misleading ballast and does not have any value anymore. An apathic population is then the best for authoritarian governments to control.

The character and possibilities of propaganda are directly influenced by the repertoire of means and tools which can be used for dissemination. During the reign of Pope Gregory XV, when the Sacred Congregation for the Propagation of the Faith was founded, the main instrument of communication was word of mouth. Literature was the prerogative of the narrowest layers of society. By the second half of the nineteenth century, however, the mass printing of newspapers had begun and would become one of the tools in the arsenal of propagandists. A similar shift was seen with the advent of cinema, radio, and television among the general public. It is not an accident that the golden era of propaganda is associated with the first half of the twentieth century's world war period, when most of the abovementioned media underwent a massive boom.

A similar boom accompanied the onset of the Internet and social media especially. These are not solely exploited for propaganda purposes—now termed digital propaganda—but also for the repression and oppression of citizens in the form of blackmail, harassment, and coercion of those opposing the regime (Pearce 2015). The possibilities of the current information environment have given people almost unlimited access to information, which makes censorship more difficult. It has also given rise to the new phenomenon of online journalism (Bor 2014) and citizen journalism (Atton 2009; Goode 2009; Kaufhold et al. 2010; Lewis et al. 2010). They represent a big challenge for us because these types of journalism contribute to the increased amount of information—albeit, sometimes of disputable quality and accuracy—in the information environment. For the recipients of news, this democratisation of journalism, as well as the abundance of information and its sources, are ambiguous. They also empower the potential of digital propaganda, which, thanks to these developments, uses the massive peer-to-peer replication of ideas and active participation in the spread of propaganda. It decreases the necessity for centralised structures to maintain or accelerate the propagation of particular ideas. Propagandists may enjoy the advantage of the decentralised structure of social media by orchestrating campaigns with broad impact while the source remains difficult to identify (Farkas and Neumayer 2018; Sparkes-Vian 2018). Using trolls and bots for astroturfing, the simulation of public support, is one of the consequences of the development of social media technologies. This specific aspect is discussed further in Chapter 2.

1.2.1 Manipulation Is the Backbone of Propaganda

As was already implied, the concept of manipulation is crucial for propaganda. All propaganda is manipulative, and it would be nonsense to speak of non-manipulative propaganda (O'Shaughnessy 2004, 18). Manipulation can acquire different meanings depending on the sector and context in which it is applied. It acquires the broad and somewhat blurred semantic field of the term, the negative intention of the speaker, and the covert character of influence (Akopova 2013). Manipulation can take many different forms and can be applied through the use of manipulative techniques. Propaganda manipulation is often concerned with information, information systems, and the networks people use. Propaganda manipulates individuals in terms of processing people's consciousness as well. Data can be manipulated by changing its meaning or content. This kind of manipulation is the least noticeable and, therefore, the most difficult to detect. There are dozens of manipulative techniques of propaganda and persuasion (see Pratkinis and Arons 2001; Bernays 2004; Shabo 2008). To mention at least some of those most often described by scholars and used by propagandists, we can name the appeal to fear, blaming, demonisation, fabrication, labelling or name-calling, relativisation, and the use of manipulative pictures or videos.

The appeal to fear benefits from the fact that emotions are the backbone of propaganda. Thus, fear belongs among the most common emotions exploited by propagandists (Baines et al. 2020). Several underlying fears frequently present in propaganda can be identified: the fear of rejection, powerlessness, and, most significantly, the fear of death (Shabo 2008). The appeal to fear employs audiences' worry about the unknown or their bad experiences with the target group or principles. These fears are one of the most potent motivations behind people's behaviour and attitudes. Blaming, as a manipulative technique, pinpoints the enemy responsible for the event or situation. Propagandists often oversimplify complex problems by pointing out a single cause or a single enemy who can be blamed for it (even if not responsible at all). For everything, from unemployment to natural disasters, blaming the enemy can help the propagandist achieve his or her agenda (Shabo 2008). Demonisation is used to dehumanise the opponent. It usually employs similar tools to labelling— though in a more straightforward way. The aim is to picture the opponent as an enemy not just with a different point of view but also not even human. Such a technique is frequently used in armed conflicts in order to remove the fear from soldiers who are meant to kill the adversary's soldiers (men killing men). When depicting the enemy in a dehumanised way, equating humans with animals, it psychologically makes the situation easier. Fabrications are false information presented as true statements (Syed 2012). They usually take the form of misleading or downright false information presented as verified information. Labelling (or name-calling) is the use of negative words to disparage an enemy or an opposing view. Labelling can take many different forms depending on the circumstances, but they all, rather than making a legitimate argument, attack the opposition on a personal level. They also often appeal to the audience's preconceptions and prejudices (Domatob 1985; Shabo 2008). Relativisation serves to weaken either the opponent's merits or damage a preferred actor. It is usually used to pacify emotions when (from the propagandist's point of view) something bad is happening. It explicitly contains criticism of the opponent or trivialises the problem. Manipulative video and pictures represent one of the most apparent manipulative techniques here. In the context of this edited volume, we consider video or picture as manipulative if it shifts audiences' perception of the subject, or if it presents a collage or somehow modified media.

A common denominator of most manipulative techniques is emotions. They represent a crucial part of human existence, and they are an important factor in different processes through which every individual goes. In 2010, neuroscientist Antonio Damasio used his research to confirm a major psychological theory. In decision-making, emotions play a very important role and are perhaps even more decisive than logic. To blame is the part of the brain responsible for the formation of emotions—without it, we would not be able to make even simple decisions (Damasio 2010). The importance of emotions can be further demonstrated by prejudice—our associations awaken different emotions, and our strong social attitudes are emotionally supported. Frequently, manipulative techniques target fear and feelings of uncertainty. The reaction of some political actors to the 2015 European migration crisis was an excellent example of manipulation that fed people's (natural) fears, for example, creating connections between immigrants and terrorists/criminals. When subjectively feeling unsafe and unstable, an individual is more susceptible to manipulation as the need for personal safety belongs among basic personal needs.

Propagandists do not produce deceptive messages through linguistic manipulation with an emotional appeal or accents only, but also by manipulating the information as a whole or the context in which the information is presented. We can distinguish among four primary methods: biasing published information, ambiguously presenting information, manipulation through the amount of information published, and presenting irrelevant information to the discourse (McCornack 1992, 4). With the developments described above, with the shift from persuasion to relativisation, we can observe a shift from the first two manipulation forms to the latter two mentioned: manipulation of the amount of information and presenting irrelevant information to the discourse.

1.3 Disinformation

In the last decade, likely mentioned even more than propaganda was the term disinformation. Disinformation can be perceived as a part of the larger conceptual realm of propaganda. It deploys lies, but not always and not necessarily. Therefore, we can say not all propaganda is disinformation, but all disinformation is propaganda (O'Shaughnessy 2020, 55). The intense debate about the dangers of spreading disinformation and propaganda was revived in 2014 in the context of the Russian Army's occupation of the eastern part of Ukraine and the annexation of Crimea. However, like propaganda, disinformation is also not a new phenomenon. For decades, the concept of disinformation had been exclusively related to intelligence activities around the world. A classic example of a disinformation campaign in this regard is Operation INFEKTION, a disinformation campaign run by the KGB, the Soviet intelligence service, in the 1980s. The campaign was designed in order to undermine the credibility of the United States and foster anti-Americanism. The campaign planted the idea that the United States had invented the HIV virus in the laboratories of the Department of Defense as a biological weapon. The term disinformation, however, only began to penetrate the media lexicon and the general public starting in the 1980s. In February 1992, David C. Berliner presented a paper dedicated to educational reforms in the 'era of disinformation' (Berliner 1992).

The aim of disinformation is not necessarily to persuade, to make people change their mind. According to its purpose, we can distinguish among four categories of disinformation (O'Shaughnessy 2020, 58–59):

1. Acquiescence, not belief: The purpose of disinformation is to create, sustain, and amplify divisions within a rival political party, a government, a coalition. In this sense, disinformation is a strategy of political control.
2. Sow division: Disinformation as a national strategic tool with the aim of sabotaging international consensus—a weapon against a hostile nation or coalition. It becomes therefore a method of leveraging advantage in international relations.
3. Sow confusion: The aim is to perplex—everything and nothing is believable anymore, which is the precondition for political paralysis. Lying is a strategy. The object is not to create belief but to spread confusion.

4. Raise doubt: The spread of doubt is a very effective genre of disinformation since credible phenomena can seldom be proven absolutely. There is always the possibility of doubt.

Disinformation includes a broad scale of false, fake, inaccurate, or misleading information or messages which are generated, presented, and disseminated with the aim of confusing the recipient of the information or causing public damage. Disinformation is based on three necessary characteristics (Fallis 2015), and we can speak of disinformation only if all features are fulfilled. First of all, disinformation is information, information which represents some part of the world as being a certain way. Although some authors consider information only what is true (Dretske 1983), we do not have to have a philosophical discussion on the meaning of information since we can accept the view that information provides us content that is either true or false (see Chapter 6). The fact is, we perceive information firstly and consider or evaluate it subsequently. And only in some cases, the second characteristic defines disinformation as misleading information, which means it creates false beliefs. Thirdly, disinformation is not accidental in its misleading nature; there is an intentional attempt to provide an audience with information which creates false beliefs. The intention to deliberately disseminate false information is crucial to the characteristic because it differentiates disinformation from other forms of inaccurate messages, such as misinformation.

The intention is also reflected in the term *disinformation campaign*, which refers to the systematic usage of misleading information and the series of acts leading to desired goals. A disinformation campaign is the focused, controlled, and coordinated dissemination of disinformation in order to influence the opponent's decision-making process or to achieve political, economic, or other advantages (Kragh and Åsberg 2017). It means the systematic and deliberate manipulation of an audience regardless of whether the audience is represented by the general public or a specific segment of the population, such as politicians.

1.3.1 What Disinformation Is and What It Is not

In discussions among politicians or in the general public, we can encounter overuse of the term disinformation. In addition to cases which fulfil the characteristics described above (intentionally misleading information), other cases are sometimes referred to as disinformation as well. Not only do politicians use the term disinformation as labelling, which serves to discredit presented information, an argument, or even the bearer of information, but marking a statement or argument as disinformation has also become a heated point of discussion in and of itself.

There is much information which does not carry true content, which can be misleading or even false. These cases, however, do not fulfil the intention to mislead; they do not have this function. An example could be information which used to be true but is not anymore (e.g. which team is leading the National Football League). However, we can distinguish between two main types of disinformation which may have this function. First is the intention to mislead as the goal—that is, they try to change the audience's mind or behaviour. The second uses the misleading message not as a goal but to benefit the author in a different way, for example, financial gain. The goal of disinformation in such cases is not to change the mind or behaviour of the audience but to gain a benefit resulting from this change. In health care, for instance, disinformation can be used to convince the audience of the harmfulness of drugs in order to make people use products the author wishes them to.

Categories falling within the scope of disinformation are, among others, represented by lies, audio-visual messages, or those produced and spread altruistically. It represents information which is not just out of context, presented as partly true, or incomplete but also information presented against objectively verifiable truth. Audio-visual disinformation can take the form of pictures or videos with post-production modifications or presented in a different context (place or time) than that in which it was created. Deepfakes are another example (see Chapter 2). Even altruistic misleading information can be considered disinformation; it makes no difference whether the presentation of misleading information was driven by good intentions. Conversely, barely true information cannot be considered disinformation; otherwise, the meaning of the term would be empty. False information can also be presented without the intention to manipulate; it can be accidental falsehoods. A special category represents jokes and satire, which are usually based on mendacious or incomplete information. Their intention is rather to entertain the audience than to mislead it. However, this does not mean that the abovementioned cases cannot mislead people. Even if they were not created with the purpose of misleading an audience, they can later become disinformation when they are disseminated (Table 1.1).

Table 1.1 Categories of disinformation

Disinformation	*Not disinformation*
Malicious lies	Truthful statement
Audio-visual disinformation	Accidental falsehoods
True disinformation	Jokes
Side-effect disinformation	Sarcastic comments
Adaptive disinformation	Accidental truths
Altruistic disinformation	Implausible lies
Detrimental disinformation	Satire

Source Authors, based on Fallis (2015, 415)

1.3.2 *Disinformation Versus Fake News*

Today, the term fake news has become more common than disinformation after becoming publicly known and widely used during the 2016 US presidential election at the latest. Its popularisation was due to the then presidential candidate Donald Trump, who labelled media critical of him as fake news. As a relatively new concept, it has not been given enough epistemological attention, and its understanding varies across the general public and academia (Gelfert 2018).

Some authors consider fake news to be all news which is not fact-based but, despite that, is reported as true news (Allcott and Gentzkow 2017). Others perceive fake news as news which denies the principles of quality and objective journalism (Baym 2005). However, there is difference between the media spreading fake news and so-called political media, which adjusts news coverage in such a way that it seeks to establish the political agenda of a related political party or entity (Vargo et al. 2017). Silverman claims that fake news is news which is not based on truth and is made for financial gain—typically through ad revenue. Fake news is, therefore, close to tabloid journalism, but unlike the tabloids, the profit motive, aside from the selling of the medium itself, is crucial in this definition because, according to Silverman, it should be considered propaganda when a financial motivation is missing (Silverman 2016).

Fake news is also often used as a catch-all term for all disinformation, but it is a narrower term falling within this classification (Gelfert 2018). Therefore, fake news is a kind of disinformation and can be defined as the deliberate creation and dissemination of false stories and news which are claimed to be serious news by their author.

The concept of fake news in a way responds to the fact that we rather associate disinformation with agents and governments and much of the misleading information presented in the information environment and media with other actors. Today, however, anyone with a political or economic intention can deliberately create disinformation.

1.4 Disinformation and Propaganda as a Tool to Promote Political Outcomes

Nobody, perhaps with a few exceptions, uses disinformation and propaganda just for fun. There is always some intention standing behind it, which is also the purpose of disinformation and propaganda and their inherent characteristic. State, state-sponsored, or non-state actors decide to walk the pathway of manipulation usually in order to promote its political, economic, military, or cultural interests and goals, or the actor deems it necessary to protect themselves against adversaries. Mostly, it has been undemocratic regimes and their supporters or extremist and terrorist organisations being mentioned in this context. Disinformation and propaganda give them the opportunity to use manipulative techniques and lies in order to target the hearts and minds of predefined target groups, which is after all believed to be the most important factor in any conflict.

Disinformation and propaganda based on its character are usually exercised in a planned and coordinated manner, indicating that any intentionally misleading information does not stay alone for a long time; it mostly fits into a series of actions taken to achieve someone's desired advantages and goals defined within time and place. This may not appear as misleading information at the time, but it is usually revealed later to be part of a more complex sequence of actions, supporting strategic aims. We can call it an operation, a performed action, including its planning and execution (Merriam-Webster Dictionary n.d.). More specifically, disinformation and propaganda represent major components of psychological operations.

The ability to manage and change the perceptions of a targeted audience may be considered the fourth instrument of power available to a political actor next to diplomatic, economic, and military powers (Brazzoli 2007, 223). The use of psychological operations increases the effectiveness of other instruments, and it increases one's chances in conflicts, which, contemporarily, often happens in an asymmetric environment. Psychological operations (psyops) can be defined as pre-planned activities using communication methods and other resources aimed at selected target audiences to influence and shape their emotions, attitudes, behaviours, perceptions, and interpretations of reality. Thus, by using special methods, it is possible to induce desirable responses in the target population, which, in the broader context, contributes to the fulfilment of specific objectives. Every psychological operation is based on a particular psychological theme: the main, carefully prepared narrative or ideas. The higher the target audience's receptivity—in other words, their sensitivity to specific psyops tools—the higher the probability of the whole psychological operation's success (NATO Standardization Office 2014, 2018; Vejvodová 2019; Wojnowski 2019).

The importance of psyops is based on the belief that the psychological nature of a conflict is as important as the physical (Stilwell 1996). People's attitudes and behaviours affect the course and outcome of a conflict and the nature of an environment in which a conflict takes place. For a well-conducted psychological operation, it is crucial to know the target audience, its will, and its motivation. Psyops work with these elements and aim to influence them, weakening the adversary's will, strengthening the target group's commitment, and gaining the support and cooperation of undecided groups (Vejvodová 2019). Psyops can promote resistance within a population against a regime, or it can put forward the image of a legitimate government. They have the power to demoralise or enliven a population. They can reduce or increase desired emotions among a target population. They can even support apathy, on the one hand, or radicalise, on the other. Brazzoli (2007) distinguished between hard and soft aspects of psyops: He relates the hard aspects to the creation of negative perceptions, for example, of state, government, or society in order to sow the seeds of alienation. The soft aspects relate to positive images motivating the audience to follow a lead. Both aspects have the goal of subverting the mind and influencing unconscious behaviour as decided by those who direct the operation.

It is believed that conflicts end when one side has lost the will to continue the conflict and comes to the decision that there is more to be gained or less to be lost by letting the adversary prevail. Therefore, the adversary's will is, in addition to military and economic tools or external support, a decisive factor in a conflict. In military conflicts, psychological operations achieve objectives where military force is not available, is inappropriate, or where it can be combined with the military in order to minimise expenditures and maximise effects. Psyops persuade via nonviolent means—psychological weapons of persuasion and deception. In this context, the Chinese strategist Sun Tzu is very often quoted. Sun Tzu advocated for the psychological undermining of the adversary and mentions in his *The Art of War* that one of the fundamental factors affecting war is that which 'causes the people to be in harmony with their leaders so that they will accompany them in life and unto death without fear of mortal peril' (Post n.d.). Dortbudak quotes another piece of his work when stressing that victory is rather determined by which side has influence over the other side's decisions and actions: 'To fight and conquer in all our battles is not supreme excellence; supreme excellence consists in breaking the enemy's resistance without fighting' (Dortbudak 2008).

Psyops can be divided into three types: strategic, operational, and tactical. Strategic psyops advance broad or long-term objectives. They might even be global, or at least focused on large audiences or key decision-makers. Operational psyops are conducted on a smaller scale. Their purpose can range from gaining support for an action to preparing the defined field or environment for an action. Tactical psyops are then even more limited and used to secure immediate and near-term goals.

But do not mistake psyops as connected only with the military environments and military actions. Psyops are also conducted in environments short of military conflict or declared war; they belong among the tools of political, economic, and ideological influence. They are conducted continuously to influence perceptions and attitudes in order to effectively target an audience to the benefit of the influence source. In political theory, psyops are studied mostly in the context of nondemocratic regimes, where they are based on propaganda, and where the ultimate goal is to control and manipulate the population, adversaries, or even neutral actors in and outside the regime. The same applies to extremist or terrorist organisations. Modern versions of these organisations put great emphasis on their psyops methods so as to increase fear within their target audience (Ganor 2002). Spreading fear beyond the direct target is an essential aspect of terrorism, and the development of the Internet and social media has served as a force-multiplier for terrorists. The emergence of virtual space combined with increasing technological literacy among terrorist organisations has created new opportunities for the use of psyops (Bates and Mooney 2014; Cilluffo and Gergely 1997; Emery et al. 2004). 9/11 is a classic example of terrorist psychological influence. Nevertheless, democratic regimes and actors conduct psyops as well. In comparison to undemocratic ones, however, they are short of propaganda and disinformation, which are believed to be excluded from the democratic toolbox.

Today, psychological operations are perceived as a specific part of information operations. With information operations, we are already moving more towards the area of strategic and military thinking. Nevertheless, the term *information operation* has also been integrated into civil and political communication language, mainly due to the debates over Russian and Chinese activities abroad. Information operations can be defined as activities undertaken to counter hostile information and information systems while protecting their own. It is the coordinated and integrated employment of information-related capabilities to influence, disrupt, corrupt, or usurp decision-making (United States—Joint Chiefs of Staff 2014; Miljkovic and Pešic 2019). They represent offensive and defensive measures focused on influencing an adversary's decisions, manipulating information and information systems. They also include measures protecting their decision-making processes, information, and information systems. Information operations must have specifically predefined goals and targets; therefore, careful planning is part of the process.

Information operations are conducted within an information environment in which they affect all its three dimensions: physical, informational, and cognitive. In the physical dimension, we think about information infrastructure; information collection, transmission, processing, and delivery systems and devices can be affected, as well as command and control facilities, ICT, and supporting infrastructure. This dimension also covers human beings. What is important is that the physical dimension is not connected exclusively to military or nation-based systems and processes. Even though we are considering the military arena, civilians and civil infrastructure is included in information operations as well. In the information dimension, we think of information itself and its content and flow. When command and control facilities are affected in the physical dimension, the same feature may also be targeted in the information dimension but from the perspective of the type of collected information, its quality, content, and meaning. In the information dimension, information operations target the ways information is collected, processed, stored, disseminated, and protected. Last but not least, in the cognitive dimension, information operations influence the minds of those who transmit, receive, respond to, or act upon information. The cognitive dimension means individuals and groups, their individual and cultural beliefs, norms, vulnerabilities, motivations, emotions, experiences, education, mental health, identities, and ideologies (United States—Joint Chiefs of Staff 2014; Miljkovic and Pešic 2019; Vejvodová 2019). Understanding these factors is crucial for developing the best operations in order to influence decision-makers and produce the desired effect.

From the above description, it is clear that thinking about information operations as a collection of single pieces of information would be too reductive. They are complex processes of activities integrating the effects of information activities (collection, creation, transmission, and protection) leading to influence over an adversary and the attainment of goals. Information operations integrate a wide spectrum of activities, such as psychological operations, operations security, information security, deception, electronic warfare, kinetic actions, key leader engagement, and computer network operations. All together, they target the will of adversaries, their understanding of the situation, and their capabilities.

Information activities aimed at influencing the adversary focus mainly on decision-makers who have the ability to influence the situation. Activities in this case include questioning the legitimacy of political leaders, undermining the morals of the population or, in military terms, the morals of the military, polarising society, and so on. Information activities intended to affect the understanding of the situation seek to influence the information available to the enemy for their decision-making processes. This includes disseminating disinformation, using military-scale mock-ups to fool the enemy's radar systems, deliberately leaking distorted information, destroying or manipulating information inside the opponent's information systems, and so forth. The third kind of information activities are enacted upon the enemy's abilities and are meant to disrupt their ability to understand information and promote their will. These include internet connection disruptions, physical destruction of infrastructure, and cyberattacks.

In this approach, information operations can be subdivided as *information-technical* and *information-psychological* activities. Information-technical activities represent, for example, attacks on critical infrastructure, attacks on elements of information infrastructure, or cyber-attacks. By information-psychological operations, we mean management of an adversary's perception, propaganda, disinformation campaigns, psychological operations, and deception. It is manipulation with or by information in a cognitive manner. That returns us to the reason why we classify psychological operations as a tool in information operations.

Let's move for a moment to another relevant term often mentioned by political representatives and decision-makers when discussing disinformation and propaganda, typically in relation to elections, the promotion of particular interests in society, the external polarisation of society through existing inner conflict lines, or in relation to the question of national security—influence operations. *Influence operations* are coordinated, integrated, and synchronised activities which use diplomatic, informational, intelligence, psychological, communication, technical, military, cultural (identity-based), or economic tools in order to influence the attitudes, behaviour, and decisions of a predefined target audience so that the audience supports the goals of the actor performing the influence operations. In principle, influence operations aim to promote, undercut support, or a combination of both in order to create a space which can be filled with a desired solution. They can be developed in peacetime, in times of crisis, conflicts, and post-conflict periods (Brangetto and Veenendaal 2016; Larson et al. 2009). They are carried out in both physical and digital space. Notoriously used as an example of influence operations is the rivalry between the Russian Federation and United States. With its origin in the Cold War, it continues currently through the partial use of previously tested patterns and tools as well as under new conditions generated by the onset of the online information environment and technological progress, which has been developing novel techniques and methods of exploitation and influencing. Tromblay (2018) describes aspects of influence collection as information on and exploitation of vulnerabilities outside formal diplomacy, the exploitation of lobbyists, university and academia idealism, cultural/ethnic/religious affinities (e.g. China's concept of 'overseas Chinese'—Chinese people living abroad as a block beholden to China), and the media.

Influence operations is an umbrella term for all operations in the information domain, including activities relying on so-called soft power tools. However, influence operations are not exclusively soft power tools; due to infiltration into and disruption of information systems, secret and disruptive activities are also part of influence operations. Soft power tools and influence activities overlap, but they are not synonymous. Soft power includes overt activities meant to sell an agenda. Covert influence includes activities meant to disrupt processes (Tromblay 2018). In the military field, they can be used during military operations and serve to weaken the will of the adversary, intimidate or confuse decision-makers, influence (disrupt, modify, or shut down) their information systems, weaken public support for the adversary, or attract audiences to support their activities. Victory can be achieved without firing a single bullet.

Similar to information operations, influence operations affect all three dimensions of the information environment as well. They affect information systems, the content of information, and how information affects the target audience, creating space for the implementation of disinformation and propaganda as well. Influence operations use activities with both an information-technical and information-psychological character. This may sound interchangeable with the definition of information operations; however, that would be a misleading perception. First, influence operations integrate a much broader scope of tools than information operations. Information operations are, therefore, a subset of influence operations, as already mentioned. Second, information operations are limited to military operations. Influence operations are conducted as coordinated activities in both civil and military affairs, and, in the case of civil affairs, they are performed regardless of peace or war, usually in relation to the projection of (geo)political power.

Although hierarchy and relations among defined terms may seem complicated, Figs. 1.1 and 1.2 can provide us with a clear picture; however, to understand them, it is necessary to distinguish between civil and military affairs, and between times of peace and conflict insomuch as each term may play a different role.

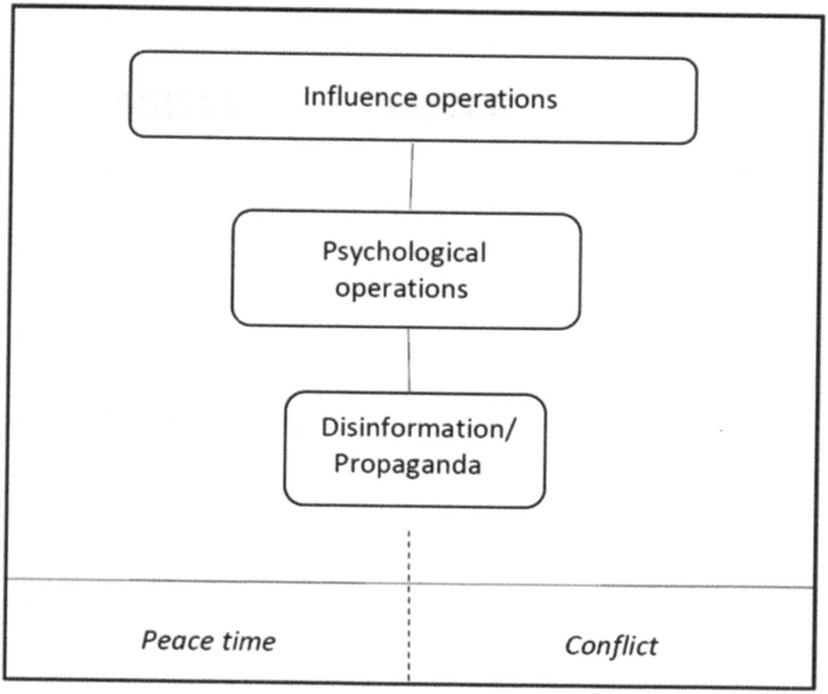

Fig. 1.1 Hierarchy of terms in civil affairs (*Source* Authors)

1.5 What Is New in the Twenty-First Century, and Where Are My Facts?

The year 2016 and the presidential election in the United States are associated not only with the advent of fake news but also the point at which we began to increasingly talk about the decline of people's concern with facts, verified sources, and truthful information. More and more, people believe widely circulating conspiracy theories, lies, and manipulation. This phenomenon is known as the post-truth era, which, not coincidentally, became the Oxford Dictionary's 2016 word of the year. Post-truth can be described as a manifestation of a 'qualitatively new dishonesty on the part of politicians who appear to make up facts to suit their narratives' (Mair 2017, 3). Post-truth is leading to 'the diminishing importance

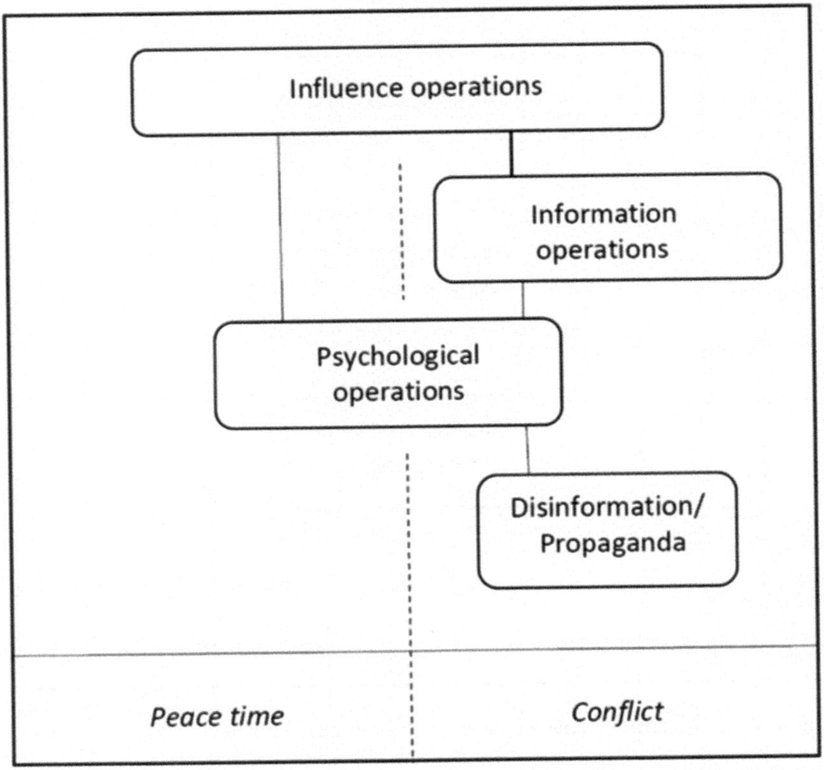

Fig. 1.2 Hierarchy of terms in military affairs (*Source* Authors)

of anchoring political utterances in relation to verifiable facts' (Hopkin, Rosamond 2017, 1–2). When voters accept such a mindset, politicians can lie to them without blushing and voters will even appreciate it. This can explain the current political situation observable in the United States and elsewhere. Presidential elections in America are the most widely followed, and this most visible case of fake news propagation has spread, in addition to other post-truth symptoms, around the world. However, a similar trend could be found in other countries even prior to 2016. This is not an issue connected only to politicians. It refers to obvious lies being routine across a section of society. The traditional standard of truthfulness has lost its importance—the distinction between factual truth and falsehood has become irrelevant; only public preferences for one set of facts matter (Kalpokas 2020, 71). Similarly, at the academic level, the role of truth and its questioning was being discussed beforehand (see Bufacchi 2020).

Today's situation is different from the cliché that all politicians lie and make promises they do not keep. Of course, politics and especially the electoral campaign periods have always been characterised by efforts of candidates to present reality framed so as to advantage them. Electoral campaigns are conducted to persuade people; they cannot be confused with education, no matter how informative they seem to be sometimes. Political communication and marketing cannot fulfil the educational role we know from the presentation of objective and impartial information. As a rule, however, political proclamations in the past bent the truth within the boundaries set by the rules of the political game in democratic contests. If politicians were caught lying, they were usually forced by party members, political competitors, the media, or the voters to explain their standpoint and provide apologies (Sismondo 2017). If they were unable to do so, they often had to give up their candidacy or elected office—Richard Nixon could tell the story.

Such a mindset is not typical of everyone anymore. There is a significant part of society—not just politicians but citizens and voters as well—which does not rely on facts for truth. Post-truth is for politics a qualitatively new game. Facts are not simply twisted or omitted to disguise reality, but, instead, new realities are discursively created to serve a political message (Kalpokas 2020, 71). The prefix *post* in post-truth does not allude to a chronological reference that something occurs *after* truth. Instead, it indicates the fact that truth is no longer essential and has been superseded by a new reality (Bufacchi 2020). Hence, we can speak about a post-truth or post-factual society. We are facing a situation in which a significant part of the population has abandoned the conventional criteria of evidence, internal consistency, and fact-seeking. In a post-truth world, the principle of honesty as the default position and moral responsibility for one's statements is something some politicians no longer hold (Higgins 2016).

Many among the electorate seem not to register the troubles stemming from the fact that politicians are lying to them. This is probably because they believe their favoured candidate's intentions are good, and they would not be deliberately misleading (Higgins 2016). Therefore, today's politics can be described as a competition to choose which 'truth' can be considered the most salient and more important. The question of which claims can be considered true and false seems to have been sidetracked, no matter how important the consequences these choices have (see Sismondo 2015). This is a prominent attribute of today's politics, and it is the essence of the post-truth era: it empowers people to choose their reality; a reality where evidence-based and objective facts are less important than people's already existing beliefs and prejudices. The phenomenon has sometimes been labelled by the buzzword term 'alternative facts'.

However, post-truth claims or so-called alternative facts do not seek to establish a coherent model of reality. Instead, they serve to distract the public from unwanted information or potentially unpopular policy actions, which as a result of the distraction can go uncommented on or unnoticed. Moreover, they are able to destroy trust in facts and reality to the point where facts no longer matter or are not even acknowledged to exist. Instead, people seek affirmations even when they know they are being misled; people wish to believe them (Colleoni et al. 2014; Lewandowsky et al. 2017). This can be amplified by politicians who incorporate misleading information and deception into their arsenal as an adequate way of gaining power. To this portion of the political establishment and society, lying is not only accepted but also rewarded. As Lewandowsky et al. (2017) add, falsifying reality is no longer about changing people's beliefs, it is about gaining and sustaining power.

Thus, the post-truth era is characterised by the shift from persuasion to relativisation, sometimes leading to apathy. It is no surprise that disinformation and propaganda have found more than favourable conditions for their development and dissemination these days, irrespective of how easy it is to find facts and evidence-based information—there are some audiences which are just not interested in them.

In the political sphere, there are frequent discussions about historical periods and interpretations of historical events. Democratic representatives and experts in the post-communist region struggle with those who present an 'alternative interpretation of history', mainly in the context of the installation of communist governments after the end of World War II with the support of the Soviet Union. For example, in Czechoslovakia, the installation of the communist regime was preceded by the abuse of political power and the intimidation of political opponents by Communist representatives. However, the current interpretation of revisionists (e.g. Communist Party representatives supported by some Russian media channels) is framed as democratic. The same could be said even of the

Holocaust, a very well-documented atrocity. We are still witnessing discussions when doubts about single aspects are expressed, or the Holocaust as a whole is denied. This perception of information, facts, and the evidence does not concern only the political views and attitudes of voters, it grows into other spheres of our lives. The growing number of people who believe in conspiracy theories, hoaxes, and disinformation in the health care or nutrition fields only prove that. We no longer wonder how many people still believe the measles vaccine causes autism. We have become used to it. A few years ago, we would not have thought that at the beginning of the twenty-first century the number of people believing the Earth was flat would be increasing. Today, however, we may be shocked by this, but it is a fact. Yes, a real fact, not an alternative fact. What do these cases have in common? Distrust of scientists, experts, and professionals and their knowledge and skills.

Relativism and the tendency to misuse, misinterpret, or question facts and research is nothing new. New is the degree and intensity with which it is happening. Discussions of facts focus on what is right and what is wrong. But for some, this is simply not relevant (Ihlen et al. 2019). An indispensable condition for a relationship among the general public, politicians, and experts, like almost all relationships in a democracy, is trust. The general public trusts politicians in their political decisions, while politicians trust experts whose knowledge provides them with the base for political decision-making. Thus, directly or indirectly, the general public must trust experts. When that trust collapses, when the public or politicians no longer trust experts, democracy itself can enter a death spiral which presents an immediate danger of decay either into mob rule or towards an elitist technocracy. Both are authoritarian outcomes (Nichols 2017, 216). While mob rule is not observable in today's democracies directly, there are cases of politicians dominating the political scene who, in their words, represent the common people and define themselves in opposition to experts (not just elites as in the case of populism). In fact, these cases are on the rise in the twenty-first century, and post-truth is one of the main causes.

What is also surprising is the high level of public tolerance for the inaccurate, misleading, or false statements of fact deniers. Since you are reading this chapter, you may not be surprised at this point that it is not unusual for these deniers of reality to appear on television screens or other media side by side with scientists. There are serious discussions about who is right and who is wrong and, moreover, whether fact deniers just have a different perspective or opinion. Indeed, the blurring of the differences between objectively recognisable facts and the presentation of one's own opinion is another typical feature of the post-truth era. 'Don't bother me with facts' is no longer a punchline, it has become a political stance. (Higgins 2016).

1.5.1 The Journey We Have Taken to the Post-Truth Era

It is obvious that the post-truth era has not appeared out of nowhere. When we consider the factors which caused its onset, we can distinguish three main categories: psychological factors affecting our daily work with information, societal changes and transformation, and technological progress affecting both the media and our lives as such. We cannot say which one of these is predominant. They are interconnected and all of them are crucial for understanding why we are dealing with the post-truth era, and why it is happening at the beginning of the twenty-first century. It is not our intention to analyse them in detail—each of them would require a book on their own—the aim of the following paragraphs is to provide readers with at least a basic introduction of them so that they can gain a better understanding of why we are dealing with post-truth now. This will also provide readers with the raison d'être of the following chapters of this edited volume.

Every human being must deal with biases when receiving and processing information and news (Nickerson 1988). No one is impervious to them; only if we are aware of them can we minimise them by knowingly changing our habits and behaviours associated with receiving news and information. Both our current views and attitudes are factors which play a significant role in how we receive new information. They have an impact on communication in general. We consciously and unconsciously try to avoid communication which contradicts our beliefs, and, on the contrary, we seek messages which confirm our already established attitudes. The new information one is able to accept tends to entrench further the fault lines of existing perspectives (O'Shaughnessy 2020, 60). When exposed to inadequate information, we often ignore it, reformulate it, or interpret it to support our existing attitudes. We also usually forget information we disagree with more quickly in comparison to the information which agrees with us. These processes are called selective exposure, selective perception, and selective memory. Selective exposure is a tendency to expose ourselves to information or news which are in line with our current attitudes while avoiding those we disagree with. Selective perception for change embodies the phenomenon of a person projecting what we want to see and hear into what we see or hear. Selective memory makes it easier for us to recall from our memory information which supports our views (see Freedman and Sears 1965; Hart et al. 2009; Stroud 2010; Zillmann and Bryant 2011).

Another principle affecting our attitude to information is cognitive dissonance. Festinger (1957) argues that if we have two or more pieces of information which are incompatible, then we feel a state of discomfort—dissonance. The information we have and believe in should be in harmony to make us feel comfortable. Therefore, in the case of any discord, we must act. Nevertheless, this state of mental discomfort does not only occur when the information we have does not match. There is also discomfort which arises after a decision is made, when there is discord between attitude and behaviour, and when there is discomfort from disappointment. The discomfort is caused by two or more relevant pieces of information, and the discomfort experienced is higher the more important the information. The state of discomfort itself is perceived as unpleasant and can be reduced, for example, by reducing the significance of non-conforming information or re-evaluating it. We can also add information which confirms our initial opinion to eliminate the discomfort (see Harmon-Jones 2002).

Confirmation bias is probably the best known and most widely accepted notion of inferential error to emerge from the literature on human reasoning (Evans 1989, 41). However, there is in fact a set of confirmation biases rather than one unified confirmation bias (see Nickerson 1998). There are often substantial task-to-task differences in these observed phenomena, their consequences, and the underlying cognitive processes we are able to identify. Generally, though, their direction is a tendency for people to believe too much in their favoured hypothesis. The term confirmation bias refers to looking for the presence of what we expect as opposed to looking for what we do not expect, to an inclination to retain or a disinclination to abandon a currently favoured hypothesis (see Jones, Sudden 2001; Knobloch-Westerwick and Kleinman 2012).

Societal changes represent the second category affecting our perception of information and news. It is natural for human beings to evolve and change. Likewise, the values and conventions which prevail in society evolve and change. This is nothing new or a characteristic purely found in recent decades or the last century. However, the specific changes play to the cards of post-truth. First of all, in Western democracies, there has been an observable decline in civic engagement, trust, and goodwill since the 1960s. Values which have encouraged people to discuss, exchange opinions, and seek consensus are increasingly less relevant to people. This trend leads us to stay in contact with people with similar attitudes, social status, political views, and hobbies. With our enclosure into social bubbles, there has also been a shift of values and life goals among the majority of people. The will to help the environment or interest in the philosophy of life has declined significantly since the 1970s. On the other hand, the importance of being well-off financially has risen over the same period (Twenge et al. 2012). Although we may have seen increased environmental concern in recent years, the question is how this trend will be affected by the COVID-19 pandemic and the subsequent economic development of individual countries. We cannot predict since this text is being written in the middle of the pandemic.

These changing life goals have unexpectedly been accompanied by growing inequality. As Lewandowsky et al. (2017) note, it is a paradox that at the same time as money has become more prominent, real income growth for young Americans has largely stagnated since the 1960s. Nor is this a problem for youth in just the United States. It is something the younger generation must deal with in most of the democracies. The ability to become independent and acquire their own housing is more difficult for millennials than to the generation of their parents. This generation gap leading to inequality is associated with affective political polarisation, which means that members of political parties tend to view members of their political party more positively and those of opposing parties more negatively than ever before (see Abramowitz and Webster 2016). Party affiliation or, more precisely, ideological preference is also the link to another societal effect: politically asymmetric credulity. Recent studies have shown that there are cognitive and psychological differences between liberals and conservatives in the way they access information and evaluate their relevance or trustworthiness: conservative voters tend to believe in disinformation and false information more often than liberal voters (see Jost 2017). This societal effect is represented by a declining trust in science as already mentioned above. Naturally, when considering individual specific cases of trust in disinformation and alternative facts, not all of these societal effects or changes must be present or fulfilled. However, looking at the current political developments on the national and international level, it is not easy to free oneself of the impression that these are often exemplary cases of the effects mentioned here.

Last but not least, there are technological changes. Probably the most visible technological development affecting our perception of information are the changes in the global media landscape which have led to fragmentation. The advent of the Internet, especially Web 2.0, produced sources of information tailored to each user's needs and wishes. In light of the fractionalisation of the media landscape into echo chambers (e.g. Jasny et al. 2015), many people believe their opinions, however exotic or unsupported by evidence, to be widely shared, thereby rendering them resistant to change or correction (Lewandowsky et al. 2017). Thus, alternative facts have increasingly moved in from the outskirts of public discourse. Conspiracy theories and disinformation gain more attention from mainstream audiences than ever before (Webb and Jirotka 2017). If traditional and mainstream media does not provide us with the information confirming our opinion and biases, we can look for media which does provide it—even if it is bullshit. Furthermore, this heterogeneity contributes to the incivility of political discourse. The media is trying to supply more shocking news or frame them in ever catchier ways to get our attention.

Social media is a phenomenon in and of itself. It polarises society through algorithms which embody the essence of its functioning. Functionality based on the logic of consumer behaviour, where we are offered products and services which are evaluated as attractive to us based on our previous behaviour, can be appreciated when talking about goods. However, it is highly problematic in the field of news and political content. Users are presented with content which reflects their view of the world (O'Shaughnessy 2020); therefore, they are less and less confronted by other views. The willingness to speak to people with a different opinion is declining. Because why should we even bother to do so? In order to filter inconvenient information (or data smog), people naturally tend to belong to an 'information group'—people who are 'marked by allegiance to particular types and sources of information, to particular modes of problem perception and solution' (Marshall et al. 2015, 23). Belonging to an information group saves our time. Consciously or not, we are getting closed in our filter bubbles or echo chambers—communities where we like to confirm our opinion regardless of whether it is based on real facts or not—without being exposed to counter arguments (Ihlen et al. 2019).

Since we are like-minded people in these echo chambers, the chance that someone will question false information is declining. People tend to believe their opinions are widely shared regardless of whether or not they are actually widely shared (Lewandowsky et al. 2017). When people believe this, they are more resistant to changing their minds, less likely to compromise, and more likely to insist on their own views (Leviston et al. 2013). Of course, people can belong to more than one information group, hearing more than one echo chamber with varying degrees of commitment or awareness (Marshall et al. 2015, 24). Another effect connected to social media is the roughness of discussions. We do not see those with whom we are conversing with on social media. It is, therefore, easier to slip into rougher language. In the same way, trolls and bots have a similarly vulgarising effect.

Until now, the focus has mainly been on users, citizens, or voters. However, the technological giants of the online world have also had an undeniable impact on the current situation, as demonstrated in the strengthening effects of algorithms. In addition to social media platforms like Facebook, YouTube, and Twitter, Google and its targeted ads are among the most influential. It is enough for a user to read an article on a disreputable website a few times, and search engines and ads already recommend similar resources to them. As with shopping behaviour, when receiving information, the Internet players offer 'similar products'. Therefore, paradoxically a small number of technological 'superpowers' have come to dominate the global spread of information and affect not only the way we consume information but also what information and from what sources (Webb and Jirotka 2017).

1.5.2 *Infodemic—Post-Truth on Steroids*

The year 2020 and the COVID-19 pandemic has brought—among other things—a further acceleration of the spread of misleading information. Misleading health information, such as 'guaranteed' advice and tips on how to treat the disease, has become a new issue in particular (Lilleker et al. 2021). The term 'infodemic' has become widespread, highlighting the danger of the misinformation phenomenon throughout the management of virus outbreaks since it has the ability to even accelerate the spread of the novel coronavirus by empowering reluctance towards the social response. The pandemic has shown how crucial and important a role social media plays in the new information environment (Cinelli et al. 2020, 2). Users increasingly see trusted sources of information within their peer networks and further share their statements. As that information is further spread, it often increases in its perceived legitimacy. This method of sharing and validating information contrasts with methods implemented by mass media, who have specialised knowledge and specific responsibilities related to information verification and sharing. During the COVID-19 pandemic, individuals have, not surprisingly, been turning to this new digital reality for guidance (Limaye et al. 2020, 277). We can see this trend all around the world, with countries and even supranational organisations, such as the European Union or the World Health Organisation (WHO), having faced it (see Lilleker et al. 2021).

It would not be correct to state that social media has served exclusively the dissemination of misleading information. There were numerous cases when social media helped to empower and support hospital staff as well as information campaigns on epidemiological recommendations or governmental measures. The latter two especially represent a battlefield where social media has met mass media and fought for the audience's attention, for the privilege of who gets to inform the general public. Even though users share information on social media, 'old school' techniques of (political) communication have proved that they do not yet belong in the scrapheap. Mass media has played a crucial role mainly in two aspects: (1) mediation of press conferences and speeches of government members to the masses, and (2) the selection of experts who provide comments based on their expertise.

The phenomenon, which is not new but has been boosted by the pandemic, is the comments and statements of self-proclaimed experts or authorities with expertise from fields not correlated to the pandemic. These statements have been widely circulated on social media and have often undermined the official statements made by the government. 'Scientific misinformation has been actively propagated as a means to destabilise trust in governments and as a political weapon' (Limaye et al. 2020, 277), and mass media, at least to some degree, has played the role of moderator, returning the debate to acceptable norms with eligible speakers. Although social media has strengthened its power during the pandemic, mass media has shown itself to be crucial if verified and reliable information is needed. Nevertheless, even mass media has not gone without blemish and has been criticised, for example, for providing space to 'erroneous' experts.

*****

People usually hear what they want to hear because they get their news exclusively from sources whose bias they agree with. A source provides the framing for the information. It tells the consumer whether the information is likely to be agreeable and conform to expectations (Marshall et al. 2015, 24). It is not decisive how trustworthy the source is according to the objective criteria—we recognise the source as trustworthy when it provides likeable 'facts', no matter how 'alternative' they are. Although some authors expect that echo chambers boosted by computer algorithms to select news on Web 2.0 (and social media especially) will have an effect on both solid news and fake news (see Sismondo 2017), recent data shows that disinformation and lies spread faster and to a broader audience than truth—a product of the different predominant emotions both types of news evoke (Vosoughi et al. 2018). However, no matter what side people choose, whether to trust facts or alternative facts, both ways play into approaches which treat voters as people to be manipulated rather than convinced (Sismondo 2017).

Lies and bullshit have always been among us, but technologies, such as social media; the growth of so-called alternative media; and even bots have elevated them to a common cause, which a part of our society is unashamed of, elevating it even to a political attitude. Verifying information and debunking lies and disinformation is then perceived as a restriction on freedom of speech and the enforcement of political attitudes to the detriment of others. All these trends have encouraged politicians to strategically target their supporters with radical and, in some cases, even extremist messages. At a time when people are overwhelmed with information, the political struggle is often won not by the politician who is able to compromise and use substantive reasoning, but the one whose tweets and Facebook statuses are more visible and striking. And while you are reading the explanation of what the post-truth era is, more and more people argue on Facebook about blatant lies which are presented and defended as their opinion.

1.6 Conclusion

On the previous pages, we tried to explain what propaganda and disinformation are, how they differ from other forms of false or misleading information, and how they fit into the broader concept of influence operations. The way we receive information and news has changed radically over the past decade, which is also linked to the emergence of the post-truth era or, more recently, the so-called infodemic. Although there is a lack of consensus on the universally accepted definition of propaganda, the individual definitions are characterised by standard features: (1) systematically and intentionally disseminated (2) ideas and information (3) are inaccurate, distorted, false, or omitted (4) and intended to influence or manipulate the public (5) to harm the opponent. Disinformation represents a conceptually more straightforward phenomenon (intentionally misleading information). However, it is often confused with other forms of deception.

The form and strategy of propaganda are influenced by the means which propaganda can use—propaganda depends on the tools and channels of information dissemination on offer. Today, it has taken the form of using the Internet and social media so anyone can write what they want, anyone can be a journalist, or, more generally, be a creator of popular content. This means, among other things, an overloading of the information environment and the individual as well. Laswell's, Ellul's, and Taylor's definitions of propaganda as introduced in this chapter remain valid, but the nature of the information environment and the means through which we can use in it have changed, affecting the strategies that lead to the fulfilment of those still valid goals for which both propaganda and disinformation are used. Manipulative techniques remain the same, although the frequency varies in the use of particular techniques. What does not change is the essential role of emotions.

Today's propaganda and disinformation do not necessarily aim to persuade; another strategy used is the effort to overload a targeted audience with information and thus induce relativisation, which suits the post-truth era. In the post-truth era, three primary shifts can be identified: (1) a lie is elevated to political opinion, and if the facts do not fit into our vision of the world, we choose other, alternative facts which do; (2) technologies accelerate our enclosure into echo chambers and opinion ghettos; and, paradoxically, (3) politicians who benefit from post-truth rely on people's tendencies to believe that others are telling (at least mostly) truth, and they exploit it. Moreover, the post-truth era is often characterised by an intertwining of political ambitions and politicians with propaganda narratives and disinformation.

The question is which came first, the chicken or the egg? Are the information overloading and relativisation strategies a characteristic of the post-truth era or were they just an advantageous condition which facilitated the onset of the post-truth era? Did the post-truth era enable this strategy to be applied, or did the use of the strategy lead to its development? The purpose of this chapter was not to answer such questions but instead seek to highlight that these new strategies respond to the fact that society has access to nearly unlimited information which is affected by strategies of applied propaganda and disinformation. It is challenging to control or even stop the flow of information unless we create a downright new and controllable information environment. Thus, the new method of manipulation is to create the illusion that things are not as they seem, that there are always alternative facts for everyone. With the change in the information environment, so too have the strategies changed. We have moved from persuasion to manipulation through the sheer amount of information and the presentation of information irrelevant to the discourse and, therefore, to its relativisation.

Bibliography

Abramowitz, A. I., & Webster, S. (2016). The Rise of Negative Partisanship and the Nationalization of U.S. Elections in the 21st Century. *Electoral Studies, 41*(March), 12–22. https://doi.org/10.1016/j.electstud.2015.11.001.

Akopova, A. S. (2013). Linguistic Manipulation: Definition and Types. *International Journal of Cognitive Research in Science, Engineering, and Education, 1*(2), 78–82.

Allcott, H., & Gentzkow, D. (2017). Social Media and Fake News in the 2016 Election. *Journal of Economic Perspectives, 31*(2), 211–236.

Atton, C. (2009). Alternative and Citizen Journalism. In K. Wahl-Jorgensen & T. Hanitzsch (Eds.), *The Handbook of Journalism Studies* (pp. 265–278). New York and London: Routledge.

Bates, R. A., & Mooney, M. (2014). Psychological Operations and Terrorism: The Digital Domain. *The Journal of Public and Professional Sociology, 6*(1). https://digitalcommons.kennesaw.edu/cgi/viewcontent.cgi?article=1070&context=jpps. Accessed 22 Mar 2020.

Baym, G. (2005). The Daily Show: Discursive Integration and the Reinvention of Political Journalism. *Political Communication, 22*(3), 259–276.

Berliner, D. C. (1992, February). Educational Reform in an Era of Disinformation. *Annual Meeting of the American Association of Colleges for Teacher Education*. San Antonio, TX, USA. https://files.eric.ed.gov/fulltext/ED348710.pdf. Accessed 22 Mar 2020.

Bernays, E. L. (1947). The Engineering of Consent. *The Annals of the American Academy of Political and Social Science, 250*(1), 113–120. https://doi.org/10.1177/000271624725000116.

Bernays, E. L. (2004). *Propaganda*. New York: IG Publishing.

Bor, S. E. (2014). Teaching Social Media Journalism: Challenges and Opportunities for Future Curriculum Design. *Journalism & Mass Communication Educator, 69*(3), 243–255. https://doi.org/10.1177/1077695814531767.

Brangetto, P., & Veenendaal, A. M. (2016). *Influence Cyber Operations: The Use of Cyberattacks in Support of Influence Operations*. Tallinn: NATO CCD COE Publications.

Brazzoli, M. S. (2007). Future Prospects of Information Warfare and Particularly Psychological Operations. In L. Le Roux (Ed.), *South African Army Vision 2020: Security Challenges Shaping the Future African Army* (pp. 217–234). Pretoria: Institute for Security Studies.

Bufacchi, V. (2020). Trutp, Lies and Tweets: A Concensus Theory of Post-Truth. *Philosophy and Social Criticism*, 1–15. https://doi.org/10.1177/0191453719896382.

Cilluffo, F. J., & Gergely, C. H. (1997). Information Warfare and Strategic Terrorism. *Terrorism and Political Violence, 9*(1), 84–94.

Cinelli, M., Quattrociocchi, W., Galeazzi, A., Valensise, C. M., Brugnoli, E., Schmidt, A. L., et al. (2020). The COVID-19 Social Media Infodemic. *Scientific Reports* 10.

Colleoni, E., Rozza, A., & Arvidsson, A. (2014). Echo Chambers or Public Sphere? Predicting Political Orientation and Measuring Political Homophily in Twitter Using Big Data. *Journal of Communication, 64*(2), 317–332. https://doi.org/10.1111/jcom.12084.

Damasio, A. (2010). *Self Comes to Mind: Constructing the Conscious Brain*. New York: Pantheon.

Domatob, J. (1985). Propaganda Techniques in Black Afrika. *International Communication Gazete, 36*(3), 193–212.

Dortbudak, M. F. (2008). *The Intelligence Requirement of Psychological Operations in Counterterrorism*. Monterey: Naval Postgraduate School. https://calhoun.nps.edu/bitstream/handle/10945/3856/08Dec_Dortbudak.pdf?sequence=1&isAllowed=y. Accessed 22 Mar 2020.

Dretske, F. I. (1983). Précis of Knowledge and the Flow of Information. *Behavioral and Brain Sciences, 6*(1), 55–90.

Ellul, J. (1973). *Propaganda: The Formation of Men's Attitudes*. New York: Vintage Books.

Emery, N. E., Earl, R. S., & Buettner, R. (2004). Terrorist Use of Information Operations. *Journal of Information Warfare, 3*(2), 14–26.
Evans, J. S. B. T. (1989). *Bias in Human Reasoning*. Hillsdale, NJ: Erlbaum.
Fallis, D. (2015). What Is Disinformation? *Library Trends, 63*(3), 401–426.
Farkas, J., & Neumayer, C. (2018). Disguised Propaganda from Digital to Social Media. In J. Hunsinger et al. (Eds.), *Second International Handbook of Internet Research* (pp. 1–17), Springer.
Festinger, L. (1957). *A Theory of Cognitive Dissonance*. Stanford, CA: Stanford University Press.
Freedman, J. L., & Sears, D. O. (1965). Selective Exposure. *Advances in Experimental Social Psychology, 2,* 57–97. https://doi.org/10.1016/S0065-2601(08)60103-3.
Ganor, B. (2002). *Terror as a Strategy of Psychological Warfare*. International Institute for Counter-Terrorism. https://www.ict.org.il/Article/827/Terror-as-a-Strategy-of-Psychological-Warfare#gsc.tab=0. Accessed 22 Mar 2020.
Gelfert, A. (2018). Fake News: A Definition. *Informal Logic, 38*(1), 84–117.
Goode, L. (2009). Social News, Citizen Journalism and Democracy. *New Media & Society, 11*(8), 1287–1305. https://doi.org/10.1177/1461444809341393.
Guilday, P. (1921). The Sacred Congregation de Propaganda Fide (1622–1922). *The Catholic Historical Review, 6*(4), 478–494.
Harmon-Jones, E. (2002). A Cognitive Dissonance: Theory Perspective on Persuasion. In J. P Dillard & M. W. Pfau (Eds.), *The Persuasion Handbook: Developments in Theory and Practice* (pp. 99–116). London: Sage. http://dx.doi.org/10.4135/9781412976046.n6.
Hart, W., Albarracin, D., Eagly, A. H., Brechan, I., Lindberg, M. J., & Merrill, L. (2009). Feeling Validated Versus Being Correct: A Meta-Analysis of Selective Exposure to Information. *Psychological Bulletin, 135*(4), 555–588. https://doi.org/10.1037/a0015701.
Higgins, K. (2016). Post-Truth: A Guide for the Perplexed. *Nature, 540*(9). https://doi.org/10.1038/540009a.
Hopkin, J., & Rosamond, B. (2017). Post-Truth Politics, Bullshit and Bad Ideas: 'Deficit Fetishism' in the UK. *New Political Economy, 23*(6), 641–655.
Ihlen, Ø., Gregory, A., Luoma-aho, V., & Buhmann, A. (2019). Post-Truth and Public Relations: Special Section Introduction. *Public Relations Review, 45*(4), 1–4. https://doi.org/10.1016/j.pubrev.2019.101844.
Jasny, L., Waggle, J., & Fisher, D. R. (2015). An Empirical Examination of Echo Chambers in US Climate Policy Networks. *Nature Climate Change, 5,* 782–786. https://doi.org/10.1038/nclimate2666.
Jones, M., & Sugden, R. (2001). Positive Confirmation Bias in the Acquisition of Information. *Theory and Decision, 50,* 59–99. https://doi.org/10.1023/A:1005296023424.

Jost, J. T. (2017). Ideological Asymetries and the Essence of Political Psychology. *Political Psychology, 38*(2), 167–208. https://doi.org/10.1111/pops.12407.
Kalpokas, I. (2020). Post-Truth and the Changing Information Environment. In P. Baines, N. O'Shaughnessy, & N. Snow (Eds.), *The Sage Handbook of Propaganda* (pp. 71–84). London, Thousand Oaks, New Dehli and Singapore: Sage.
Kaufhold, K., Valenzuela, S., & Gil de Zuniga, H. (2010). Citizen Journalism and Democracy: How User-Generated News Use Relates to Political Knowledge and Participation. *Journalism and Mass Communication Quarterly, 87*(3–4), 515–529. https://doi.org/10.1177/107769901008700305.
Knobloch-Westerwick, S., & Kleinman, S. B. (2012). Preelection Selective Exposure: Confirmation Bias Versus Informational Utility. *Communication Research, 39*(2), 170–193.
Kragh, M., & Åsberg, S. (2017). Russia's Strategy for Influence Through Public Diplomacy and Active Measures: The Swedish Case. *Journal of Strategic Studies, 40*(6), 773–816.
Larson, V. E., et al. (2009). *Foundation of Effective Influence Operations.* A Framework for Enhancing Army Capabilities: RAND Corporation.
Lasswell, H.D. (1927). The Theory of Propaganda. *American Political Science Review*, 627–631. https://doi.org/10.2307/19455515.
Leviston, Z., Walker, I., & Morwinski, S. (2013). Your Opinion on Climate Change Might Not Be as Common as You Think. *Nature Climate Change, 3,* 334–337. https://doi.org/10.1038/nclimate1743.
Lewandowsky, S., Ecker, U. K. H., & Cook, J. (2017). Beyond Misinformation: Understanding and Coping with the "Post-Truth" Era. *Journal of Applied Research in Memory and Cognition, 6*(4), 353–369.
Lewis, S. C., Kaufhold, K., & Lasorsa, D. L. (2010). Thinking About Citizen Journalism: The Philosophical and Practical Challenges of User-Generated Content for Community Newspapers. *Journalism Practice, 4*(2), 163–179. https://doi.org/10.1080/14616700903156919.
Lilleker, D., Coman, I., Gregor, M., & Novelli, E. (2021). *Political Communication and COVID-19: Governance and Rhetoric in Times of Crisis*. London and New York: Routledge.
Limaye, R. J., Suaer, M., Ali, J., Bernstein, J., Wahl, B., Barnhill, A., et al. (2020). Building Trust While Influencing Online COVID-19 Content in the Social Media World. *The Lancet Digital Health, 2*(1), e277–e278.
Mair, J. (2017). Post-Truth Anthropology. *Anthropology Today, 33*(3), 3–4.
Marshall, J. P., Goodman, J., Zowghi, D., & da Rimini, F. (2015). *Disorder and the Disinformation Society*. London and New York: Routledge.
McCornack, S. A. (1992). Information Manipulation Theory. *Communication Monographs, 59*(1), 1–16. https://doi.org/10.1080/03637759209376245.

Merriam-Webster Dictionary. (n.d.). *Operation*. https://www.merriam-webster.com/dictionary/operation. Accessed 22 Mar 2020.

Miljkovic, M., & Pešic, A. (2019). Informational and Psychological Aspects of Security Threats in Contemporary Environment. *TEME, 43*(4), 1079–1094.

NATO Standardization Office. (2014). *Allied Joint Doctrine for Psychological Operations. Allied Joint Publication—3.10.1.* Brussels: North Atlantic Treaty Organization, NATO Standardization Office.

NATO Standardization Office. (2018). *NATO Glossary of Terms and Definitions. AAP-06.* Brussels: North Atlantic Treaty Organization, NATO Standardization Office.

Nichols, T. (2017). *The Death of Expertise*. New York: Oxford University Press.

Nickerson, R. S. (1998). Confirmation Bias: A Ubiquitous Phenomenon in Many Guises. *Review of General Psychology, 2*(2), 175–220.

O'Shaughnessy, N. (2004). *Politics and Propaganda: Weapons of Mass Seduction*. Manchester: Manchester University Press.

O'Shaughnessy, N. (2016). *Selling Hitler: Propaganda & The Nazi Brand*. London: Hurst & Company.

O'Shaughnessy, N. (2020). From Disinformation to Fake News: Forward into the Past. In P. Baines, N. O'Shaughnessy, & N. Snow (Eds.), *The Sage Handbook of Propaganda* (pp. 55–70). SAGE: London, Thousand Oaks, New Dehli and Singapore.

Orwell, G. (1949). *1984*. London: Secker and Warburg.

Pearce, K. E. (2015). Democratizing Kompromat: The Affair Dances of Social Media for State-Sponsored Harassment. *Information, Communication & Society, 18*(10), 1158–1174. https://doi.org/10.1080/1369118X.2015.1021705.

Post, J. M. (n.d.). *Psychological Operations and Counterterrorism*. https://www.pol-psych.com/downloads/JFQ%20Psyops%20and%20counterterrorism.pdf. Accessed 22 Mar 2020.

Pratkanis, A., & Aronson, E. (2001). *Age of Propaganda: The Everyday Use and Abuse of Persuasion*. New York: Holt Paperbacks.

Shabo, M. E. (2008). *Techniques of Propaganda & Persuasion*. Clayton: Prestwick House.

Shenk, D. (1997). *Data Smog: Surviving the Information Glut*. New York: Harper Collins.

Silverman, C. (2016). This Analysis Shows How Viral Fake Election News Stories Outperformed Real News on Facebook. *Buzzfeed*. https://www.buzzfeed.com/craigsilverman/viral-fake-election-news-outperformed-real-news-on-facebook?utm_term=tgEkrDpr#.dvkvJ3DJ. Accessed 22 Mar 2020.

Sismondo, S. (2017). Post-truth? *Social Studies of Science, 47*(1), 3–6. https://doi.org/10.1177/0306312717692076.

Smith, B. L. (2019). Propaganda. *Encyclopaedia Britannica*. https://www.britannica.com/topic/propaganda. Accessed 20 Mar 2020.

Sparkes-Vian, C. (2018). Digital Propaganda: The Tyranny of Ignorance. *Critical Sociology, 45*(3), 393–409.

Stilwell, R. D. (1996). Political-Psychological Dimensions of Counterinsurgency. In F.L Goldstein & B. F Findley (Eds.), *Psychological Operations: Principles and Case Studies* (pp. 319–332). Alabama: Air University Press.

Stroud, N. J. (2010). Polarization and Partisan Selective Exposure. *Journal of Communication, 60*(3), 556–576. https://doi.org/10.1111/j.1460-2466.2010.01497.x.

Syed, M. (2012). On War by Deception-Mind Control to Propaganda: From Theory to Practice. *ISSRA Papers*, 195–214.

Taylor, P. M. (2003). *Munitions of the Mind: A History of Propaganda from the Ancient World to the Present Era*. Manchester and New York: Manchester University Press.

Tromblay, E. D. (2018). *Political Influence Operations: How Foreign Actors Seek to Shape U.S. Policy Making*. Lanham: Rowman & Littlefield.

Twenge, J. M., Campbell, W. K., & Freeman, E. C. (2012). Generational Differences in Young Adults' Life Goals, Concern for Others, and Civic Orientation, 1966–2009. *Journal of Personality and Social Psychology, 102*(5), 1045–1062. https://doi.org/10.1037/a0027408.

United States—Join Chiefs of Staff. (2014). Joint Publication 3–13: Information operations.

Vargo, C., Lei, G., & Amazeen, M. (2017). The Agenda-Setting Power of Fake News: A Big Data Analysis of the Online Media Landscape from 2014 to 2016. *New Media & Society, 20*(5), 2028–2049.

Vejvodová, P. (2019). Information and Psychological Operations as a Challenge to Security and Defence. *Vojenské rozhledy, 28*(3), 83–96.

Vosoughi, S., Roy, D., & Aral, S. (2018). The Spread of True and False News Online. *Science, 359*(6380), 1146–1151. https://doi.org/10.1126/science.aap9559.

Webb, H., & Jirotka, M. (2017). Nuance, Societal Dynamics, and Responsibility in Addressing Misinformation in the Post-Truth Era: Commentary on Lewandowsky, Ecker, and Cook. *Journal of Applied Research in Memory and Cognition, 6*(4), 414–417. https://doi.org/10.1016/j.jarmac.2017.10.001.

Wojnowski, M. (2019). Presidential Elections as a State Destabilization Tool in the Theory and Practice of the Russian Info-Psychological Operations in the 20th and 21st Century. *Przegląd Bezpieczeństwa Wewnętrznego, 11*(21), 311–333.

Zillmann, D., & Jennings, B. (2011). *Selective Exposure to Communication*. London: Routledge Communication Series.

CHAPTER 2

Propaganda and Disinformation Go Online

Miroslava Pavlíková, Barbora Šenkýřová, and Jakub Drmola

2.1 Introduction

What is the future of political propaganda? Is the future 'now'? In Ukraine, information warfare was made public, and a discussion about new forms of propaganda dissemination subsequently appeared. Human controlled accounts manipulating online content at the same time emerged in the Russian–Ukrainian conflict. The so-called Kremlin trolls tried to influence domestic as well as Ukrainian audiences in favour of the Russian framing of the confrontation. The Ukrainian side, for its part, also attempted to utilise the Internet as a non-kinetic weapon. The Ukraine Information Army was founded by the Ministry of Information Policy as an initiative aiming to fight the Russian trolls, and every Ukrainian citizen

M. Pavlíková (✉) · B. Šenkýřová · J. Drmola
Department of Political Science, Faculty of Social Studies, Masaryk University, Brno, Czech Republic

J. Drmola
e-mail: jdrmola@mail.muni.cz

M. Gregor and P. Mlejnková (eds.), *Challenging Online Propaganda and Disinformation in the 21st Century*, Political Campaigning and Communication,
https://doi.org/10.1007/978-3-030-58624-9_2

was able to become a member of the group, a tactic aimed at debunking the disinformation spread by the trolls.

Another sign of the times as regards technology development and propaganda usage was the 2016 US presidential election and the ensuing allegations about Russian state interference. Russia conducted complex influence operations with the use of cyberspace, where propaganda played a significant role. A massive campaign of robotised accounts spreading content hit social media. Precisely chosen target groups became the objective of this upgrade to the Ukrainian Internet's former Kremlin trolls. Shortly thereafter, a scandal with the company Cambridge Analytica appeared. After the Brexit referendum, it was revealed that the consulting company had misused holes in the data protection of Facebook users to produce micro-targeted political campaigns all around the world—the company's services had been hired by state actors on various levels. What is more, we are now reading about the threat of the so-called deep-fakes and their ability to perfectly deceive a target audience. Could future propaganda and information manipulation like these examples decide elections?

A new information environment, driven largely by the growth in the Internet, is rapidly changing the economic, social, and political landscape. Given the exponential growth in both Internet use and the availability of news, it is no wonder this new form of communication brings new tools and methods for media manipulation. The aim of this chapter is therefore to introduce and describe changes in the information environment and the newest tools and trends identified in the context of information manipulation and propaganda at the beginning of the twenty-first century. The technology of disinformation and propaganda has been going through significant changes since the end of the Cold War. Together with changes in society and the very meaning of information, we could nowadays talk about an information society (Webster 2006), information economy (a society that produces more information then goods) (Zhang 2017), or an information-centric society. The societal changes have also applied to the security and military domain. Although the importance of information dates to classic military theorists like Sun Tzu, its connection with the rapid emergence of new technologies has profoundly changed the way conflict and war is waged. Terms like information warfare or the weaponisation of information (see Toffler and Toffler 1981) have become a vital part of today's security and military discourse.

Sun Tzu would agree that information has always been an extremely dangerous weapon. However, at the start of the twenty-first century, we are witnessing very turbulent times due to high-speed technological development and the expansionary potential of virtual space. The chapter therefore begins with a reflection on the information environment and the infosphere. The focus is put on the development of the information environment, because that is the decisive factor affecting what tools can be used and in what way information can be manipulated. The issues related to the information environment and the efforts of countries to protect it is illustrated by the cases of two undemocratic countries, China and Russia. These countries are more prone to believe disinformation and propaganda to be suitable parts of a toolset in the protection and promotion of their interests, and efforts to control the information environment go hand in hand with it. Through such examples we can demonstrate the importance of the information environment (and its protection), and also how far regimes can go in their obsession to control the flow of information given the current circumstances. How different information environments can work as well as how they can prevent the public from being informed within a regime will be described, but also, conversely, how they can openly spread information outside a regime.

The second part of the chapter is focused on technological disinformation and propaganda tools in online space. This part depicts the shift from human-made trolling to bot activities and highly personalised, precisely targeted, emotion-adaptive artificial intelligence. The following section briefly confirms that it is not only actors with political or ideological goals using disinformation and propaganda—a frequent motive for deploying them is in fact profit. Another change observed in the context of online disinformation and propaganda is that of businesses implementing manipulative activities in political communication, as can be seen in the example of the 2016 US presidential elections and Cambridge Analytica; and let us not also forget the crucial role social media platforms, such as Facebook, played as well. Technology companies will therefore be subsequently covered. In the final part, we move closer to the future, focusing on deepfake technology, which can be seen as a future tool of new online propaganda. Although deepfakes are a very new disinformation technology, we can already explore it through some examples (fake videos of Barack Obama and Donald Trump, fake profile pictures on LinkedIn, and the FaceApp data privacy case). Although deepfakes represent new technology, we argue that they mark the next step in the gradual professionalisation of information manipulation rather than a revolutionary new phenomenon.

The aim of this chapter is not to provide readers with an exhaustive list of 'high-tech technologies' but rather to point out the main directions of modern propaganda and disinformation developments.

2.2 Information Environment

The key element all propaganda and disinformation are based on is information. Since the development of technology such as radio and television, the importance of information and its value has been changing. In the 1950s, when television broadcasts entered the daily lives of people in the developed world, the perception and need for new information began to be a new requirement in their lives. The word information (having Latin roots and a Greek origin) is used in two basic contexts: the act of moulding the mind and the act of communicating knowledge (Capurro and Hjørland 2005, 351). The action of *informing*, therefore, refers to the shaping of mind or character, education, and teaching (Oxford English Dictionary). According to the OECD there are three conceptions of information: information as knowledge, information as economic activity, and information as technology (Godin 2008, 256). In our chapter we will deal with all of these conceptions. As a society in which information and information technology have a powerful influence on everyday social life (OECD, *A Framework document in* Godin 2008, 268), we often use the term 'information society'. Similar to information itself, this concept is not clear and generally accepted. It is worth pointing out here that one of the approaches to defining information society is the fulfilment of these five criteria: technological (connected with technology innovation since 1970), economic (in the context of the information economy), occupational (informational work), spatial (change in the organisation of time and space), and cultural (information in everyday life—TV, emails, etc.) (Webster 2006, 8).[1]

The definition of information as it relates to the information economy is 'grounded more in the production and exchange of information than

[1] According to Webster (2006, 8), there is also a sixth definition. However, '… its main claim is not that there is more information today (there obviously is), but rather that the character of information is such as to have transformed how we live'.

physical goods' (Mazarr et al. 2019, 3). Moreover, in some studies, information society is used instead of information economy (Atik 1999, 121). According to OECD information economy 'refers to the implications of information technologies on the economy, [and] on firms' performance (productivity, profitability, employment)' (Godin 2008, 268). Godin's three conceptions here demonstrate that information and information technologies are, today, the main commodities of international business.

The information environment, where all these processes take place, is both a vaguely and complexly understood concept. Media and communication studies often use terms like 'press system', 'media system', and 'mass communication system'. However, the way in which media systems are constructed and developed is not homogenous (anymore). Moreover, these concepts do not integrate all the actors and ways of interpersonal communication, which we can see today. Therefore, the concept of information environment provides a better understanding of the 'battleground' where propaganda and disinformation fight for our attention and affection. The information environment consists of three dimensions: cognitive, informational, and physical (US Joint Chiefs of Staff 2006). The information environment throughout most of the twentieth century was one in which people could easily identify the place, time, and space information was related to; however, this became more difficult (if not impossible) with the advent of the Internet in the late 1980s. This shift not only made it difficult for consumers to identify where and when information was initially released, but even identifying the producer became challenging. Another way of conceiving this change is that cyberspace and social networks became intertwined with (or started overlapping) the information environment (Porche et al. 2013, 12).

The integral part of the information environment is the infosphere. Sometimes, these two terms are used synonymously. However, in our view, these two concepts are more complex, and, therefore, we will define the infosphere separately. The term was devised by Boulding in 1970. He notes that 'the infosphere then consists of inputs and outputs of conversation, books, television, radio, speeches, church services, classes, and lectures as well as information received from the physical world by personal observation. … It is clearly a segment of the sociosphere in its own right, and indeed it has considerable claim to dominate the other segments. It can be argued that development of any kind is essentially a learning process and that it is primarily dependent on a network of information flows' (Martens 2015, 332). Similar to the information environment, the infosphere used to be controlled by only a few television channels and shows (Mazarr et al. 2019, 25). Regularly published newspapers and the continuous broadcasting of radio and TV stations were supplemented by the Internet, where access to the information is more a question of the users' will, deciding for themselves when and where they wish to consume it. In these terms, and given the permanently changing environment and society, infosphere could be defined as 'the ongoing process of producing, disseminating, and perceiving information in a society, including media, data-based algorithmic processes, and information exchange in networks' (Mazarr et al. 2019, 7). In other words, in today's information environment, 'the direct links between time and place, on the one hand, and the individual as a producer and consumer of the content, on the other hand, have long since disappeared' (Brikše 2006). This shift has increased the space and possibilities for the production of media manipulation. This also applies to the infosphere, whose challenges we will discuss later.

In the context of today's information environment, cyberspace, which is essential but difficult to define, is often mentioned. The word cyberspace was first used by writer William Gibson in 1982 in the short story 'Burning Chrome'. In the absence of a widely accepted definition of cyberspace, each sector defines the term in accordance with its own needs. In recent years, however, there has been a trend to call everything related to networks and computers 'cybernetic' (Lorents and Ottis 2010). In addition to the Internet and computer networks, we also include telecommunication networks, embedded processors, and drivers in cyberspace. For example, Lorents and Ottis (2010) attempted to create a general definition of cyberspace as a virtual world which would be valid in all sectors. According to them, cyberspace represents a time-dependent set of interconnected information systems and human users interacting with these systems. Although cyberspace is independent of geographical boundaries, it falls within the jurisdiction of a state located in that territory. However, even this division is unclear and legally difficult to grasp, as will be shown later in this chapter. At the same time, it makes it challenging to enforce legal offences and crimes committed by individual users in cyberspace.

State and non-state actors endeavour to protect their cyberspace. These efforts, called cybersecurity, can be represented by the concepts of IT security and electronic information system security. There are de facto two approaches to cybersecurity as a discipline: the technical and social science approaches. The first deals mainly with the practical side—the actual repelling of cyber attacks, their analysis, the implementation of technically oriented security solutions, and more, i.e. the logical and physical layer of cyberspace—while the latter explores the social layer of the problem.

Because information technology is hugely dynamic, attackers are continually inventing new techniques of malicious activity. Those that were up to date five years ago appear to be outdated today and have been replaced by more sophisticated methods. This development in cyberspace requires flexible responses from the security community. Knowing the source of the attacks is more important than knowing the attack technique. Although cyber threat techniques change over time, the actors usually remain the same (Secureworks 2017).

2.3 Challenges in Today's Information Environment

As the technology developed (through the spread of different broadcast methods), so too did the infosphere change. Nowadays, the infosphere could be characterised by many (not only) new problematic trends, including 'the fragmentation of authority, the rise of silos of belief, and a persistent trolling ethic of cynical and aggressive harassment in the name of an amorphous social dissent' (Mazarr et al. 2019, 2). It means that today the infosphere is determined by:

- networked dynamics and the role of viral spread of information
- broad-based sensationalism in news and other media
- fragmentation of the infosphere
- concentration of information platforms
- the effect of self-reinforcing echo chambers
- the role of influencers
- the emergence of a 'trolling ethic' on the Internet
- the explosive growth of data collection on individuals and groups. (Mazarr et al. 2019, 19)

All of these characteristics influence how the information environment is perceived and could indicate the main future challenges (largely in the context of online propaganda, cyber attacks, and information warfare). In what follows, we will focus on examples of how state or non-state actors react to changes in the infosphere by controlling the information environment. However, the main challenges will be the new tools used in the current information environment. This approach is called hostile social manipulation, and it uses techniques like trolling or deepfake learning.

The Internet, its development, and its expansion is generally tied to freedom of speech (see Chapter 4) and the process of democratisation (Whitehead 2002; Grugel and Bishop 2013). Take, for example, the significant role it played in the events surrounding the Arab Spring (see Wolfsfeld et al. 2013; Khondker 2011). However, together with Internet development and information dissemination, the tendency towards information control has grown as well. Nondemocratic actors appear nervous due to the flow of information, which is almost impossible to stop given the ease of accessibility. They are afraid of an erosion in their political power and, therefore, search for methods of controlling the situation as much as possible—via censorship or manipulation. An example of these tendencies is the contemporary absence of visible political changes in authoritarian regimes, which indicates that Internet censorship helps these regimes consolidate (Tang and Huhe 2020, 143).

Such a situation is evident in China, where the Internet is censored, monopolised by the state, and filled with manipulative content (see Freedom House Report: China, 2018). Starting in 1997, when the Internet began to be widely used in China, the government passed laws and regulations providing control over ownership connected with all Internet services and media, Internet content, and all behaviour on the Internet (Lu and Zhao 2018, 3297; Thim 2017). Later, in 2014, a new Office of the Central Leading Group for Cyberspace Affairs (CAC), controlled by the General Secretary of the Communist Party of China, was established. This office controls the regulation of the Internet with its justification being cybersecurity (Lu and Zhao 2018, 3297). In 2016, China passed the so-called Cybersecurity Law, which strengthens the role of the state in cyberspace and emphasises security over freedom of speech (Qi et al. 2018).

Internet regulation in China is layered in three levels (King et al. 2013, 3). The first is the Great Firewall of China, meaning the specific information environment in which only some websites are allowed. In fact, it means most foreign websites are blocked. This censorship does not allow people to be in connection with people or media from outside of China. The second type is keyword blocking, which makes publishing a text (whether on websites or social media) impossible when a user writes banned words or phrases. The third level can be called 'hand censoring', and, unlike the previous two types, this one is employed after the publication of information. While the first two methods of censorship are automatic or technical, the latter is carried out by people; there are thousands of censors reading, marking, and prohibiting content on the Internet. A special type of hand censor is people focusing on content production. One of the known examples is the so-called 50 Cent Army of Chinese Internet trolls. They are paid by the government to write comments favouring the Chinese communist regime (Farrell 2016).

Despite its geographical distance, China's operation within the information environment can constitute a threat to the Euro-Atlantic space. Today, discussions about new, fifth-generation information infrastructure (5G) and its provision in Europe and the United States are occurring. The affair became prominent in 2019 when a Pentagon report dedicated to 5G infrastructure mentioned the security risk connected with the Chinese intelligence community (mainly the company Huawei). Based on this report, Huawei was placed on an entity list which prohibited American companies from selling their goods to them (without special government permission). The risks resulting from a 5G network were discussed by many governments in Europe as well—especially in the context of national security. Since Huawei is tied to the Chinese regime, there is concern about its approach to the information environment (see Chapter 7 for the example of the Czech Republic). The distrust originates mostly from the strong connection between the Chinese government (especially secret services) and technology providers such as Huawei or ZET. There is apprehension over China's potential use of the 5G network for influence operations. However, despite evident pressure, Huawei still cooperates and has signed contracts to supply 5G in many countries (Segev et al. 2019).

Besides China, Internet censorship and content adjustments also occur in Syria, India (Steen-Thornhammar 2012, 227–228), North Korea, Cuba (Cheng et al. 2010), and Russia. Cuba and North Korea use the mosquito-net model whereby the governments support the inflow of foreign investment (even in the IT business), but they block the inflow of foreign values, ideas, and culture (Cheng et al. 2010, 660). In North Korea, access to the Internet is limited and available only to elites (Cheng et al. 2010, 650).

The Russian approach is characterised instead by censorship and intimidation rather than limited access (Maréchal 2017, 31). However, Russia does have its liberal loopholes—the development of RuNet, the Russian-language community on the Internet, was from the beginning mainly about academic sharing and development (Bowles 2006). Nonetheless, it still attempts to widen its Internet environment surveillance. The new Russian information policy is notably connected with the start of the 2010s and the accumulation of power into Vladimir Putin's hands.

State-controlled communication providers have a significant role in Russia, which allows the state, through its secret services, to have easy access to Internet traffic (Freedom House Report: Russia, 2014). The legislature is also a powerful tool in Internet regulation (see legislative measure No. 428884-6, the so-called Bloggers Law; legislative measure No. 553424-6 about data storage; or a legislative measure No. 89417-6 2012 concerning children's protection against malicious Internet content). All these legal measures have attempted or enabled the state to better control Internet content, its regulation, and repression against dissent. Moreover, the laws are flexible in their application and can target a wide spectrum of subjects unfavourable to the regime.

The specificity of the emerging form of RuNet lies in its strong ties with the government and its relation to the Russian national identity. RuNet has been defined as 'a totality of information, communications, and activities which occur on the Internet, mostly in the Russian language, no matter where resources and users are physically located, and which are somehow linked to Russian culture and Russian cultural identity' (Gorny 2009 in Ristolainen 2017, 118). The idea of RuNet and the isolation of the Internet in the Russian context is connected with the idea of Russian sovereign space and challenges to the 'US dominated world' (Ristolainen 2017, 124). Tensions between Russia and the West (represented especially by NATO and the United States) started to deepen, with a peak during the Ukraine crisis and the 2016 US presidential election interference. On 12 May 2019, a bill was adopted which confirmed the control and isolation of the Russian language Internet space from the rest of the Internet as of 2020 (The Moscow Times 2019).

The Russian approach to Internet regulation and online propaganda can be described through the concept of hybrid warfare. Russia uses advantages in the information environment because the low price and simplicity make it available. Instead of regular warfare, it builds on irregularity to counterweigh possible asymmetry in confrontation.

Control over the information environment has multiple benefits for undemocratic regimes. First of all, there are the economic reasons. The

Internet and its development are crucial for the economic development of a country, which might be the main legitimating factor for authoritarian countries (Kalathil and Boas 2003, 144). However, for modern strategic communication, in order to control the minds and opinions of citizens and, therefore, support for the regime's fundamentals, it is important to control and censor the Internet. As examples from Russia and China show, it is easier to establish a sovereign information environment for all of these variables. Jiang (2010, 72–73) offers a theoretical explanation called 'authoritarian informationalism'. It is based on Internet development and regulatory model. Individual responsibilities are emphasised over individual rights; maximum economic benefit and minimal political risk for the one-party state are also stressed. Jiang explains the concept through the Chinese case. Authoritarian informationalism in China combines elements of capitalism, authoritarianism, and Confucianism (Jiang 2010, 82). Jiang further claims that authoritarian informationalism describes the future reality of its information environment because it is based not only on extending control but also on enhancing its legitimacy (mainly based on trust in government and economic success).

These characteristics pertaining especially to authoritarian countries have produced new threats for the democratic world as well as their own civilians. The authoritarian regimes tend to control their own information environment inside the country and, at the same time, interfere in the outside environment so as to reduce the power of information which might be endangering the regime and running against its interests. In the following sections, the latest technological tools and tactics of propaganda and manipulation will be approached. They are the tools used to control and manipulate the information environment. What looked like science fiction in the 1970s has become a reality today or will in a few years' time.

2.4 From Trolls to Bots

In 2015, there was an article called 'The Agency' published in the *New York Times* (Chen 2015). This occurrence could mark the moment interest began in the new wave of Internet propaganda, especially for the Western world. The article by Chen presented the wider public with the existence of the so-called Kremlin trolls and their organisation. 'The Agency', believed to be linked to Putin's administration, refers to one of the first publicly known 'troll farms' (*Financial Times* 2019). This one, located in St. Petersburg, Russia, was employing mostly young Russians who were uninterested in politics. As part of their job description, they were supposed to spread propaganda regarding the ongoing Russia–Ukrainian conflict without any personal interest.

This agency represents a new tool of propaganda strictly linked to the online world: *trolls*. With advantages for propagandists and disadvantages for receivers, trolls, sometimes referred to as hybrid trolls (Hannah 2018), are persons who aim to spread or destroy a particular narrative. Their primary role is to dominate the discussion on social media or in discussion forums; to overwhelm it with various contributions, often not even related to the topic of discussion; and to vulgarly offend opponents' opinions and discourage them from further discussion using these practices (for a larger explanation of the term and its role in cyberspace, see Nycyk 2017). In this case, trolls are acting as a force multiplier for driving home Russian messages (Giles 2016, 9). As leaked documents proved, paid trolls from St. Petersburg received worksheets every day with indications of the topics they should cover and discourse they should use.

The story of trolls from St. Petersburg is connected to an inconspicuous administrative building in the area of Olgino where mostly young people without any significant political stance work basically as copywriters. However, the content they were producing was strictly oriented to the framing of the ongoing political situation in Russia and Ukraine. This is in marked contrast to what would be seen three years later when trolls with the same background conducted sophisticated complex influence operations, including classical trolling, fake website making, local news outlet impersonation, cooperation with Russia's military service (StopFake 2019), and the production of micro-targeted campaigns.

Besides the Ukraine conflict, the troll's operations were spotted in the Baltics a few months later—according to research from the NATO StratCom Centre of Excellence, the activities of the St. Petersburg troll farm were evident in Latvia (Spruds et al. 2016). Finnish investigative journalist Jessikka Aro also revealed[2] Kremlin troll activities in Finland, which helped to publicise the issue; however, her investigation also resulted in massive cyberbullying directed towards her (Aro 2016; Rose 2019).

[2] Aro's case went even further. The most aggressive trolls/cyberbullies ended up in Finnish court, and three people were consequently sentenced (Staudenmaier 2018).

What might have seemed like regional information operations evolved into a supranational conflict and propaganda campaign. St. Petersburg's trolls became known by its official business name, the Internet Research Agency (IRA). The IRA was found to have interfered in the 2016 US presidential election (US Department of Justice 2019), but Howard et al. (2018) noticed that the targeting of US society by the IRA had begun much earlier. Engagement of IRA trolls was further proved in the 2016 Brexit referendum campaign (Bastos and Mercea 2018; Field and Wright 2018) as well as in the 2017 German general election and the debate which followed a mosque shooting in Canada (Al-Rawi and Jiwani 2019). The Kremlin trolls' interference in the US election demonstrated just how sophisticated this form of online propaganda could be, and how its operational abilities, scope, and intensity are growing (Inkster 2016; Badawy et al. 2019; Kreiss 2019).

The trolls had been covering a wide range of topics, mostly with the potential to divide public society. To illustrate, they massively covered topics connected to black American culture as well as veterans' issues and gun rights in the US election campaign. Targeted groups were sometimes contradictory, such as covering anti-refugee as well as pro-immigration reform content, yet they were deliberately selected with a focus on message receptivity (Yonder 2018; Howard et al. 2018). The case illustrates one of the main characteristics of these online information operations: the sowing of uncertainty, chaos, and the fragmentation and polarisation of society, as opposed to the propagation of a particular ideology.

As demonstrated above, the issue of trolls is closely tied to pro-Kremlin individuals and groups in European discussions, because these are the most active propaganda actors influencing the Euro-Atlantic region. However, we can identify many other organised groups of trolls all around the world, for example, the above-mentioned Chinese 50 Cent Army producing content for its own citizens to support the regime (see Farrell 2016). During the Brexit referendum, it was not only Russian trolls who interfered, Iranian trolls operating on Twitter took part as well (Field and Wright 2018). In 2018, Twitter and Facebook shut down hundreds of fake accounts of Iranian government origin. The trolls promoted Iranian political interests focusing on anti-Saudi, anti-Israeli, and pro-Palestinian themes as well as topics targeting US politics (Titcomb 2018). Trolling groups have even emerged in Europe. One example is the extreme-right group Reconquista Germanica, focusing on German politics and sympathising with the far-right party Alternative for Germany (Ebner 2018).

The emergence of troll campaigns was not expected, and, in the beginning, shared content could have been easily confused with real users blogging. Yet, while the phenomena of online troll activities have been recently unveiled, their tactics have already developed, and their sophistication is growing. The evolution of trolling has not been restricted to only geographic expansion and better targeting, its robotisation and automatisation is also taking place.

Automated propaganda or robotic propaganda is based on the activities of *bots*—programmes automatically producing content that should look like that of real users, interact with humans online, and produce manipulative content on social media, especially on Twitter, Facebook, and Instagram (see The Computational Propaganda Project 2016; Gorwa and Guilbeault 2018; Nimmo 2019). Originally, they were used as a supplementary tool for trolls, with bots spreading the content produced by trolls and genuine pro-government users.

Low costs, availability, and scaling through automatisation (Woolley and Howard 2016, 7) have shown that bots alone can help governments, political parties, or other interest groups to manipulate an audience's opinions. Naturally, the main difference between trolls and bots lies in bots' ability to coordinate tweeting about the same issue thousands upon thousands of times a day (see Gorwa and Guilbeault 2018, 10). In many examples, the programmers who deploy bots work as pure mercenaries. They are ideologically apolitical and motivated strictly by money (Woolley and Howard 2016, 10).

By using online bots, propaganda can produce the impression of a strong grassroots campaign and, therefore, attract new supporters or encourage higher activity among existing ones—a practice called astroturfing (see Zhang et al. 2013; Spruds et al. 2016; Kollanyi et al. 2016). Twitter represents an ideal platform for this strategy; a large amount of bots and real users were actively in favour of Donald Trump's and Hillary Clinton's Twitter campaigns (with hashtags '#MAGA' and '#ImWithHer') as well as the Brexit referendum. Through a high frequency of tweeting and coordinated activity, bots are able to shift and distort 'trending' topics, messages, and posts with hashtags. It is usual for bots to 'hijack' hashtags. Popular and trending hashtags are exploited with the intention of getting more visibility and attention even though the content shared by bots does not have to be connected to the topic of a hashtag anyhow (Woolley and Guilbeault 2017). Take, for example, the coordinated hijacking of Twitter hashtags during the 2017 Florida high school shooting. Trending hashtags like #NRA, #shooting, #Nikolas, #Florida, and #teacher were hijacked by political bots, mostly originating in Russia (Frenkel and Wakabayashi 2018).

Bots are also reusable. Sleeping botnets, a system of bots, can be inactive or focused on non-political spamming for sometime. When it is needed, they can be activated to spread political and manipulative content. Therefore, one group of bots can be used during multiple political campaigns by different actors with various ideologies (Neudert 2017). Besides that mentioned above, bots are deployed as part of various strategies to manipulate opinion. They can also maintain coordinated intimidation, participate in surveillance against citizens or regime opponents (Pavlíková and Mareš 2018), help block certain content through coordinated complaints to providers, or be used as a tool for search engine optimisation (SEO) (Zhdanova and Orlova 2019, 53–54).

Troll and bot activities spreading particular narratives should not all be perceived as strictly directed by governments. The specificity of contemporary online propaganda is its participatory character (see Wanless and Berk 2017); there is, besides attempts to manipulate audiences, the co-option of members from this audience to active engagement in propaganda too. Manipulation by trolls and bots is also used by political parties or individual politicians, particularly during election campaigns.

Bot activities can be massively enhanced by new technologies based on artificial intelligence (AI). The Atlantic Council defines this phenomenon as the integration of artificial intelligence into machine-driven communication tools for use in propaganda—MADCOM (Chessen 2017). MADCOM uses machine learning, deep learning, and chatbots. When machine learning is combined with big data, a very powerful propaganda tool emerges (Chessen 2017). Campaigns become highly personalised based on information about recipients' activities in virtual space and information shared in virtual space about family, friends, political preferences, demographic data, and hobbies and, therefore, precisely targeting people's individual characters and, what is more, precisely targeting vulnerabilities and detecting emotions in real time. These sophisticated technologies, when linked to private companies willing to be hired by governments, parties, or even individuals, may bring radical inputs into decision-making processes or voter behaviour.

2.5 Blurring the Lines Between Politics and Business

In the information society, boundaries between politics and business are being blurred. The line between public relations and propaganda has always been rather fuzzy and their development has been closely connected for at least a century (see Bernays 1928). In this chapter we will introduce how the strategies and technologies more recently developed by the business sector are now also used by political manipulators while, simultaneously, propaganda has become a profitable business. This can be considered a typical trait of an information society and economy, as detailed earlier in this chapter, in which information is the primary business commodity and source of power and political influence. In this sense, just as the information and information technologies became valuable for business, they also became valuable to political competition. At present, developed countries face a problematic lack of political programmes and political values, e.g. populism is on the rise. At the same time, traditional means of political competition (such as distinct values and ideologies) are today becoming increasingly supplemented (or even displaced in some cases, one might argue) by business-powered influence campaigns. Crucially, technological proliferation and the resultant data accumulation is enabling these efforts, both in terms of their large scale and also precise targeting.

The Internet Research Agency (IRA), originally a hybrid between a private subject and a state-controlled organisation, once again provides an example. At some point, it gradually shifted from the use of trolls to more precise information campaigns based on accurate group targeting, which has been more typical for business. As analysis of the US election interference shows, the IRA was thoughtfully focusing on segments of social media users based on race, ethnicity, and geographical division, and it ran multiple ad campaigns targeting different groups (Howard et al. 2019). Its strategy had two stages. The first was focused on the narratives of a specific group as a clickbait strategy to drive traffic to the IRA's pages. The second was to manipulate the audience by posting content to these pages (Howard et al. 2019, 18–19). The case of the IRA emphasises complexity and level of online manipulation threats which lie at the border between state propaganda and the business model, merging both and learning from each.

There is also a growing trend today of cyber troops being deployed primarily as a tool of mass (yet targeted) influence. The character of bots, their reusability and effectivity, has led to the formation of IT propaganda mercenaries. Woolley and Howard (2018, 10) mention programmers who deploy bots for hire and who are purely money-oriented, without any political affiliation. These can be equally deployed to influence potential customers as much as potential voters.

Besides cyber mercenaries, there are whole companies participating in online political manipulation (without connection to a government as it was with the IRA). An example from the Brexit campaign shows that big companies can be powerful in opinion-forming and can lead to huge political consequences. New technologies using micro-targeting, machine learning, deep learning, and big data—mostly from social media providers with weak user data security—are able to manipulate opinions to advance ideological viewpoints (Neudert 2017). Connections between campaigners for leaving the European Union and the companies Cambridge Analytica and Aggregate IQ doing 'psychological warfare' (Cadwalladr and Townsend 2018) formed the opinions of Britons during the Brexit referendum.

Cambridge Analytica promoted itself as a hi-tech consultant using data to micro-target population groups with precisely designed messages. However, according to accusations, the company harvested the data of 50 million Facebook users to set up the campaign (Cadwalladr and Graham-Harrison 2018). Christopher Wylie, a former employee and whistle-blower, later stated that the company 'exploited Facebook to harvest millions of people's profiles. And built models to exploit what [Cambridge Analytica] knew about them and target their inner demons' (ibid.). While political actors have been hiring private businesses for public relations for decades, these micro-targeting propaganda campaigns, which have proven especially effective at manipulating a targeted audience, have only been enabled by for-profit technologies deployed exclusively by business actors since they require some form of access to massive amounts of private customer and/or user data in order to operate.

Cambridge Analytica did not operate only in the United Kingdom but in many other countries during important elections, mostly in Africa or the United States (Solomon 2018). However, the example of the Brexit referendum campaign and its consequences emphasises the scope of the overlap between politics and business. Moreover, this internal form of propaganda took place in a democratic state. It emphasises that two cherished attributes of democracies—freedom of speech and economic freedom—can also make them more vulnerable.[3]

2.6 Deepfake as a Future Tool of Online Propaganda?

The Internet offers a platform to anonymously spread manipulative content which—through use of new dissemination technologies—is so easy that anybody is able to produce it. Depersonalised and anonymous accounts can enable and amplify their hostile messaging. What has always been challenging for manipulation was the credibility and trustworthiness of the information. Nevertheless, with new forms of manipulation techniques and new technologies, including artificial intelligence, this issue seems likely to be overcome very soon. In 2017, a new tool usable for propaganda was made available: the so-called 'deepfake' (see Parkin 2019). The reason why this new phenomenon came to be studied was the introduction of new deep learning technology. As one of its uses, this technology could alter and replace the faces of people in videos with believable results. Even more importantly, it is no longer an exclusive tool of IT engineers and enthusiasts, but a tool that is becoming available to the wider public.

The deepfake is a combination of two expressions: *deep learning* (a product of artificial intelligence) and *fake news* (false content, see Chapter 1). The term refers to false audiovisual content generated by artificial intelligence which is so credible that the average viewer is unable to recognise it as a product of artificial intelligence or falsified content (Chesney and Citron 2018a). Software using modern deep learning technology combs through a large amount of data (videos, images, or audio tracks), analyses them, and over time learns to recognise regularities, such as intonation, facial expressions, voice colour, or gestures. These AI systems have two elements: generator and discriminator. The basic function of the generator might be to create a new video—a fake video clip. Thereafter, the discriminator is asked to test if the video is real or fake. Based on the discriminator's evaluation, which identifies what the fake parts are, the generator learns what to avoid in the next

[3] Naturally, online internal state propaganda in nondemocratic regimes takes different forms. Botsman (in: Jiang and King-wa 2018) describes Beijing's propaganda as 'Big data meets Big brother' (plus Big profit).

video clip. When a generator produces an acceptable level of output, the videos are again 'fed' to the discriminator. The process is repeated so the generator gets better at creating videos and the discriminator gets better at analysing them. These two parts of the system are also called a generative adversarial network (GAN) (Yuzeun and Lyu 2018, 47; Robinson 2018, 18; What Is It 2019, n.d.; Giles et al. 2019).

While discussing deepfakes, many people might be familiar with the 'face swap', as an example, when the face of another person who does not initially appear in a video is added into the scene replacing someone else. It is a simpler method of creating this type of fake video, and it is widely used in pornographic content. However, what is possible by using deep learning technology and what is correctly indicated as a deepfake is the generation of custom content based on the analysis of accumulated data (as opposed to simply swapping two pieces of pre-existing content). This type is not only more sophisticated but also represents a greater security threat because, with sufficient data, it can realistically simulate any expression of any person (e.g. influential politicians).

The first huge scandal connected with deepfake technology was the distribution of pornographic videos with faces of celebrities like Gal Gadot or Emma Watson, who were not involved in the production (Chesney and Citron 2018b; What Is It 2019, n.d.). The fake or manipulated videos and photoshopped stills are there for decades and more are being produced all the time. With the expansion of social media, which provides perfect source material to train the algorithms, there are numerous examples of fake photos and fake videos which could affect the security and well-being of celebrities and citizens alike.

Among the most famous examples of a fake video (which started the public discussion about deepfake) is a 'phone call' between Barack Obama and Donald Trump. In 2016, NBC's *The Tonight Show* aired a scene featuring Jimmy Fallon dressed up as Donald Trump and on a phone call with Dion Flynn, who was dressed up as Barack Obama. This scene was remade in 2019 when a similar video was uploaded onto YouTube by a user called James. This time, however, the video was created through the deep machine learning model and viewers had the impression of watching the real faces of Donald Trump and Barack Obama. Their gestures and voices were almost indistinguishable from those of the real presidents (Parkin 2019). Along with the increasing quality of deepfake videos comes a growing concern that the abuse of such a tool will lead to attacks on politicians, which could be especially harmful during elections. Danger arises from the fact that today, there is no readily available software which could quickly and reliably detect these videos as fake (Schellmann 2017).

However, deepfake technologies are not just videos. Another use of the technology was demonstrated in the case of a fake Kate Jones LinkedIn profile photo. Jones' profile differed from 'ordinary' fakes in many ways—style, precision of the profile, but mainly in the use of deepfake technology. Instead of a copy of a photograph or a stolen photograph from a real person, Jones' fake profile used a unique photo, which was a computer-generated artefact made by machine learning algorithms. This made it more difficult for real LinkedIn users to recognise that the account was fake and many of them accepted the connection requests from Jones. Requests were accepted even by the US Defence Attaché to Moscow, a top-ranking US State Departmental official,[4] and other professionals (Giles et al. 2019, 4–5). The profile was detected as fake in June 2019, three months after its creation. The purpose of the fake profile as well as its creators remain unknown. This 'faked authenticity' is a cause for concern, as the erosion of standard and easily accessible methods for verifying accounts (such as reverse-searching the photos) makes distinguishing fake profiles from real ones more difficult.

Another tool connected with deepfake threats in 2019 was the application FaceApp. The app is based on AI algorithms that can swap faces in videos. FaceApp shows that using tools employing artificial intelligence can be so simple that anyone can do so using a smartphone. It does not need any sophisticated hardware systems or a team of specialists and experts. In addition to funny videos, the app can be used to produce fake videos (Dickson 2018). Another threat FaceApp presents lies in the data privacy field. In 2019, when celebrities posted their photos generated by this app on social media, starting the 'FaceApp challenge', the app became famous and widespread among dozens of millions of users. As it turned out later, the company responsible for the app came from Russia, and the app's privacy policy is unclear; users do not know if the company is collecting their data or selling it to third parties, or possibly harvesting their data to train even better deep learning algorithms for future deployment. Moreover, this type of application could be a tool for

[4] Authors of the research did not mention the names of officers.

the future politically oriented goals of some organisations (see Wondracz 2019; Libby 2019). With the company based in Russia and in the context of information warfare, the case is more relevant—a US investigation into the app and its data handling was started in July 2019 (Wondracz 2019).

Deepfake technology is also not focused exclusively on visual content. A necessary part of any (video) content is the sound as well, and it is even easier to manipulate audio than video. Two of the main projects dealing with deepfake technology in the audio environment include 'Project VoCo' created by Adobe, which is nicknamed 'Photoshop for Audio' (Wardle and Derakhshan 2017, 76), and the second is the widespread tool Lyrebird, which is focused on deep learning and neural networks and is used to synthesise the human voice (Dickson 2018). Lyrebird represents another example of an easy-to-use app; it needs just a one-minute recording to start imitating the voice of a person.

To conclude, based on the aforementioned research and the examples, there is a growing threat to many institutions, organisations, and other interests, as well as to society as a whole. What follows is an introduction to the main threats facing these groups separately, although it is important to state that each threat for one group is connected with the consequences facing another. From the view of government, deepfakes present multiple dangers. One is in military and national security: deepfake technology could generate false instructions and orders. From this perspective, deepfakes could be used as a form of disinformation supporting strategic, operational, and even tactical deception (Giles et al. 2019, 14; Chesney and Citron 2018b, 1783). At the same time, deepfake technology could support disinformation connected with the credibility of military services or intelligence agencies. Besides existing disinformation, which attempts to change real events (for example, Russia's information warfare), deepfake technologies could produce disinformation or authentic-looking news about an event which did not happen (or has yet not happened), for example, an attack against civilians in Iraq (Giles et al. 2019, 15; Chesney and Citron 2018b, 1783; Westerlund 2019, 40). All of these events could thus have consequences internationally—in international relations and diplomacy.

Moreover, deepfakes could also have an impact on democracy and trust in information spread by media and social media. For democracy, this manifests mainly in terms of elections (fake and manipulative political campaigns created by deepfake technology), the credibility of politicians (as was illustrated in the case of Obama), or the credibility of institutions (attacks against judges, policemen, etc.). Another threat to democracy is connected with credibility and trust in media. Deepfake technology causes challenges not only for citizens in recognising what is real and what is fake, but also for journalists (for example, which eyewitness videos are real) (Chesney and Citron 2018b, 1779; CNN 2019, n.d.; Westerlund 2019, 42). The distrust could be even more dangerous than the deepfake itself. This distrust in media, news, and information can be called an 'information apocalypse' or 'reality apathy' (Westerlund 2019, 43).

For companies, the main threats are connected with credibility and privacy, mainly as it concerns transparency and data privacy. There are also dangers that some deepfakes will initiate fatal decisions based on totally false information (fake news, fake voice mails, etc.) which seems to be real. The threat of credibility is mainly connected with reputation (of companies or their leaders), which could be very easily damaged by deepfake technology (for example, by some fake impropriety videos). Another threat is connected with the manipulation of the market or manipulation of the decision-making process. Deepfake technologies could produce records which could be used for blackmailing or which would cause panic on the market (for example, news about a bankruptcy, etc.) (Westerlund 2019, 43).

For individuals, the first possible implication is anyone could be the target of manipulation, abuse, blackmailing, and so forth; this risk is higher for people who are celebrities, politicians, and the like. The second implication is that all content produced by us could be used as input for the creation of a deepfake (Giles et al. 2019, 17). This point is then connected with privacy and data protection. In connection with individuals, we also could point out that deepfake technology could be easily used in the abuse of children by child predators (Westerlund 2019, 43) or cause a public panic.

It is impossible to mention all the possible threats deepfake technology poses as the list is unlimited, but it is a real threat to the entirety of society. It is obvious that everyone is potentially a target of deepfake products, and, based on this, there are many challenges for researchers, politicians, and other experts to face. One of the challenges will be in the legal context of data privacy, data protection, and so forth. Another will be for IT experts to find tools for the detection and recognition of deepfake content (see Fraga-Lamas and Fernández-Caramés 2019; Nelson et al. 2020). And, last but not least, is a challenge not only connected with deepfake recognition but also with other kinds of information manipulation: increasing the public's media literacy (Parkin 2019). However, it is important to note, that these threats stemming from deepfakes are not really novel. All the negative impacts on various institutions and parts of the society already exist and are posed by 'old' forms of faked content: primarily text and pictures. Deepfakes are simply expanding this to videos as well by making it so much easier to produce them. Just as it was possible to create doctored images long before using Photoshop and similar software, it was possible to create doctored videos before the advent of deepfakes. However, these technologies do make it massively easier, which leads to greater proliferation and production of such content. Whereas in previous decades manipulated videos were quite rare, in the coming decades they will probably become commonplace. The volume itself will become a problem. This prevalence will probably further erode public trust in information, making it easier for anyone seeking to destabilise and undermine society through the use of propaganda and information warfare.

2.7 Summary

The evolution of manipulative propaganda techniques goes hand in hand with technological development. With propaganda's 'going online', it uses voluntary as well as paid cyber troops, backed by the state and business, and primitive as well as sophisticated tools. Online propaganda manipulates people's behaviour in both nondemocratic and democratic countries. In nondemocratic regimes, the aim is to influence citizens and strengthen the regime. However, such countries can also have offensive aspirations against other state actors. As Russia's recent activities have shown, online propaganda and manipulation can be an important tool in power confrontation.

The current trends of modern online disinformation and propaganda activities were presented in this chapter from different perspectives. First was a focus on the information environment in the context of propaganda usage. New trends in nondemocracies, widened through the lens of the Russian example, were introduced. In Russia, the restriction of the Internet is still evolving. As mentioned, the newest example is RuNet, an isolated environment as of 2020 which manifests the 'digital sovereignty' of Russia. However, it does not mean that Russia or other 'isolated' countries will not influence and use propaganda tools upon others. Recent manipulative Russian activities in Europe and the United States have demonstrated how sinister a virtual offensive can be.

The second part of the chapter was dedicated to the newest technological tools of online disinformation and propaganda and their fast evolution. Examples of troll and bot behaviour demonstrated how these originally primitive actors were able to evolve and become an important part in complex influence operations. Not long after the revelations of Russian influence activities in Europe and the United States, a new strategy in propaganda and manipulation appeared. The affairs surrounding the company Cambridge Analytica presented what influence the combination of big data, deep learning, and micro-targeting can have on voter behaviour. Moreover, Cambridge Analytica was hired primarily by actors in democracies, not undemocratic regimes, and not as a result of a confrontation between state powers.

In the last part, a new, future tool which may influence coming propaganda campaigns was introduced. Deepfake technology is based on artificial intelligence, and it is very likely that proliferation of this technology could be extremely serious as it relates to the credibility of all audio and video recordings (Schellmann 2017). The most concerning is its wide availability combined with speed and ease of production, leading to a trust-eroding deluge of deepfake videos.

In summary, the changing online environment and new tools using artificial intelligence (MADCOMs), deep learning, big data, and micro-targeting might be the future of propaganda and disinformation dissemination. However, given the quickly changing environment and rapid technological development, it is frankly not easy to predict what comes next. At present, it might seem that disinformation tools and propaganda capabilities are developing faster than countermeasures (Schellmann 2017). There is need for better threat recognition on the state level (see Chapter 7) as well as legal and strategic adjustments. Better technical abilities and understanding of defending actors are also needed. Media as well as technology organisations have a huge part to play in combating propaganda as well. They need to cooperate with state actors and realise that they also have a civil responsibility even if they work for business. Finally, there is an important role for society itself and particularly academia (see Chapter 8). Academics should still educate themselves about new technological developments and their possible consequences on propaganda even if it might be uneasy for their field of study. Their findings should be heard and discussed, especially by authorities who have the power to take decisive steps.

Bibliography

Al-Rawi, A., & Jiwani, Y. (2019). Russian Twitter Trolls Stoke Anti-Immigrant Lies Ahead of Canadian Election. *Public Radio International*. https://www.pri.org/stories/2019-07-26/russian-twitter-trolls-stoke-anti-immigrant-lies-ahead-canadian-election. Accessed 20 Mar 2020.

Aro, J. (2016). The Cyberspace War: Propaganda and Trolling as Warfare Tools. *European View, 15*(1), 121–132. https://doi.org/10.1007/s12290-016-0395-5.

Atik, H. (1999). *The Characteristics of the Information Economy*. Erciyes University Faculty of Economics and Administrative Sciences, Department of Economics.

Badawy, A., Addawood, A., Lerman, K., & Ferrera, E. (2019). Characterizing the 2016 Russian IRA Influence campaign. *Social Network Analysis and Mining, 31*(9). https://doi.org/10.1007/s13278-019-0578-6.

Bastos, M. T., & Mercea, D. (2018). The Public Accountability of Social Platforms: Lessons from a Study on Bots and Trolls in the Brexit Campaign. *Philosophical Transactions of the Royal Society A: Mathematical, Physical and Engineering Sciences, 376*. https://doi.org/10.1098/rsta.2018.0003.

Bernays, E. (1928). *Propaganda*. New York: H. Liveright.

Bowles, A. (2006). The Changing Face of the RuNet. In H. Schmidt, K. Teubener, & N. Konradova (Eds.), *Control + Shift: Public and Private Usages of the Russian Internet* (pp. 21–33). Norderstedt: Books on Demand.

Brikše, I. (2006). *The Information Environment: Theoretical Approaches and Explanations*. https://www.szf.lu.lv/fileadmin/user_upload/szf_faili/Petniecciba/sppi/mediji/inta-brikse_anglu.pdf. Accessed 26 Oct 2020.

Cadwalladr, C., & Graham-Harrison, E. (2018, March 17). Revealed: 50 Million Facebook Profiles Harvested for Cambridge Analytica in Major Data Breach. *The Guardian*. https://www.theguardian.com/news/2018/mar/17/cambridge-analytica-facebook-influence-us-election?CMP=share_btn_tw. Accessed 20 Mar 2020.

Cadwalladr, C., & Townsend, M. (2018, March 24). Revealed: The Ties That Bound Vote Leave's Data Firm to Controversial Cambridge Analytica. *The Guardian*. https://www.theguardian.com/uk-news/2018/mar/24/aggregateiq-data-firm-link-raises-leave-group-questions. Accessed 20 Mar 2020.

Capurro, R., & Hjørland, B. (2005). The Concept of Information. *Annual Review of Information Science and Technology, 37*(1), 343–411. https://doi.org/10.1002/aris.1440370109.

Chen, A. (2015, June 7). The Agency. *The New York Times*. https://www.nytimes.com/2015/06/07/magazine/the-agency.html. Accessed 20 Mar 2020.

Cheng, C., Kyungmin, K., & Ji-Yong, L. (2010). North Korea's Internet Strategy and Its Political Implications. *The Pacific Review, 23*(5), 649–670. https://doi.org/10.1080/09512748.2010.522249.

Chesney, R., & Citron, D. K. (2018a). Deepfakes and the New Disinformation War: The Coming Age of Post-Truth Geopolitics. *Foreign Affairs, 97*(6), 147–155.

Chesney, R., & Citron, D. K. (2018b). Deep Fakes: A Looming Challenge for Privacy, Democracy, and National Security. *LAWFARE blog*.

Chessen, M. (2017). *The MADCOM Future: How Artificial Intelligence Will Enhance Computational Propaganda, Reprogram Human Culture and Threaten Democracy and What Can Be Done About It*. Washington: Atlantic Council.

CNN. (2019). Deepfake Videos: Inside the Pentagon's Race Against Deepfake Videos. *Cable News Network*. https://edition.cnn.com/interactive/2019/01/business/pentagons-race-against-deepfakes/. Accessed 20 Mar 2020.

Dickson, B. (2018, July). When Ai Blurs: The Line Between Reality and Fiction. *PC Magazine*, pp. 114–125.

Ebner, J. (2018, March 6). Forscherin schleust sich bei Hasskommentatoren ein - und erlebt Erschreckendes. *Online Focus*. https://www.focus.de/politik/experten/gastbeitrag-von-julia-ebner-hass-auf-knopfdruck-wenn-die-verbreitung-von-hass-computerspiel-charakter-bekommt_id_8554382.html. Accessed 19 Mar 2020.

Farrell, H. (2016, May 19). The Chinese Government Fakes Nearly 450 Million Social Media Comments a Year: This Is Why. *The Washington Post*. https://www.washingtonpost.com/news/monkey-cage/wp/2016/05/19/the-chinese-government-fakes-nearly-450-million-social-media-comments-a-year-this-is-why/. Accessed 19 Mar 2020.

Field, M., & Wright, M. (2018, October 17). Russian Trolls Sent Thousands of Pro-Leave Messages on Day of Brexit Referendum, Twitter Data Reveals. *The Telegraph*. https://www.telegraph.co.uk/technology/2018/10/17/russian-iranian-twitter-trolls-sent-10-million-tweets-fake-news/. Accessed 19 Mar 2020.

Financial Times. (2019, September 30). US Treasury Hits 'Putin's Chef' with New Sanctions.

Fraga-Lamas, P., & Fernández-Caramés, T. M. (2019). *Fake News, Disinformation, and Deepfakes: Leveraging Distributed Ledger Technologies and Blockchain to Combat Digital Deception and Counterfeit Reality* (Working Paper). Cornell University. https://arxiv.org/abs/1904.05386.

Freedom House. (2014). *Freedom on the Net: Russia*. https://freedomhouse.org/report/freedom-net/2014/russia. Accessed 20 Mar 2020.

Freedom House. (2018). *Freedom on the Net: China*. https://freedomhouse.org/report/freedom-net/2018/china. Accessed 20 Mar 2020.

Frenkel, S., & Wakabayashi, D. (2018, February 2). After Florida School Shooting, Russian 'Bot' Army Pounced. *New York Times*. https://www.nytimes.com/2018/02/19/technology/russian-bots-school-shooting.html. Accessed 20 Mar 2020.

Giles, K. (2016). *The Next Phase of Russian Information Warfare*. Riga: NATO Stratcom CoE.

Giles, K., Hartmann, K., & Mustaffa, M. (2019). *The Role of Deepfakes in Malign Influence Campaigns*. Riga: NATO Stratcom CoE. https://www.stratcomcoe.org/role-deepfakes-malign-influence-campaigns?fbclid=IwAR25Hbld-nb7nOaVmoW8AAnMLkiPxh8HoRRpjluIBhNWckD0yNZ8AJA1Sxg. Accessed 19 Mar 2020.

Godin, B. (2008). The Information Economy: The History of a Concept Through Its Measurement, 1949–2005. *History and Technology, 24*(3), 255–287. https://doi.org/10.1080/07341510801900334.

Gorwa, R., & Guilbeault, D. (2018). Unpacking the Social Media Bot: A Typology to Guide Research and Policy. *Policy & Internet*. https://doi.org/10.1002/poi3.184.

Grugel, J., & Bishop, M. L. (2013). *Democratization: A Critical Introduction*. London: Palgrave Macmillan.

Hannah, J. (2018). Trolling Ourselves to Death? Social Media and Post-Truth Politics! *European Journal of Communication, 33*(2), 214–226. https://doi.org/10.1177/0267323118760323.

Howard, P. N., Ganesh, B., Liotsiou, D., & Kelly, J. (2018). *The IRA and Political Polarization in the United States, 2012–2018*. University of Oxford: Computational Propaganda Research Project. https://comprop.oii.ox.ac.uk/wp-content/uploads/sites/93/2018/12/The-IRA-Social-Media-and-Political-Polarization.pdf. Accessed 19 Mar 2020.

Howard, P. N., Ganesh, B., & Liotsiou, D. (2019). *The IRA, Social Media and Political Polarization in the United States, 2012–2018*. University of Oxford: Computational Propaganda Research Project. https://comprop.oii.ox.ac.uk/wp-content/uploads/sites/93/2018/12/The-IRA-Social-Media-and-Political-Polarization.pdf. Accessed 19 Mar 2020.

Inkster, N. (2016). Information Warfare and the US Presidential Election. *Survival, 58*(5), 23–32. https://doi.org/10.1080/00396338.2016.1231527.

Jiang, M. (2010). Authoritarian Informationalism: "China's Approach to Internet Sovereignty". *SAIS Review, 30*(2), 71–89. https://doi.org/10.1353/sais.2010.0006.

Jiang, M., & King-wa, F. (2018). Chinese Social Media and Big Data: Big Data, Big Brother, Big Profit? *Policy and Internet, 10*(4), 372–392. https://doi.org/10.1002/poi3.187.

Kalathil, S., & Boas T. C. (2003). *Open Networks, Closed Regimes: The Impact of the Internet on Authoritarian Rule*. Carnegie Endowment for International Peace, Washington, DC.

Khondker, H. H. (2011). Role of the New Media in the Arab Spring. *Globalization, 8*(5), 675–679. https://doi.org/10.1080/14747731.2011.621287.

King, G., Pan, J., & Roberts, M. E. (2013). How Censorship in China Allows Government Criticism but Silences Collective Expression. *American Political Science Review, 107*(2), 1–18. http://j.mp/2nxNUhk. Accessed 20 Mar 2020.

Kollanyi, B., Howard, P. N., & Woolley, S. C. (2016). *Bots and Automation over Twitter During the U.S. Election: Data Memo.* University of Oxford: Computational Propaganda Research Project.

Kreiss, D. (2019). From Epistemic to Identity Crisis: Perspectives on the 2016 U.S. Presidential Election. *The International Journal of Press/Politics, 24*(3), 383–388. https://doi.org/10.1177/1940161219843256.

Libby, K. (2019, July 17). Giving Your FaceApp Selfie to Russians Is Really Bad Idea. *Popular Mechanics*. https://www.popularmechanics.com/technology/security/a28424868/faceapp-challenge-security-risks/. Accessed 20 Mar 2020.

Lorents, P., & Ottis, R. (2010). Cyberspace: Definition and Implications. In *Proceedings of the 5th International Conference on Information Warfare and Security* (pp. 267–270). Reading: Academic Publishing Limited.

Lu, J., & Zhao, Y. (2018). Implicit and Explicit Control: Modeling the Effect of Internet Censorship on Political Protest in China. *International Journal of Communication, 12,* 3294.

Maréchal, N. (2017). Networked Authoritarianism and the Geopolitics of Information: Understanding Russian Internet Policy. *Media and Communication, 5*(1), 29–41. http://dx.doi.org/10.17645/mac.v5i1.808.

Martens, B. (2015). An Illustrated Introduction to the Infosphere. *Library Trends, 63*(3), 317–361.

Mazarr, M. J., Bauer, R. M., Casey, A., Heintz, S., & Matthews, L. J. (2019). *The Emerging Risk of Virtual Societal Warfare: Social Manipulation in a Changing Information Environment* (p. 2019). Santa Monica, CA: RAND Corporation.

Nelson, S. D., Simek, J. W., & Maschke, M. (2020). Detecting Deepfakes. *Law Practice: The Business of Practicing Law, 46*(1), 42–47.

Neudert, L.-M. N. (2017). *Computational Propaganda in Germany: A Cautionary Tale* (Working Paper No. 2017.7). University of Oxford: Computational Propaganda Research Project. http://blogs.oii.ox.ac.uk/wp-content/uploads/sites/89/2017/06/Comprop-Germany.pdf. Accessed 7 November 2019.

Nimmo, B. (2019). *Measuring Traffic Manipulation on Twitter*. University of Oxford: Computational Propaganda Research Project. https://comprop.oii.ox.ac.uk/research/working-papers/twitter-traffic-manipulation/. Accessed 7 Nov 2019.

Nycyk, M. (2017). *Trolls and Trolling: An Exploration of Those That Live Under the Internet Bridge*. Australia: Brisbane.

OED Online. (2020, October 21). "information, n.". Oxford University Press. https://www.oed.com/viewdictionaryentry/Entry/95568.

Parkin, S. (2019, June 22). The Rise of the Deepfake and the Threat to Democracy. *The Guardian*. https://www.theguardian.com/technology/ng-interactive/2019/jun/22/the-rise-of-the-deepfake-and-the-threat-to-democracy. Accessed 7 Nov 2019.

Pavlíková, M., & Mareš, M. (2018). Techniky robotické propagandy na sociální síti Twitter [Techniques of Robotic Propaganda on Twitter Network]. *Právo a Technologie, 9*(18), 3–28. https://doi.org/10.5817/RPT2018-2-1.

Porche, I. R., Paul, Ch., York, M., Serena, Ch. C., Sollinger, J. M., Axelband, E., et al. (2013). The Information Environment and Information Warfare. In *Redefining Information Warfare Boundaries for an Army in a Wireless World* (pp. 11–18). RAND Corporation.

Qi, A., Guosong, S., & Zheng, W. (2018). Assessing China's Cybersecurity Law. *Computer Law & Security Review, 34*(6), 1342–1354. https://doi.org/10.1016/j.clsr.2018.08.007.

Ristolainen, M. (2017). Should 'RuNet 2020' Be Taken Seriously? Contradictory Views About Cyber Security Between Russia and the West. *Journal of Information Warfare, 16*(4), 113–131. https://www.jstor.org/stable/26504121.

Robinson, O. (2018). *Malicious Use of Social Media: Case Studies from BBC Monitoring*. Riga: NATO Stratcom CoE. https://www.stratcomcoe.org/malicious-use-social-media-case-studies-bbc-monitoring. Accessed 7 Nov 2019.

Rose, H. (2019, May 29). Jessikka Aro, the Journalist Who Took on Russian Trolls. *The Sunday Times*. https://www.thetimes.co.uk/article/jessikka-aro-the-journalist-who-took-on-russian-trolls-fv0z5zgsg. Accessed 7 Nov 2019.

Schellmann, H. (2017, December 5). The Dangerous New Technology That Will Make Us Question Our Basic Idea of Reality. *Quartz*. https://qz.com/1145657/the-dangerous-new-technology-that-will-make-us-question-our-basic-idea-of-reality/. Accessed 9 Nov 2019.

Secureworks. (2017). Cyber Threat Basics, Types of Threats, Intelligence & Best Practices. https://www.secureworks.com/blog/cyber-threat-basics. Accessed 18 Feb 2020.

Segev, H., Doron, E., & Orion, A. (2019). *My Way or the Huawei? The United States-China Race for 5G Dominance*. The Institute for National Security Studies, Tel Aviv University. INSS Insight, no. 1193. https://www.inss.org.il/publication/my-way-or-the-huawei-the-united-states-china-race-for-5g-dominance/?offset=2&posts=2219&fbclid=IwAR1VgdtXd2msdotNHsOaCm_lkvyz_XFp4nDM0w0gjapp1DMIPdcVfQamTwE. Accessed 10 Jan 2020.

Solomon, S. (2018, March 22). Cambridge Analytica Played Roles in Multiple African Elections. *Voa*. https://www.voanews.com/africa/cambridge-analytica-played-roles-multiple-african-elections. Accessed 8 Nov 2019.

Spruds, A., Rožulkalne, A., & Sedlenieks, K. (2016). *Internet Trolling as a Hybrid Warfare Tool: The Case of Latvia*. Riga: NATO CoE.

Staudenmaier, R. (2018, October 18). Court in Finland Finds Pro-Kremlin Trolls Guilty of Harassing Journalist. *Deutsche Welle*. https://www.dw.com/en/court-in-finland-finds-pro-kremlin-trolls-guilty-of-harassing-journalist/a-45944893-0. Accessed 8 Nov 2019.

Steen-Thornhammar, H. (2012). Combating Censorship Should Be a Foreign Policy Goal. In J. Perry & S. S. Costigan (Eds.), *Cyberspaces and Global Affairs*. Burlington, VT: Routledge.

StopFake. (2019, June 9). Figures of the Week. https://www.shorturl.at/eNT04. Accessed 9 Nov 2019.

Tang, M., & Huhe, N. (2020). Parsing the Effect of the Internet on Regime Support in China. *Government and Opposition, 55*(20), 130–146. https://doi.org/10.1017/gov.2017.39.

The Computational Propaganda Project. (2016). *Resource for Understanding Political Bots*. http://comprop.oii.ox.ac.uk/research/public-scholarship/resource-for-understanding-political-bots/. Accessed 10 Nov 2019.

The Moscow Times. (2019, May 1). *Putin Signs Internet Isolation Bill into Law*. https://www.themoscowtimes.com/2019/05/01/putin-signs-internet-isolation-bill-into-law-a65461. Accessed 7 Nov 2019.

The State Duma. (2012). Legislative Measure No. 89417-6 2012, On Children's Protection Against Malicious Internet Content.

The State Duma. (2014a). Legislative Measure No. 428884-6, The Bloggers Law.

The State Duma. (2014b). Legislative Measure No. 553424-6, About Data Storage and Telecommunication Providers.

Thim, M. (2017). *Čínský internet pod rostoucí kontrolou* [The Chinese Internet Under Increasing Control]. Praha: AMO.

Titcomb, J. (2018, August 22). Facebook and Twitter Delete Hundreds of Fake Accounts Linked to Iran and Russia. *The Telegraph*. https://www.telegraph.co.uk/technology/2018/08/22/facebook-twitter-delete-hundreds-fake-accounts-linked-iran-russia/. Accessed 10 Nov 2019.

Toffler, A., & Toffler, H. (1981). *The Third Wave*. New York: Bantam Books.

U.S. Department of Justice. (2019). *Report on the Investigation into Russian Interference in the 2016 Presidential Election*. https://www.justice.gov/storage/report.pdf. Accessed 8 Nov 2019.

U.S. Joint Chiefs of Staff. (2006, December). *The National Military Strategy for Cyberspace Operations*. Washington, DC.

Wanless, A., & Berk, M. (2017). Participatory Propaganda: The Engagement of Audiences in the Spread of Persuasive Communications. In *Proceedings of the Social Media and Social Order, Culture Conflict 2.0 Conference.*

Wardle, C., & Derakhshan, H. (2017). *Information Disorder: Toward an Interdisciplinary Framework for Research and Policy Making.* Council of Europe. https://rm.coe.int/information-disorder-toward-an-interdisciplinary-framework-for-researc/168076277c. Accessed 6 Nov 2019.

Webster, F. (2006). *Theories of the Information Society.* Cambridge: Routledge.

Westerlund, M. (2019). The Emergence of Deepfake Technology: A Review. *Technology Innovation Management Review, 9*(11), 39–52.

What Is It. (2019). *Deepfake (Deep Fake AI).* https://whatis.techtarget.com/definition/deepfake. Accessed 6 Nov 2019.

Whitehead, L. (2002). *Democratization: Theory and Experience.* Oxford: Oxford University Press.

Wolfsfeld, G., Elad, S., & Sheafer, T. (2013). Social Media and the Arab Spring: Politics Comes First. *The International Journal of Press/Politics, 18*(2), 115–137. https://doi.org/10.1177/1940161212471716.

Wondracz, A. (2019, August 6). Experts Warn to Stay Away from Data-Hoarding FaceApp—as 'Self-Absorbed' Selfies Could Lead to Devastating Privacy Breaches. *Daily Mail.* https://www.dailymail.co.uk/news/article-7324955/FaceApp-warning-experts-raise-concerns-privacy.html. Accessed 6 Nov 2019.

Woolley, S. C., & Guilbeault, D. (2017). *Computational Propaganda in the United States of America: Manufacturing Consensus Online* (Working Paper No. 2017.5). University of Oxford: Computational Propaganda Research Project.

Woolley, S. C., & Howard, P. N. (2016). Automation, Algorithms, and Politics| Political Communication, Computational Propaganda, and Autonomous Agents—Introduction. *International Journal of Communication, [S.l.], 10,* 9. ISSN 1932-8036.

Woolley, S. C., & Howard, P. N. (2018). *Computational Propaganda: Political Parties, Politicians, and Political Manipulation on Social Media.* Oxford, UK: Oxford University Press.

Yonder. (2018). *The Disinformation Report.* https://www.yonder.co/articles/the-disinformation-report/. Accessed 6 Nov 2019.

Yuzeun, L., & Lyu, S. (2018). *Exposing DeepFake Videos by Detecting Face Warping Artifacts.* Computer Vision Foundation. http://openaccess.thecvf.com/content_CVPRW_2019/papers/Media%20Forensics/Li_Exposing_DeepFake_Videos_By_Detecting_Face_Warping_Artifacts_CVPRW_2019_paper.p. Accessed 6 Nov 2019.

Zhang, Y. C. (2017 [2016]) The Information Economy. In J. Johnson, A. Nowak, P. Ormerod, B. Rosewell, Y. C. Zhang. Non-Equilibrium Social Science and Policy. Understanding Complex Systems. Springer, Cham. https://doi.org/10.1007/978-3-319-42424-8_10.

Zhang, J., Carpenter, D., & Ko, M. (2013). Online Astroturfing: A Theoretical Perspective: Completed Research Paper. In *Conference: 19th Americas Conference on Information Systems, AMCIS 2013—Hyperconnected World: Anything, Anywhere, Anytime.*

Zhdanova, M., & Orlova, D. (2019). Ukraine: External Threats and Internal Challenged. In S. Woolley & P. N. Howard (Eds.), *Computational Propaganda: Political Parties, Politicians, Political Manipulation and Social Media.* Oxford: Oxford University Press.

CHAPTER 3

Propaganda and Disinformation as a Security Threat

Miroslav Mareš and Petra Mlejnková

3.1 Introduction

The present-day attention being paid to disinformation campaigns is a sensitive matter for politicians, decision-makers, and the media in many countries, particularly in Western liberal democracies. It has also caused huge interest among academics and security experts. Specific political forms of disinformation have a strong impact on societies in the digital age. Some authors, when speaking of the most recent developments, even use the term ***post-digital era***, which refers 'to a state in which the disruption brought upon by digital information technology has already occurred' (Albrecht et al. 2019, 11).

M. Mareš · P. Mlejnková (✉)
Department of Political Science, Masaryk University, Brno, Czechia
e-mail: mlejnkova@fss.muni.cz

M. Mareš
e-mail: mmares@fss.muni.cz

M. Gregor and P. Mlejnková (eds.), *Challenging Online Propaganda and Disinformation in the 21st Century*, Political Campaigning and Communication,
https://doi.org/10.1007/978-3-030-58624-9_3

Modern propaganda and disinformation campaigns continue in line with the deep historical traditions and legacies of subversive propaganda. This new dimension of subversive propaganda is characterised by the use of disinformation in cyberspace with the goal of undermining societal cohesion while valuing consistency and the loyalty of citizens in order to legitimate political representation. Various actors have recently labelled this phenomenon a security threat, including international security organisations in the Euro-Atlantic area. However, it is very difficult to create efficient countermeasures. A tension between freedom of speech and limits on false and/or hateful messages is growing. New internal norms of internet providers, laws against disinformation and fake news, or institutional adaptation of security architecture to the new propaganda environment are being broadly discussed.

The aim of this chapter is to describe and explain how the spread of propaganda and disinformation constitutes a security threat. After a short historical contextualisation, we analyse the impact of this threat from various security dimensions. Then we categorise ‘rogue’ governmental and non-governmental actors who are responsible for the mass dissemination of disinformation in the contemporary world, including their strategies and tactics. These actors can be successful only in a situation where the adversary is vulnerable. Due to this fact, we also outline the vulnerability of contemporary societies and their information systems in the context of the described threats. Finally, we briefly deal with defence and protection against this new propaganda and disinformation threat dimension on a national as well as international level.

3.2 Propaganda and Disinformation from the Point of View of Security Analysis

Propaganda and disinformation have long historical traditions with roots in the ancient era. They were and are widespread in various interconnected security dimensions. Traditionally, they were connected with various military conflicts and regime security (within the context of homeland security, including the pre-Westphalian era). In modern times, they have also served ‘political warfare’, in the sense of overthrowing an adversary without direct use of military or domestic forces. They can be aimed at the broad population with the goal of destroying moral and the loyalty of the citizenry, which can accept the interests of an adversary. Within these realistic contexts are specific disinformation and propaganda 'weapons' of one side of the conflict and, at the same time, the perceived threat of the conflict's other side, which causes defensive and offensive countermeasures. Propaganda and counter-propaganda, the spread of disinformation, and defence against them are two sides of the same coin.

In his short analysis of the use of propaganda in conflicts, Haroro J. Ingram, described the use of propaganda from the ancient Mesopotamian empires to the twenty-first century's War on Terror (he deals intensively also with propaganda in the First World War, the Second World War and the Cold War). Ingram summarised his findings with the following words: 'The historical evolution of propaganda during conflict has been driven by the interplay of three persistent factors: (1) advancements in communication technologies, (2) developments in military technologies and strategies, and (3) the changing relationship between the political elite and the people' (Ingram 2016, 34).

The military dimension of disinformation and propaganda has throughout history accompanied propaganda and disinformation campaigns organised by the governmental forces of various regimes for the purposes of their own homeland security. These campaigns have been aimed mostly against domestic ideological, religious, or ethno-national opponents and their foreign supporters. However, many persuasive activities with propagandistic elements were and are focused on other internal threats, such as corruption, organised crime, health threats, and the prevention of disasters. Conversely, subversive political forces have also used propaganda and disinformation with the goal of undermining a ruling regime, for instance, the well-known terrorist concept of 'propaganda by deed' (Campion 2015), or the many resistance movements and revolutionary forces which have had their own propaganda divisions (Shultz 1989).

From the perspective of security, the military and regime dimensions were dominant until the end of the twentieth century. As mentioned above, however, recently we have been able to see the intervention of disinformation and propaganda in all security sectors defined by the Copenhagen School—military, political, economic, societal, and environmental sectors (Buzan et al. 1998). This approach works within these five security sectors, but also in a more specific analytical framework, with a specific focus on information security.

In some contemporary conceptual models, the information dimension is incorporated as an equal part along with other categories. The political, military, economic, social, informational, and infrastructure (PMESII) model is the most important representation of this approach. It was developed in 2000 by US military experts during a war game (McFate et al. 2012, 94) and, in the current era, it is used for—among other things—the analysis of hybrid warfare. From this model, the military, political, economic, civilian, and informational (MPECI) model was derived (Cullen and Reichborn-Kjennerud 2017, 4). The information dimension is, of course, very closely interconnected with other dimensions (and it is itself broader than 'only' disinformation and propaganda).

If we return to the traditional military and homeland security dimensions, we can work primarily with the security concepts of propaganda, deception, and destructive false flag operations in which disinformation is located where they overlap (Fig. 3.1).

Propaganda is a broader category than disinformation (see Chapter 1). It can be based on true information, on the spread of positive messages about real success, or the threat of real weapons or atrocities with the aim

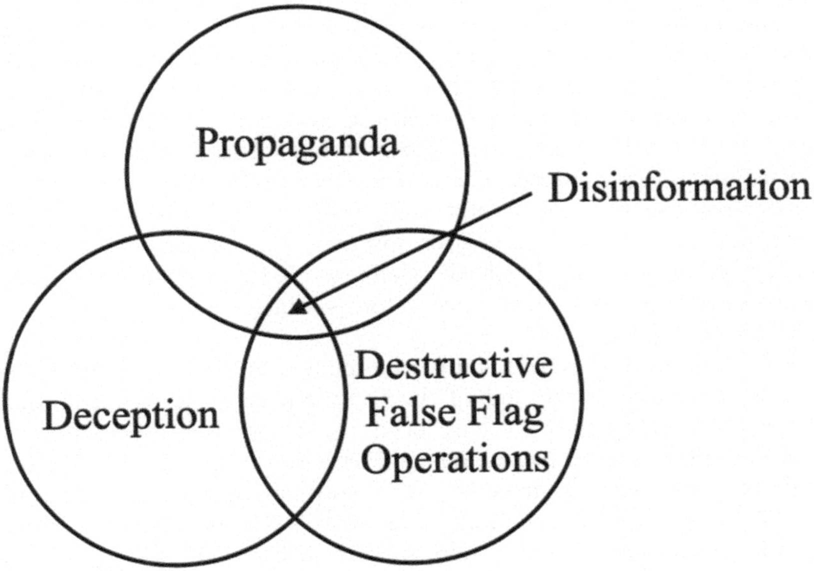

Fig. 3.1 Disinformation within the context of propaganda, deception, and destructive false flag operations (*Source* Authors)

of influencing a targeted population. Disinformation should, in the propagandistic context, serve the spread of false or incomplete and misleading news and information with the goal of weakening cohesion and the resolve of an adversary so as to provide efficient policy while this policy contrasts with the interests of the actor spreading the disinformation. Disinformation can also cause decisions to be made in error due to the poor assessment of a situation.

This last context is also included in the concept of deception aimed towards an adversary. Deception is also a broader category which, according to Gerwehr and Glenn, includes the subcategories (1) camouflage/concealment and demonstration/feint/diversion, (2) display/decoy/dummy, (3) mimicry/spoofing, (4) dazzling/sensory saturation, (5) disinformation/ruse, and (6) conditioning/exploit (Gerwehr and Glenn 2000, 30–31). Disinformation is also an inherent part of false flag operations, defined as a 'diversionary or propaganda tactic of deceiving an adversary into thinking that an operation was carried out by another party' (Pihelgas 2015, 6).

If we look to destructive false flag operations, disinformation is their crucial element; however, they are also a broader category, which also includes the preparation and execution of the operation itself (with military forces, special secret police units, terrorist commandos, hacker-groups, etc.). Disinformation can be spread only among the limited number of involved actors or the broader public. Both variants can be demonstrated in cases from the 'pre-internet' era. The Kámen Action (referring to 'stone' in the Czech language) can be used as an example of the first category. At the turn of the 1940s/1950s, the Czechoslovak communist secret police, State Security (StB; Státní bezpečnost), created false checkpoints and US forces facilities, including staff dressed in US uniforms or playing American secret service agents, close to the German border. People escaping with the help of controlled human smuggling networks from communist Czechoslovakia across the 'Iron Curtain' to Western Germany were transported to this false border. During the interrogations, the communist police received important data about domestic resistance (Jandečková 2018). The operation was top secret and disinformation about the false building and staff was aimed only at the victims of this operation. A representative case of the second category (with an impact on the broader public) is the commando attack of the German Security Service (SD; Sicherheitsdienst) led by Alfred Naujocks in Gleiwitz (at that time in Germany, now in Poland) on 31 August 1939.

Members of the commando captured a radio station and, under the false flag of Polish nationalists, they broadcasted an anti-German proclamation. This incident served as one of the excuses for Hitler's invasion of Poland on 1 September 1939 (Runzheimer 1962). The false message was spread across the radio waves, and information about this incident was misused by German propaganda. In the internet era, cyberattacks under a false flag aimed at specific persons (among others reasons, for the purposes of blackmail) are representative of the first category, and mass attacks on websites in a foreign country, led in fact by government military experts pretending to be non-governmental hacktivists and the like, are representatives of the second category (Pihelgas and Tammekänd 2015).

Deception and propaganda are, in the abovementioned sense, also part of ***information operations*** and ***psychological operations*** (psyops). These terms are used with more or less overlapping meanings (Cowan and Cook 2018) and were discussed in Chapter 1 of this volume. Some authors also work with the concept of ***political warfare*** (Lord and Barnett 1989, xi). Recently, ***hybrid war*** (or warfare) has been a 'buzzword' referring to the security-related impact of disinformation.

In various historical eras, specialised governmental bodies or parts of non-governmental organisations and movements (including resistance organisations) were established with propagandistic tasks, with some even specialising in disinformation campaigns. The (in)famous example is the creation of the Disinformation Office (Dezinformbyuro) in the Main Intelligence Directorate (GRU; Glavnoye razvedyvatelnoye upravleniye) of the Soviet Union in 1923. The first of its important operations was aimed to discredit the Russian priest Kirill Vladimirovitch among Russian emigrants in Germany (Zhirnov 2003).

International cooperation in the spread of disinformation is also possible. The specialised disinformation department of the Soviet civilian secret service Committee for State Security (KGB; Komitet Gosudarstvennoy Bezopasnosti) was established in 1959. During the Cold war, it served as a model for the creation of similar bodies in satellite secret services throughout the Eastern Bloc, and it cooperated with them. A defector from the Czechoslovak StB Ladislav Bittman, following his emigration to the United States, informed about these facts (Bittman 1972). After the fall of communism, he published a book in the Czech language warning of continuing disinformation operations against Western interests (Bittman 2000).

The strong efforts of various actors in history to create their own disinformation and propaganda activities have also led to defences against them. Targeted military attacks, special forces raids, or various attacks, including sabotage and terrorism, against enemy sources of propaganda have been carried out—recently, the possibilities of hacking and cyberwarfare can be used. Various forms of legal restrictions, such as draconic punishments, were reactions to propagandistic help given to enemies and even just reading or listening to foreign propaganda. These penalties were typical of many historical eras, mostly in non-democratic regimes, such as in Nazi Germany and the occupied territories during the Second World War. However, during wars and other crisis situations or as a protection against extremism, democracies also have limited freedom of speech in relation to the spread of false news and infiltration by foreign propaganda (Capoccia 2005, 58). Moreover, some lesser or non-formalised restrictions aimed at the spread of propaganda and disinformation in public spaces (schools, public television, etc.) can be efficient. Technologies can be used against the spread of propaganda too, for example, radio interference during the Cold War or, recently, the blocking of internet websites. Besides repressive measures, counter-propaganda and public education could also eliminate the impact of an adversary's propaganda.

(1) Direct military and other violent actions against sources (including cyberattacks); (2) repressive legal; (3) societal; and (4) technological measures; (5) counter-propaganda; and (6) public education are symptoms of the securitisation of propaganda and disinformation issues. Securitisation is understood as 'the move that takes politics beyond the established rules of the game and frames the issue either as a special kind of politics or as above politics' (Buzan et al. 1998, 23). According to Ralf Emmers, 'The act of securitization is only successful once the relevant audience is convinced of the existential threat to the referent object' (Emmers 2007, 114).

This constructivist approach is difficult to test in many recent polarised societies with a fragmented political and expert spectrum. However, we can observe a strong wave of attention paid to the new forms of propaganda and disinformation in the context of the growing importance of social media, most recently in relation to the development of artificial intelligence. This wave includes clear elements of securitisation—at least in the sense of creating specialised strategies and institutions as a result of political debates, despite the fact that the public's acceptance of various measures has been ambiguous—mostly in cases concerning the limitations of free speech on the Internet.

In summary, propaganda and disinformation have strong historical traditions, and their legacies are continuously transferred into the contemporary era, which is typical of new technological opportunities (Internet, social media, artificial intelligence). These phenomena have an impact on various sectors of external and internal security. The new forms of communication and media have created a new threat dimension and caused their securitisation. Furthermore, since these phenomena have been affecting a broad range of sectors, there are also a variety of actors (both old and new) playing in the disinformation and propaganda game.

3.3 Contemporary 'Rogue' Propaganda and Disinformation Actors

Propaganda is used by many governmental and non-governmental actors in the contemporary world. Therefore, when dealing with propaganda and disinformation as specific security threats, we should identify those actors who use these instruments with the intention of destabilising the peaceful development of the international community, democracy, and democratisation on a global scope. This identification of threat-actors is based on the Western liberal democratic value system. Of course, from the point of view of authoritarian and populist political forces, the democratic propaganda struggle is perceived as a threat to their own political interests. With respect to the abovementioned democratic values and interconnected reflexion in recent respected scientific literature (Hartig 2016; Galeotti 2016; Scheidt 2019) and the security policy of the Euro-Atlantic community and their allies, there are several important 'rogue' actors which have carried out recent propaganda and disinformation threats worth specifying.

These actors are in some categories interconnected, but some of them act independently of others. It is also impossible to identify a *unified global disinformation front*. Moreover, the interdependence of some actors is also fact (see below). Were we to analyse the relationships of various actors to the governmental or non-governmental spheres, we would see an unclear and flexible border between them. Some disinformation campaigns are organised by governmental actors (including special secret service branches), while others include the involvement of non-state, but pro-governmental forces. The interconnection of various actors with ideological streams (e.g. the Far Right) can cause non-governmental actors in one country to support governmental actors in other countries via fake news campaigns (e.g. a campaign on behalf of the Italian minister of the interior, Matteo Salvini, by the Western Far Right in 2018–2019).

If we look into the analysis of how disinformation is spread, we can identify:

1. Original sources/creators of disinformation (for example, a secret service disinformation branch);
2. Primary communication channels of disinformation (for example, ideologically/regime motivated media with a global impact, false flag websites, profiles on social media, etc., primary influencers);
3. Secondary intentional channels of disinformation (non-serious media, secondary influencers, trolls directly or freely connected with the political interests of the disinformation source); and
4. Targeted audience (the broader public in one or more countries—people from this category believe the content is true, and they can further spread the original disinformation and modify their political behaviour according to the interests of the disinformation source, for example, in regard to electoral preferences).

The specific categorisation of media-actors who can spread disinformation in all the abovementioned forms is very broad and includes all types of media communication channels in the contemporary world.

A highly developed system of propaganda and disinformation has been created in Russia. It continues in line with the 'active measures' of the Soviet Union. The structure of this propaganda and disinformation system is partially covert; however, with help of many indicia, its basic contour could be outlined. After twenty years under Vladimir Putin, Russia can be characterised as a modern authoritarian regime (Mochťak and Holzer 2017, 37). Its domestic legitimisation as well as its foreign policy combine nationalist and imperial elements with the legacies of Russian expansionist politics and selected traditions of the Soviet past—mostly glorification of the Soviet victory in the Second World War, which is used to justify recent Russian interference in the politics of foreign countries.

Propaganda and disinformation are important elements of this policy, and they are well organised within the Russian political and security system. The modern era of this phenomena, related to social media in cyberspace, started at the beginning of the twenty-first century's second decade. At that time, the governmental use of trolls was aimed against internal opponents of the Russian regime (Benkler et al. 2018, 247). After the start of Ukrainian crisis at the turn 2013/2014, Russian propaganda reoriented its main interest towards foreign countries. The country's recent propaganda and disinformation machine consists mostly of the following (and, of course, interconnected) parts:

1. Government institutions are responsible for prefabrication and the primary spread of propaganda messages and disinformation, including specialised branches of Russian secret services (as a part of its active measures)—the internal civilian Federal Security Service (FSB; Federalnaya sluzhba bezopasnosti), the civilian Foreign Intelligence Service (SVR; Sluzhba vneshney razvedki), and the military's Main Directorate (GU; Glavnoye upravlenie) of the General Staff of the Armed Forces, which is still known under the abbreviation of its Soviet predecessor, the GRU (Galeotti 2016). Specific false actors can also be regular military units playing the role of a fake resistance in other countries, such as the 'little green men' from the Russian army covertly posing as the Crimean Home Guardians during the crisis in 2014 (Buchar 2017, 101–102).
2. Government-run media with domestic and global impact is presented in both Russian or foreign languages (mostly via the television broadcaster RT, including its internet dimension, and the news agency Sputnik) (Ramsay and Robertshaw 2019).
3. Domestic supporters of the Russian regime on Russian territory act openly or covertly on behalf of pro-Kremlin propaganda (private pro-Kremlin media, influencers, trolls, and internet vigilantes from pro-Putin groups, such as the Nashi, etc.).
4. Supporters from Russian diasporas around the world act openly or covertly on behalf of pro-Kremlin propaganda (pro-Kremlin media in the diaspora, influencers, active trolls discussions in the hosting countries, etc.).
5. Foreigners intentionally support the Russian regime (e.g. ideological supporters of Russian Eurasianism, Pan-Slavists, paid agents, etc., with their own media, trolls, influencers, etc.).

6. Foreign or domestic actors unintentionally support the Russian regime, spreading the regime's propaganda and disinformation for their own purposes; they are targeted and misused by Russian governmental and pro-governmental actors (for example, the esoteric scene's inclination towards conspiracy theories).

Some actors can be subsumed under more than one of the abovementioned categories. Probably the most important symbol of the modern Russian disinformation struggle is the Internet Research Agency (IRA; Agentstvo internet issledovaniya), known broadly as the Russian troll farm. Founded in 2013, its goal is to spread propaganda and disinformation with the help of employees working as trolls (see Chapter 2) on various social networks. It is organised through pro-Putin's oligarchic structures; however, the influence of Russian secret services in its activity is extremely likely (Spruds et al. 2016, 16–17).

Another important actor in the spread of disinformation and propaganda is the global white nationalist (or far right) movement, with its own media and communication channels. Of course, to use of the term 'actor' is problematic due to its internal heterogenous character; however, it serves the analytical aims in our chapter. The traditional neo-Nazi and neo-Fascist Far Right has been using the Internet since the 1990s to spread their traditional conspiracy theories, including their infamous Holocaust denying. The location of many such websites in the United States is typical due to different limits of freedom of speech (see Chapter 4). The establishment of the now oldest neo-Nazi website, Stormfront, in the mid-1990s is a good example (Fromm and Kernbach 2001, 29–32).

This new dimension of far right actors is connected with the rise of the so-called alt–Right in the United States and many other countries as well as with anti-Islamic movements, mostly in the mid-2010s. Their communication channels—platforms such as Reddit, 4Chan, and 8Chan or specific national campaigns with organisational backgrounds like 'Reconquista Germania' or 'Infokrieg'—were or still are used for propaganda and mobilisation purposes. They serve also to support the rise of right-wing populist parties (Conway and Courtney 2018, 9). The identitarian movement is an important player in the field of modern far right propaganda, as the campaign 'Defend Europe' demonstrated during the migration crisis (Gattinara and Froio 2019).

A large part of far right propaganda and disinformation platforms has recently been, intentionally or unintentionally, connected with the pro-Kremlin propaganda machine. The far right German journalist Manuel Ochsenseiter is an example. Editor of the journal *Zuerst!*, he was invited on RT several times as an expert (Shekhovtsov 2017). On the other hand, not all far right media is supportive of the recent Russian regime, such as the neo-Nazi platforms supporting the Ukrainian Far Right. These neo-Nazi connections are used in Russian propaganda with an aim to discredit Ukraine (Mareš 2017, 34).

Chinese propaganda meanwhile works relatively autonomously. The Communist Party of China has deep historical legacies, and its propaganda posters and other traditional propaganda forms are popular (Mittler 2008); today, though, their impact is limited. Chinese propaganda was for many years focused on its domestic audience (including oppressed minorities involved in the Taiwan issue). In the twenty-first century, however, the globalisation of persuasive Chinese propaganda can be observed (Edney 2014, x).

Disinformation spread was previously not a widespread Chinese instrument; however, this changed during the 2019 Hong Kong crisis. Massive use of artificial intelligence is expected from China in this field in the future (Howard and Bradshaw 2019). Various Chinese governmental and partisan institutions are involved in propaganda campaigns, among others the Ministry of State Security, the Publicity Department of the Communist Party of China (CPCPD), and China Network Television (CNTV). Helpers from Chinese communities in various countries and from China's political and economic allies are used in a global propaganda struggle (under the leadership of Chinese embassies) (Rawnsley 2013, 154). The public diplomacy and propaganda are interconnected by branches of the Confucius Institute, a global actor 'partly funded by the Office of Chinese Language Council International (Hanban), an organisation under the authority of the Chinese Ministry of Education' (Hartig 2016, 2).

Huge attention is paid in the contemporary world to the propaganda of Islamic extremists. We can also see in this case a very heterogenous spectrum of propagandistic actors. The quasi–legal propaganda is partly supported by the governments of some Islamist countries (e.g. by Saudi Arabia in the Sunni Islam world and by Iran in the Shia Islam world). It is provided by various organisations, centres, and influencers, such as imams, rappers, foreign fighters, and so forth, usually with the help of various internet platforms (within the context of the so-called global virtual *umma*). Anti-Western conspiracies are propagated in this environment. Militant jihadist organisations have their own media branches responsible for the spread of propaganda in various languages, including journals and videos with atrocities, terrorist guidelines, and battle experiences. The media landscape of the so-called Islamic State is an example (Wejkszner 2016, 133–169).

A specific actor in the phantom Islamic groups claiming responsibility for attacks committed by another group or incidents which, in fact, have no connection to terrorism (technological accidents, nature catastrophes) or spread false threats. The Abu Hafs Al Masri Brigades, for example, claimed responsibility for a blackout in the US northeast in August 2003 (Carmon 2004). However, such claims and threats can also be expressed by real terrorist groups within threatening campaigns, including Daesh (Myre and Domonoske 2017).

Disinformation and propaganda are also connected to many far leftist organisations and media. The delimitation between the Far Left and the Far Right is in many cases questionable because some propaganda and disinformation media are focused on various protests streams in society; the German journal *Compact* is an example (Schilk 2017). Recently, the global fight in media and politics over climate changes has included elements of propaganda and disinformation on both sides of the conflict (American Institute of Biological Sciences 2017; Sakas and Fendt 2019).

There are many other particular issues which involve propaganda and disinformation actors in the contemporary world. However, generally, we can observe the involvement of state, state-sponsored, and non-state actors as well as a rise in specialised actors conducting propaganda campaigns in relation to specific topics considered important to political and economic subjects. The structure of propaganda and disinformation actors can be extremely heterogenous as the spectrum of pro-Russian or far right 'disinformation machines' shows. Various individual actors can play their own role in strategic propaganda and disinformation campaigns, and they can use varieties of tactical approaches within this struggle.

3.4 Strategies and Tactics of Contemporary Disinformation and Propaganda

It is generally understood that using disinformation and propaganda is not done for altruistic reasons or good-natured intentions. Normatively said, it is a dirty approach, and it is basically cheating the target population (see Chapter 1). Nevertheless, the following words do not serve to discuss under which conditions it might be justifiable and legitimate to use disinformation and propaganda. The ensuing paragraphs instead show in more detail the problem with disinformation and propaganda as regards its impact on recipients of this misleading and manipulative content. As we know, disinformation and propaganda may affect every individual in different ways, and they can be constructed even with a goal of targeting a single person—a rather expensive strategy but with a high gain under certain conditions. In the context of the broader population, we can also identify potential harms, threats which are relevant in terms of building a resilient society and the protection of democracy, democratic values, and the stability and legitimacy of a political regime.

A substantial volume of disinformation damages democracy by aiming to undermine trust in the democratic system, which consists of political institutions and constitutional and political officials. Disinformation narratives seek to create the impression that political representatives betray their voters and misgovern or to create an atmosphere where everyone lies, and nobody can be trusted. Just imagine the consequences of doctored video or audio capturing law enforcement officials discussing possible ways of abusing their powers or accepting bribes.

Specifically, disinformation plays a very conspicuous role during elections, entering the public discourse with increased frequency and aiming to influence voters and the outcome of the elections. The most known case might be the 2016 US presidential elections; an investigation into Russian election meddling is, as of this writing, still in process. Attempts to manipulate election results were also observed in Germany in favour of the far right Alternative for Germany, which got media support from the Russian state television channel Rossiya-1, broadcasting in Russia; from RT; and from Sputnik, which reported positively only about this political party (Institute for Strategic Dialogue 2017). Another documented case comes from the Czech Republic, where very shortly before the 2017 national parliamentary elections, an online media disinformation website produced a story about national lithium supplies, accusing a governing coalition party, the Social Democrats, of selling the state's interest to Australia and secretly embezzling the contract revenue to the benefit of the political party coffers. Political opponents intensively disseminated this disinformation. Based on the survey, around six per cent of voters were influenced by this disinformation when making their choice (Median 2017).

Such phenomena are also abused in the contamination of public debates and the promotion of hateful narratives within them. They have great and dangerous potential to disrupt democratic discourse and increase or escalate tensions between various groups in the population, be they political, social, ethnic, or religious. False information about the migration crisis, terrorist attacks in Europe, or support for radical Islam are obvious examples. Existing conflicts in society may be artificially increased in order to destabilise the society. This happens through the radicalisation of discussion and the radicalisation of the attitudes and beliefs of recipients. They are then more willing to leave behind facts and expert knowledge, and they are more prone to accept 'alternative facts'—not necessarily only in politics either; radicalisation may happen in any area of discussion, such as the economy, culture, or health issues.

In politics, when the radicalisation of public discourse happens and is met with an undermined trust in political institutions and political representatives of the system, such circumstances usually lead to a search for alternatives: anti-system political alternatives, represented typically by far right and far left political parties who, in general, take advantage of the decreasing trust of mainstream political parties, and, in the post-truth era, they also actively seek opportunities to relativise and manipulate through misleading information. European far right political parties, specifically, are very often considered Trojan horses of pro-Kremlin propaganda machinery and active transmitters of pro-Kremlin narratives in their combat against the European Union, the United States, and globalisation and in the promotion of nativist politics (Laruelle 2015; Polyakova et al. 2016, 2017, 2018; Shekhovtsov 2017). Marine Le Pen, leader of the French party National Rally (formerly the National Front) has praised Vladimir Putin many times as a true patriot and a defender of European values and the Christian heritage of European civilisation. Representatives of Italy's The League have been referring to Russia as an example of how to protect national identity (Klapsis 2015). In Slavic countries, such as the Czech Republic, Slovakia, or Serbia, this is also accelerated by a belief in the necessity for unification among Slavic nations, while in Orthodox countries, such as Greece and Bulgaria, the link stands on the religious connection. Outside of official political representation, there are vigilante or paramilitary actors (Bjørgo and Mareš 2019) who undermine trust in the state as the provider of security and protection, and they take power into their hands in order to provide public order and public safety. Europe encountered such a phenomenon during the migration crisis, for example, with the Soldiers of Odin, an anti-immigrant and white supremacist movement operated in the northern countries. In central Europe, there has been an active paramilitary movement using the rhetoric of Slavic blood, such as the Slovenskí branci (Slovak recruits), with connections to the Russian military environment. Without attempting to substitute state competences, they are often ideologically motivated and supportive of current Russian geopolitics, including the dissemination of pro-Kremlin propaganda and disinformation.

The process of radicalisation leading to violent extremism is another large agenda and security threat. The role of propaganda as a tool for recruitment used by subversive (terrorist and extremist) organisations has been widely described in literature (Rabasa and Benard 2015; MacDonald et al. 2016; Vacca 2019; Littler and Lee 2020). Such actors have learned that they have the power to affect the beliefs and attitudes of individuals through the design of proper narratives targeting people's feelings and needs. Neo-Nazi organisations make certain to share national socialist propaganda materials from the Third Reich, and they create new materials, such as videos, music, computer games, or pamphlets with political content. And, of course, the case of Daesh is a must-mention example of a terrorist organisation's propaganda machine, which upgraded this activity to an extremely professional level and made 'communication' activities a key part of obtaining its goals. Subversive actors are extremely well aware of the power of well–designed propaganda in spreading fear and, therefore, weakening and demoralising the adversary, but also recruiting those who search for protection due to this spreading fear—though not exclusively. Recruitment has multiple layers and spreading fear is only one of them. It is a kind of negative motivation. The positive one is based on recruitment through positive narratives, images of a happy life, and the creation of (shared) identities, community, and togetherness. Individuals get radicalised and recruited for different reasons, and ideological motives are only one of many including identity reasons, social and economic deprivation, stigmatisation, marginalisation, discrimination, ethnocultural tension, desire for higher status, and feelings of injustice which might turn into moral outrage and feelings of revenge (Bjørgo and Horgan 2009; Schmid 2013). These individuals might be vulnerable in the face of manipulation. Neo-Nazi organisations recruit a number of people simply due to their hope of gaining friends. Similarly, Daesh recruited several women because of the hope they would gain a husband and a family; they were persuaded that that is what they would receive by joining.

Identity reasons play a special role in radicalisation and recruitment. Propaganda often uses techniques of manipulation with stress upon group identity: bandwagoning to persuade individuals to join and take the course of action everybody else is taking, the plain folks technique of convincing through appeals to common sense and common people, and the false dilemma, which pushes individuals to decide where they stand—choosing the other side or being neutral means siding with the enemy (and you must decide right now because it is a matter of our future existence!!!). Propaganda works with the gap between Us and Them. Simply said, propaganda needs an enemy, even if this enemy is invented. The creation of internal and external threats is achieved by seeking out blameworthy groups (O'Shaughnessy 2004) because it is easier to define who we are by what are we not and unifying ourselves against threats—irrespective of the world around us. People know what they hate but are more ambivalent about their preferences (O'Shaughnessy 2004).

The development of the Internet and social media has influenced the radicalisation and recruitment processes in such a way that it has opened new ways of getting attention to vulnerable individuals across the world. The Internet and social media brought new methods of connecting and influencing collective identification processes (Caiani and Parenti 2013). The current system of algorithms close users in social bubbles with regard to connections and in information bubbles as to the content they consume. The attempts to personalise and display online content as much as possible based on a user's online activity therefore has a dark side whereupon users are enclosed within small universes, sometimes not even remotely close to reality. Zeynep Tufekci talks about YouTube as a perfect tool for radicalisation in the broad sense. She describes how YouTube offers the user more and more radical and extreme content in order to gain the maximum amount of our attention. Searching and watching videos about Donald Trump led to videos about Holocaust denial and white supremacists; videos about running led to videos dedicated to ultramarathons. Thus, there are also technical aspects which, due to our natural curiosity about the unknown, can lead in the direction of disinformation and propaganda (Tufekci 2018). Combined with an echo chamber filled with like-minded users providing individuals the illusion of mass agreement, users are given more confidence, provoking them to speak more radically in the online space. In some cases, this might also result in an increasing motivation to become involved in offline acts, such as criminal activity, violence, or even terrorism.

After all, misleading information also has the potential to endanger public security. Increasing conflicts within society, radicalisation, or sowing distrust are only a small step away from situations endangering public health or life. It is rather easy to create panic with a gunshot, and disinformation and doctored materials can work similarly in the virtual world. Chesney and Citron (2018) cite an example of intentional disinformation issued by the Russian Internet Research Agency, which claimed that there had been a chemical disaster in Louisiana and an Ebola outbreak in Atlanta. The real damage caused by this disinformation was ultimately minimal as both stories lacked proof, and the facts were easy to verify. However, deepfake videos can potentially substantially improve the plausibility of disinformation.

The use of intentionally misleading information could also pose a danger to national security, disrupt international relations, and undermine diplomacy. Because of disinformation, pressure could then be created to respond rapidly, causing damage to international relations and increasing the likelihood of a conflict erupting. International relations could be disrupted.

As the Internet, social media, and data collection methods have developed, so too have the goals of disinformers and propagandists progressed and transformed, no longer limited to just the dissemination of manipulative information, manipulative content, and narratives. The current possibilities of data collection regarding internet users and a target audience allow propaganda and disinformation to be focused beyond influencing attitudes and behaviour to controlling networks among contacts, interconnections between people in virtual space, and the strength of these interconnections. The ultimate victory is not limited anymore to narrative spreading but gaining control over the network through narratives which can be spread. With knowledge of the structure and configuration of a network, the technological environment of the Internet makes it easy to manipulate in an intended way, reconfiguring links among users and trusted networks. Using military terminology, defeat is when one has lost control over one's own network. It is possible to influence with whom users communicate, which users they meet virtually, and who is considered a trusted source. It is easily possible to identify, for example, anti-system users and influence them. Natural connections can be manipulated, they can be intentionally connected together, and the mutual connection can be intentionally intensified. Once a group is identified as being locked in a social bubble with almost no influence on the majority society, again it is possible to interfere and, based on data, expand and strengthen their links outside the bubble, for example, based on data concerning the leisure time activities of such users. The anti-system opposition can be artificially strengthened. This is important to keep in mind when discussing vulnerabilities because research shows that the structure of social relations among individuals influences attitudes and behaviour. According to Hwang (2019), the structure of a network can influence political affiliation, health habits, and the probability of divorce. Manipulation of network connections on a micro-level may affect the structure of attitudes, the behaviour of a target group, or even society as a whole.

All in all, the grand strategy of actors creating disinformation campaigns and propaganda is to exploit all the possible vulnerabilities of individuals, as well as the vulnerabilities of the system—on a psychological, cognitive, and technical level.

3.5 Defence and Protection Against Propaganda and Disinformation

The recent scope of the above analysed threats connected with disinformation and propaganda have also caused a counter-reaction. Various measures have been adopted by national governments, international organisations, and non-governmental organisations as well as by private companies in order to increase the resilience of societies. The reaction to the spread of Islamism has increased since the mid-2000s (mostly under the umbrella of countering online radicalisation). Ten years later, the new form of Russian hybrid and political warfare has led to a resolute answer in several European and North American countries and on the international level. However, the perception of the threat intensity differs among various countries and actors (Scheidt 2019, 19).

The involvement of defence institutions in the process of countering propaganda and disinformation proves the importance of this issue from the point of view of contemporary security policy. The traditional concept of *psychological defence* has won new importance in countries under the attack of 'political warfare 2.0' (Rossbach 2017). The new necessity for psychological defence is strongly thematised in Sweden and Estonia. According to the Estonian government, psychological defence stands on informing society and increasing the information level about activities against the constitutional order and social values. The concept is meant to be proactive in order to preventively increase the resilience of society in possible times of crisis (Červeňová 2019; Kaitseministeerium 2017). With regard to Sweden, Rossbach (2017) talks about three components: counteracting deception and disinformation, including propaganda (everything hostile); ensuring that government authorities can communicate with the public in any crisis, including war; and strengthening the population's will to defend the country. Information and psychological operations, influence operations, and resilience against hybrid threats are again important matters of the defence agenda (Janssen and Sünkler 2019).

The civilian sector has reacted to this new threat dimension in various ways. New persuasion and education campaigns have been launched by governments and engaged non-governmental organisations from the civil society sphere. Fact-checking and trust-enhancing initiatives have been founded (Steering Committee on Human Rights, Council of Europe 2019, 37–40), including projects to improve individual media and digital literacy and the capability to recognise fake news (Permanent Mission of the Czech Republic to the UN, OSCE and Other International Organizations in Vienna 2017). The strengthening of serious media in the fight against disinformation has also become an important element (Brodnig 2019, 96). New legal and internal restrictions have been adopted, including new rules and actions by, among others, Facebook and Twitter against Chinese disinformation (on measures and countermeasures, see Chapters 7 and 8) (Reuters 2019). Arguments supporting the need to empower resilience can be heard and read almost on a daily basis. One of them was a survey conducted in March 2019 using a representative sample of a thousand adults from the Czech Republic. Among other findings, the data showed that only 23 per cent knew correctly that search internet engines provide different results when entering the same keyword by different users so that advertisements differ for different users. Only 35 per cent knew correctly that what we see on our Facebook walls is filtered based on our behaviour on this social network (Gregor and Mlejnková 2019).

In sum, the main evidence of securitisation in response to the recent wave of propaganda and disinformation on the governmental (including intergovernmental) level are:

- Parts of strategic security concepts and similar materials (or even specialised documents), which include the labelling of this issue as a security threat and a description of countermeasures, for example, the Czech Republic's *National Security Audit* from 2016 (Vláda České republiky 2016);
- New legal norms and voluntary conduct aimed at countering disinformation, for example, the European Union's Code of Practice on Disinformation (European Commission 2018);
- Redirection of traditional security institutions and the establishment of new specialised institutions countering propaganda and disinformation (recently, mostly in defence against hybrid threats), such as the establishment of the European Centre of Excellence for Countering Hybrid Threats (2017);
- Research into and the acquisition of specialised technological tools against disinformation and propaganda, including defence and protection against artificial intelligence in the service of these phenomena, for instance, the software programme Propaganda Web Crawler created at Masaryk University in 2019 (Pančík and Baisa 2019), the automatic fact-checking tool of the Swedish government and its public broadcaster, or a tool currently being planned by a cyber unit of the German army which can identify propaganda and detect the influence of artificial intelligence over the public (Kommando Cyber- und Informationraum, n.d.);
- Investigations into propaganda and disinformation which can harm national interests and/or law-violating interference, for example, the investigation of the US Senate into Russian interference in the 2016 US election (Select Committee on Intelligence, United States Senate 2019); and
- Real operations against adversarial propaganda and disinformation, such as Estonia's ongoing use of blockchain to fight fake news since 2019 (Krusten 2019).

3.6 Conclusion

Propaganda and disinformation are perceived as a threat, and reference objects are thus dependent upon security interests. If we focus—from a realistic perspective—on states as the most important actors of international policy, we can identify sovereignty, regime stability, and the wealth of citizens as the most important protected values. The influence of propaganda and the use of disinformation with the goal of harming these interests is perceived as a security threat related to the source of such propaganda and disinformation. From the point of view of contemporary decisive political forces in Western countries (including the official policy of international organisations in the Euro-Atlantic area), the most threatening actors identified in contemporary times are the Russian and Chinese regimes and the globally active, hateful white nationalists and militant jihadists movements. And at the same time, new fields of propaganda and disinformation struggles are emerging, such as the climate debate.

The main securitisation of new forms of propaganda and disinformation, interconnected with the massive growth of people using social media, occurred in the 2010s, mostly in reaction to the jihadist mobilisation campaign during the Syrian civil war and the rise of Daesh, with the start of the Russian hybrid war against Ukraine and the coinciding intensification of Russian political warfare against the West, and recently, also with the rise of Chinese propaganda skills, including the threatening potential of artificial intelligence. However, the polarisation of internal political debates makes the activity of various political movements (mostly of the alt–Right) also a threat within the context of internal security.

Despite the many new elements of recent propaganda and disinformation campaigns (among others the possibility for the creative involvement of 'troll armies', opportunities to personalise content and reconfigure the structure of virtual relations, and the active 'grass roots' participation of the public—in terms of the active creation of propagandistic content and active dissemination), the basic substance of the threat in various stages of conflict between two or more actors remains similar to previous eras. However, with the help of terms adapted to present–day developments, we can explain the main characteristic features: During this era of political warfare, propaganda and disinformation serve to systematically weaken and destabilise the adversary, including the loyalty of citizens in democratic countries to their regimes. After escalating to hybrid warfare, the goal becomes the elimination of an efficient reaction to a mixed use of conventional and non-conventional forces (as was the case during the Crimean crisis). And finally, during a conventional conflict, the aims of propaganda and disinformation are traditional but with new means of weakening support for the war in the rear (on the 'domestic front') and destroying the moral of soldiers (on the real front line or in specific positions in military facilities, for example, drone operators, etc.). All in all, the goals in all stages are: control and domination of the information environment, destabilisation of the society or the system, promotion of specific interests, and the establishment of a new order. Radicalisation and apathy, while by-products of these aims, are very much bedfellows as well.

References

Albrecht, S., Fielitz, M., & Thurston, N. (2019). Introduction. In M. Fielitz & N. Thurston (Eds.), *Post-Digital Cultures of the Far Right: Online Actions and Offline Consequences in Europe and the US* (pp. 7–22). Bielefeld: Transcript Verlag.

American Institute of Biological Sciences. (2017). Science Community Considers Approaches to Climate Disinformation. https://www.aibs.org/bioscience-press-releases/171129_science_community_considers_approaches_to_climate_disinformation.html. Accessed 15 Feb 2020.

Benkler, Y., Faris, R., & Roberts, H. (2018). *Network Propaganda: Manipulation, Disinformation, and Radicalization in American Politics*. Oxford: Oxford University Press.

Bittman, L. (1972). *The Deception Game: Czechoslovak Intelligence in Soviet Political Warfare*. Syracuse: Syracuse University Research Corporation.

Bittman, L. (2000). *Mezinárodní dezinformace: Černá propaganda, aktivní opatření a tajné akce* [International Disinformation: Black Propaganda, Active Measures and Cover Actions]. Praha: Mladá fronta.

Bjørgo, T., & Horgan, J. (Eds.). (2009). *Leaving Terrorism Behind*. Abingdon: Routledge.

Bjørgo, T., & Mareš, M. (Eds.). (2019). *Vigilantism Against Migrants and Minorities*. Abingdon: Routledge.

Brodnig, I. (2019). *Lügen im Netz: Wie Fake-News, Populisten und unkontrollierte Technik uns manipulieren*. Wien: Brändstätter.

Buchar, J. (2017). Anexe Krymu (Annexation of Crimea). In Šír, Jan et al. (Eds.), *Ruská agrese proti Ukrajině* [Russian Aggression Toward Ukraine] (pp. 94–113). Praha: Karolinum.

Buzan, B., Wæver, O., & de Wilde, J. (1998). *Security: A New Framework for Analysis*. London: Lynne Rienner.

Caiani, M., & Parenti, L. (2013). *European and American Extreme Right Groups and the Internet*. Abingdon: Routledge.
Campion, K. K. (2015). *Under the Shadows of Swords: Propaganda of the Deed in the History of Terrorism*. Doctoral thesis. Townsville: James Cook University. https://researchonline.jcu.edu.au/48293. Accessed 14 Feb 2020.
Capoccia, G. (2005). *Defending Democracy: Reactions to Extremism in Interwar Europe*. Baltimore and London: The John Hopkins University Press.
Carmon, Y. (2004). *Assessing the Credibility of the 'Abu Hafs Al-Masri Brigades' Threats*. Washington: The Middle East East Media Research Institute. https://www.memri.org/reports/assessing-credibility-abu-hafs-al-masri-brigades-threats. Accessed 14 Feb 2020.
Červeňová, T. (2019). *Estonsko: koncept psychologické obrany*. [Estonia: Concept of Psychological Defence]. Bachelor thesis. Brno: Masaryk University.
Chesney, B., & Citron, D. (2018). Deep Fakes: A Looming Challenge for Privacy, Democracy, and National Security. Research paper available at *SSRN Electronic Journal*. https://papers.ssrn.com/sol3/papers.cfm?abstract_id=3213954. Accessed 12 Feb 2020.
Conway, M., & Courtney, M. (2018). Violent Extremism and Terrorism Online. In 2017. *The Year in Review: Network of Excellence*. Dublin: The VOX-Pol Network of Excellence in Research in Violent Political Extremism. https://www.voxpol.eu/download/vox-pol_publication/YiR-2017_Web-Version.pdf. Accessed 12 Feb 2020.
Cowan, D., & Cook, C. (2018). What's in a Name? Psychological Operations Versus Military Information Support Operations and an Analysis of Organizational Change. *Military Review*. https://www.armyupress.army.mil/Journals/Military-Review/Online-Exclusive/2018-OLE/Mar/PSYOP/. Accessed 12 Feb 2020.
Cullen, P. J., & Reichborn-Kjennerud, E. (2017). *MCDC Countering Hybrid Warfare Project: Understanding Hybrid Warfare a Multinational Capability Development Campaign Project*. London: Multinational Capability Development Campaign. https://assets.publishing.service.gov.uk/government/uploads/system/uploads/attachment_data/file/647776/dar_mcdc_hybrid_warfare.pdf. Accessed 12 Feb 2020.
Edney, K. (2014). *The Globalization of Chinese Propaganda: International Power and Domestic Political Cohesion*. New York: Palgrave Macmillan.
Emmers, R. (2007). Securitization. In A. Collins (Ed.), *Contemporary Security Studies* (pp. 109–125). Oxford: Oxford University Press.
European Centre of Excellence for Countering Hybrid Threats. (2017). *What Is Hybrid COE?* https://ec.europa.eu/digital-single-market/en/news/code-practice-disinformation. Accessed 12 Feb 2020.

European Commission. (2018). *Code of Practice on Disinformation*. https://ec.europa.eu/digital-single-market/en/news/code-practice-disinformation. Accessed 12 Feb 2020.

Fromm, R., & Kernbach, B. (2001). *Rechtsextremismus im Internet: Die neue Gefahr*. München: Olzog Verlag.

Galeotti, M. (2016). *Putin's Hydra: Inside Russia's Intelligence Services*. London: European Council on Foreign Relations. https://www.ecfr.eu/page/-/ECFR_169_-_INSIDE_RUSSIAS_INTELLIGENCE_SERVICES_(WEB_AND_PRINT)_2.pdf. Accessed 10 Feb 2020.

Gattinara, P. C., & Froio, C. (2019). Getting 'Right' into the News: Grassroots Far-Right Mobilization and Media Coverage in Italy and France. *Comparative European Politics, 17*(5), 738–758. https://doi.org/10.1057/s41295-018-0123-4.

Gerwehr, S., & Glenn, R. W. (2000). *The Art of Darkness: Deception and Urban Operations*. Santa Monica: RAND Corporation. https://www.rand.org/pubs/monograph_reports/MR1132.html. Accessed 12 Feb 2020.

Gregor, M., & Mlejnková, P. (2019). Survey on Information Resilience of the Czech Society: Data Collected by Collect Agency. Archive of the Authors.

Hartig, F. (2016). *Chinese Public Diplomacy: The Rise of the Confucius Institute*. London and New York: Routledge.

Howard, P. N., & Bradshaw, S. (2019, November 29). China Joins the Global Disinformation Order. *The Strategist*. https://www.aspistrategist.org.au/china-joins-the-global-disinformation-order/. Accessed 12 Feb 2020.

Hwang, T. (2019). *Maneuver and Manipulation: On the Military Strategy of Online Information Warfare*. Carlisle: Strategic Studies Institute.

Ingram, H. J. (2016). *A Brief History of Propaganda During Conflict*. Hague: International Centre for Counter-Terrorism. https://icct.nl/publication/a-brief-history-of-propaganda-during-conflict-a-lesson-for-counter-terrorism-strategic-communications/. Accessed 12 Feb 2020.

Institute for Strategic Dialogue. (2017). Allies: The Kremlin, the AfD, the Alt-Right and the German Elections. Press Release.

Jandečková, V. (2018). *Falešné hranice: Příběhy akce „Kámen" 1948–1951* [Fake Borders: The Story of Action "Stone" 1948–1951]. Praha: Argo.

Janssen, E., & Sünkler, S. (2019). Hybride PsyOps: Info-Kriege und Meinungswaffen als Teile modernen Konfliktaustragung. *K-ISOM, 7*(6), 72–75.

Kaitseministeerium. (2017). *National Security Concept*. http://www.kaitseministeerium.ee/sites/default/files/elfinder/article_files/national_security_concept_2017_0.pdf. Accessed 12 Feb 2020.

Klapsis, A. (2015). *An Unholy Alliance: The European Far Right and Putin's Russia*. Brussels: Wilfried Martens Centre for European Studies.

Kommando Cyber- und Informationraum. (n.d.). https://www.bundeswehr.de/de/organisation/cyber-und-informationsraum/kommando-und-organisation-cir/kommando-cyber-und-informationsraum. Accessed 20 Dec 2020.

Krusten, M. (2019). *Fighting Fake News with Blockchain, E-Estonia*. https://e-estonia.com/fighting-fake-news-with-blockchain/. Accessed 10 Feb 2020.

Laruelle, M. (Ed.). (2015). *Eurasianism and the European Far Right: Reshaping the Europe-Russia Relationship*. Lanham: Lexington Books.

Littler, M., & Lee, B. (Eds.). (2020). *Digital Extremisms: Readings in Violence, Radicalisation and Extremism in the Online Space*. Cham: Palgrave Macmillan.

Lord, C., & Barnett, F. C. (1989). Introduction. In C. Lord & F. C. Barnett (Eds.), *Political Warfare and Psychological Operations: Rethinking the US Approach* (pp. xi–xxii). Washington: National Defence Unity Press, National Strategy Information Center.

Macdonald, S., Jarvis, L., Chen, T., & Aly, A. (Eds.). (2016). *Violent Extremism Online: New Perspectives on Terrorism and the Internet*. Abingdon: Routledge.

Mareš, M. (2017). Foreign Fighters in Ukraine: Risk Analysis from the Point of View of NATO. In K. Rekawek (Ed.), *Not Only Syria? The Phenomenon of Foreign Fighters in a Comparative Perspective* (pp. 31–39). Amsterdam: IOS Press.

McFate, M., Holliday, R., & Damon, B. (2012). What Do Commanders Really Want to Know? US Army Human Terrain System Lessons Learned from Iraq and Afghanistan. In J. Laurence & M. Matthews (Eds.), *The Handbook of Military Psychology* (pp. 92–113). Oxford: Oxford University Press.

Median. (2017). *Výzkum pro volební studio ČR* [Electoral Survey for the Czech Television]. http://www.median.eu/cs/wp-content/uploads/2017/10/Vyzkum_pro_volebni_studio.pdf. Accessed 13 Feb 2020.

Mittler, B. (2008). Popular Propaganda? Art and Culture in Revolutionary China. *Proceedings of the American Philosophical Society, 152*(4), 466–489.

Mochťak, M., & Holzer, J. (2017). Electoral Violence in Putin's Russia: Modern Authoritarianism in Practice. *Studies of Transition States and Societies, 9*(1), 35–52.

Myre, G., & Domonoske, C. (2017, May 24). *What Does It Mean When ISIS Claims Responsibility for an Attack? National Public Radio*. https://www.npr.org/sections/thetwo-way/2017/05/24/529685951/what-does-it-mean-when-isis-claims-responsibility-for-an-attack. Accessed 10 Feb 2020.

O'Shaughnessy, N. (2004). *Politics and Propaganda: Weapons of Mass Seduction*. Manchester: Manchester University Press.

Pančík, J., & Baisa, V. (2019). *Propaganda Web Crawler (Software)*. Brno: Faculty of Informatics, Masaryk University.

Permanent Mission of the Czech Republic to the UN, OSCE and Other International Organizations in Vienna. (2017). *Czech Students Won 3rd Place in OSCE #UnitedCVE Peer to Peer Competition*. https://www.mzv.cz/mission.

vienna/en/latest/czech_students_won_3rd_place_in_osce.html. Accessed 10 Feb 2020.

Pihelgas, M. (2015). Introduction. In M. Pihelgas (Ed.), *Mitigating Risks Arising from False-Flag and No-Flag Cyber Attacks* (pp. 6–7). Tallin: NATO Cooperative Cyber Defence Centre of Excellence. https://ccdcoe.org/uploads/2018/10/False-flag-and-no-flag-20052015.pdf. Accessed 10 Feb 2020.

Pihelgas, M., & Tammekänd, J. (2015). The Workshop. In M. Pihelgas (Ed.), *Mitigating Risks Arising from False-Flag and No-Flag Cyber Attacks* (pp. 24–36). Tallin: NATO Cooperative Cyber Defence Centre of Excellence. https://ccdcoe.org/uploads/2018/10/False-flag-and-no-flag-20052015.pdf. Accessed 12 Feb 2020.

Polyakova, A. et al. (2016). *The Kremlin's Trojan Horses: Russian Influence in France, Germany, and the United Kingdom*. Washington: Atlantic Council. https://www.atlanticcouncil.org/in-depth-research-reports/report/kremlin-trojan-horses/. Accessed 15 Feb 2020.

Polyakova, A. et al. (2017). *The Kremlin's Trojan Horses: Russian Influence in Greece, Italy, and Spain*. Washington: Atlantic Council. https://www.atlanticcouncil.org/wp-content/uploads/2017/11/The_Kremlins_Trojan_Horses_2_web_1121.pdf. Accessed 15 Feb 2020.

Polyakova, A. et al. (2018). *The Kremlin's Trojan Horses: Russian Influence in Denmark, The Netherlands, Norway, and Sweden*. Washington: Atlantic Council. https://www.atlanticcouncil.org/in-depth-research-reports/report/the-kremlins-trojan-horses-3-0/. Accessed 15 Feb 2020.

Rabasa, A., & Benard, C. (2015). *Eurojihad: Patterns of Islamist Radicalization and Terrorism in Europe*. New York: Cambridge University Press.

Ramsay, G., & Robertshaw, S. (2019). *Weaponising News: RT, Sputnik and Targeted Disinformation*. London: King's College London. https://www.kcl.ac.uk/policy-institute/assets/weaponising-news.pdf. Accessed 20 Feb 2020.

Rawnsley, G. D. (2013). "*Thought-Work*" and Propaganda: Chinese Public Diplomacy and Public Relations After Tiananmen Square. In J. Auerbach & R. Castronovo (Eds.), *Oxford Handbook of Propaganda Studies* (pp. 147–162). Oxford: Oxford University Press.

Reuters. (2019, August 19). Factbox: Track Facebook's Fight Against Disinformation Campaigns in 2019. *Reuters*. https://www.reuters.com/article/us-facebook-disinformation-factbox/factbox-track-facebooks-fight-against-disinformation-campaigns-in-2019-idUSKCN1V91V4. Accessed 9 Feb 2020.

Rossbach, N. H. (2017). Psychological Defence: Vital for Sweden's Defence Capability. In H. C. Wiklund, D. Faria, B. Johansson, & J. Öhrn-Lundin (Eds.), *Strategic Outlook 7: Perspectives on National Security in a New Security Environment* (pp. 45–52). Stockholm: The Swedish Defense Research Agency.

Runzheimer, J. (1962). Der Überfall auf den Sender Gleiwitz im Jahre 1939. *Vierteljahrshefte für Zeitgeschichte, 10*(4), 408–426.

Sakas, M. E., & Fendt, L. (2019, December 5). The City of Denver to Falsely Report a Climate Emergency. *Colorado Public Radio*. https://www.cpr.org/2019/12/05/climate-activists-used-disinformation-and-imitated-the-city-of-denver-to-falsely-report-a-climate-emergency/. Accessed 8 Feb 2020.

Scheidt, M. (2019). *The European Union Versus External Disinformation Campaigns in the Midst of Information Warfare: Ready for the Battle?* Brugge: College of Europe. https://www.coleurope.eu/study/eu-international-relations-and-diplomacy-studies/research-publications/eu-diplomacy-papers. Accessed 12 Feb 2020.

Schilk, F. (2017). *Souveränität statt Komplexität: Wie das Querfront-Magazin COMPACT die politische Legitimationskrise der Gegenwart bearbeitet*. Münster: UNRAST Verlag.

Schmid, A. (2013). *Radicalisation, De-Radicalisation, Counter-Radicalisation: A Conceptual Discussion and Literature Review*. ICCT Research Paper. Hague: ICCT. https://www.icct.nl/download/file/ICCT-Schmid-Radicalisation-De-Radicalisation-Counter-Radicalisation-March-2013.pdf. Accessed 16 Feb 2020.

Select Committee on Intelligence, United States Senate. (2019). *Russian Active Measures Campaigns and Interference in the 2016 U.S. Election Volume 2: Russia's Use of Social Media and Additional Views*. Washington: United States Senate. https://www.intelligence.senate.gov/sites/default/files/documents/Report_Volume2.pdf. Accessed 5 Feb 2020.

Shekhovtsov, A. (2017). *Russia and the Western Far Right: Tango Noir*. London: Routledge.

Shultz, R. H. (1989). Political Strategies for Revolutionary War. In F. C. Barnett & C. Lord (Eds.), *Political Warfare and Psychological Operations: Rethinking the US Approach*. Washington: National Defence Unity Press, National Strategy Information Center.

Spruds, A., Rožukalne, A., Sedlenieks, K., Daugulis, M., Potjomkina, D., & Tölgyesi, B., et al. (2016). *Internet Trolling as a Hybrid Warfare Tool: The Case of Latvia*. Riga: NATO Starcom CoE. https://www.stratcomcoe.org/internet-trolling-hybrid-warfare-tool-case-latvia-0. Accessed 4 Feb 2020.

Steering Committee on Human Rights, Council of Europe. (2019). *Guide to Good and Promising Practices on the Way of Reconciling Freedom of Expression with Other Rights and Freedoms, in Particular in Culturally Diverse Societies*. Strasbourg: Council of Europe.

Tufekci, Z. (2018, March 10). YouTube, the Great Radicalizer. *The New York Times*. https://www.nytimes.com/2018/03/10/opinion/sunday/youtube-politics-radical.html. Accessed 20 Feb 2020.

Vacca, J. (Ed.). (2019). *Online Terrorist Propaganda, Recruitment, and Radicalization*. Boca Raton: CRC Press.

Vláda České republiky. (2016). *National Security Audit*. Prague: Ministry of Interior of the Czech Republic. https://www.mvcr.cz/cthh/clanek/audit-narodni-bezpecnosti. Accessed 4 Feb 2020.

Wejkszner, A. (2016). *Państvo Islamiskie: Narodziny nowego kalifatu?*. Warszawa: Difin.

Zhirnov, E. (2003, January 13). Desinformbyuro: 80 let sovietskoy sluzhbe desinformacyi. *Kommersant*. https://www.kommersant.ru/doc/358500. Accessed 3 Feb 2020.

CHAPTER 4

Labelling Speech

František Kasl

4.1 Introduction

Chapter 7 of this edited volume offers insight into the current measures taken by EU countries against disinformation and propaganda in the online environment. A crucial aspect of these legislative or administrative measures, which needs to be taken into consideration, is their conformity with the broader European legal framework. Over its core components loom the standards of European democratic societies jointly enshrined in the European Convention on Human Rights (hereinafter referred to as 'the Convention'; ECHR 2019a) and supported by the European Court of Human Rights (ECHR) case law (ECHR 2019b). This chapter aims to guide the reader through the current position of the ECHR on the issue of permissible tools for combating disinformation and propaganda.

F. Kasl (✉)
Institute of Law and Technology, Faculty of Law, Masaryk University, Brno, Czech Republic
e-mail: frantisek.kasl@law.muni.cz
URL: https://www.muni.cz/en/people/462266-frantisekkasl

M. Gregor and P. Mlejnková (eds.), *Challenging Online Propaganda and Disinformation in the 21st Century*, Political Campaigning and Communication,
https://doi.org/10.1007/978-3-030-58624-9_4

4.2 Disinformation in the Context of Freedom of Expression

The dissemination of propaganda and disinformation constitutes a challenging legal environment, primarily from the perspective of labelling the legal permissibility of the content as an exercise of freedom of expression.

When discussing disinformation in the context of freedom of expression, two valuable perspectives on the disseminated information often collide. Disinformation (see Chapter 1) is mostly defined based on its deceptiveness, representing the deliberately fabricated nature of the information without regard for the truth or available facts, as well as the intention of the author to mislead the audience by promoting falsehood or spreading doubt about verifiable facts (McGonagle 2017, 203). It is therefore the lack of truthfulness and the insufficient sincerity of the author's intentions which allow for the identification of disinformation among other content.

However, the category of disinformation, or fake news—a subcategory with particular relevance in this context—encompasses a broad spectrum of content, which covers topics ranging from harmless to widely impactful (Katsirea 2018, 174). As for the classification of disinformation from the freedom of expression perspective, it is the impact of the content which is relevant in establishing infringement upon the fundamental rights and freedoms of others. The ECHR has a time-proven doctrine regarding the dissemination of defamatory information by traditional media. The main distinction made here is between an untruthful allegation concerning provable facts and subjective value judgements forming opinions, critique, or speculations (Regules 2018, 15). Journalistic freedom of expression receives broad recognition as a core component of a democratic society, serving as a public watchdog.[1] Nevertheless, there are boundaries recognised through the traditionally developed ethical codes of journalism (Katsirea 2018, 171). ECHR case law therefore operates with the expectation of factual accuracy and adequate verification of sources by traditional media.[2] As such, provably false factual claims do not receive protection under the Convention (Regules 2018, 16). Broadly instructive in this

[1] Sunday Times v. the United Kingdom, no. 6538/74, §41, ECHR 1979; Observer and Guardian v United Kingdom, no 13585/88, §59, ECHR 1991.

[2] Tønsberg Blad AS and Marit Haukom v. Norway, no. 510/04, ECHR 2007; Bladet Tromsø and Stensaas v Norway, no. 21980/93, ECHR 1999.

regard is the opinion of the Venice Commission establishing a set of requirements relevant in the case of an unproven defamatory allegation of fact (Venice Commission 2004). Content falsifying history or denying the Holocaust are therefore among classical examples of unprotected untruthful expressions (Katsirea 2018, 177).

This is, however, not the usual issue of fake news or propaganda content. Rather than spreading provably false factual disinformation, the sources of such content provide a more or less sophisticated mix of abridged factual descriptions, leading emotional expressions, speculative fabulations, and other manipulative techniques introduced in detail in earlier chapters. This presents the first challenge to the classification of disinformation under the freedom of expression framework. Due to often merely partial manipulation of provable facts and the otherwise predominant role of content representing value judgements, there is limited applicability of the available case law concerning defamatory media coverage. Furthermore, given that, in general, most media news consists more of socially agreed truths and reasoned subjective opinions rather than proven absolute truths (Katsirea 2018, 176), the issue of truthfulness in disinformation is a matter of scale rather than bipolar assessment. By default, most disinformation must therefore be perceived as a protected form of expression unless proven otherwise.

A further consideration of relevance regarding the category of speech that the given disinformation represents: The ECHR developed throughout its case law an implied hierarchy of protection rendered to content depending on its purpose. There is a distinctly stronger tendency towards awarding protection to expressions of political speech over purely commercial content (Katsirea 2018, 173). This is reflected in particular through the permitted margin of appreciation—that is, the freedom of national authorities and courts to interpret and limit protection provided under the Convention.[3] It is, however, not at all clear, what level of protection in this hierarchy a particular piece of disinformation should receive given the broadness of possible form, content, and purpose constituting these expressions. Even if it can be argued that a certain portion of fake news is generated primarily with commercial, rather than political, intentions (Katsirea 2018, 174), the profit-making objective does

[3] Markt Intern and Beermann v. Germany, no. 10572/83, ECHR 1990.

not exclude the given expression from legal protection by default.[4] At the same time, despite a large portion of the most controversial disinformation being focused on political matters, deeper and more specific examination of the particular content is required in order to determine its nature as a valued form of democratic political expression or rather of foreign propaganda constituting an abuse of the protective framework of the Convention.[5]

Lastly, the intentions of the author come into play when assessing his or her good faith in disseminating the given information. Intentions are of an internal and subjective nature; there is therefore only indirect evidence available to this effect. If one of the defining aspects of disinformation, as compared to misinformation, is the intention to deceive on the part of the author, there is inherent bad faith connected with spreading disinformation. However, this does not mean that the assessment of good faith can be done without, as suggested by Regules (2018, 16). The bad faith must be established, along with the factual falsity, in order to consider the given content unprotected disinformation. Nevertheless, proving bad faith may not be as straightforward in the case of fake news, particularly if the content is built on previous news or sources. If the intention of the author can only be indirectly verified, it is a matter of evidence which should, therefore, in a particular case exclude or permit a defence of good faith. The reliability of information and sources is increasingly relativised not just by fake news per se, but in general through the democratisation of media and the online information environment. Taking into consideration the effect of filter bubbles in online media (Flaxman et al. 2016), there is sufficient room for argumentation for the good faith basis of some fake news, reflecting the diversity of subjective perspectives and opinions freely shared in a democratic society. This then poses an additional challenge to restrictive measures against content labelled as disinformation.

To summarise this initial overview, disinformation encompasses a broad category of content which may be permissible under the Convention to a greatly varying degree. The versatility of this content upon closer inspection prevents a systematic classification; however, it does provide for three

[4] Markt Intern and Beermann v. Germany, no. 10572/83, ECHR 1990.

[5] Kuhnen v. the Federal Republic of Germany (inadmissible), no. 12194/86, ECHR 1988.

main aspects which indicate the position of specific content labelled as disinformation within the freedom of expression framework:

- Provability: Disinformation is in general not provably untrue but contains a mixture of misinterpreted factual claims and value judgements which can be classified as manipulative techniques. The assessment then depends on the provable presence of false factual claims in the particular content.
- Purpose: The scope of protection pursuant to ECHR case law is influenced by the purpose of the expression. Fake news has components of political as well as commercial speech, whereas each stands on the opposite spectrum of the hierarchy. Contextual interpretation of the purpose of the content will therefore (co)determinate the scope of protection.
- Intention of the author: The good faith of the author in the sources and purpose of the content has relevance to its protection. Even though disinformation is characterised by the bad faith of the author, there is no possible direct evidence regarding the intent of the author, and filter bubbles and other aspects of the online infosphere may today constitute sufficient evidence for a good faith defence in a particular case.

This introductory discussion provides an indication of the complexity of viewing disinformation from the freedom of expression perspective. The following sections shall provide more detailed insight into the relevant aspects hinted upon or which follow from this discussion.

4.2.1 European Convention on Human Rights

As already noted, the Convention is a prominent beacon in the European framework of fundamental rights and freedoms of an individual. Its unifying and harmonising impact on the approach to protect these values among the member states of the Council of Europe can hardly be overstated. A great deal of the central position dedicated to this framework is built on the basis of comprehensive ECHR case law, which throughout the past 60 years (ECHR 2018) has provided a guiding interpretation on the scope and application of the provisions under the Convention as well as their gradual evolving adaptation to new technological, social, and political contexts (Bychawska-Siniarska 2017, 9). The guiding role of the ECHR case law in the context of permissible freedom of expression was explicitly recognised even by the Court of Justice of the European Union (CJEU).[6] As such, the Convention and its values are an integral part of all 47 legal systems of the Council of Europe member states (Equality and Human Rights Commission 2017), which include all EU member states as well as the additional states of wider Europe. It thereby establishes the binding nature of this international treaty and its inescapable relevance for the functioning of public authorities and the decision-making of domestic courts throughout Europe (Bychawska-Siniarska 2017, 9). For all these reasons, ECHR case law deserves particular attention when considering permissible regulatory measures by European institutions towards combatting disinformation and propaganda.

It must be further noted that, despite a prolonged complex legal relationship between the application and enforcement of the Convention and the framework of the European Union (Kuijer 2018), there is a close overlap in the protection provided by these legal structures for freedom of expression. The Convention stood at the basis of the values enshrined in the Charter of Fundamental Rights of the European Union, which sets them in close alignment (Lemmens 2001). Furthermore, recent activity of the European Parliament indicates a continuing validity of efforts towards closer interconnection of these supranational legal frameworks through accession of the European Union to the Convention (European Parliament 2019). Due to this close relation and the baseline nature of the Convention, this chapter is, following other academics (Sluijs 2012, 520), predominantly limited in focus on the Convention and ECHR case law while recognising the increasing subsidiary relevance of the Charter of Fundamental Rights of the European Union as well as national constitutional or specific legislation. EU law is then taken into more explicit consideration only in the final section when discussing the existing framework for the (co)liability of hosting providers.

[6] Buivids, C-345/17, §66, CJEU 2019, ECLI:EU:C:2019:122.

4.2.2 *Freedom of Expression*

Freedom of expression constitutes one of the core elements of the Convention, enshrined in the provisions of Article 10 and stipulating broad understanding of an individual fundamental right to free expression as well as access to information. It is perceived as one of the cardinal European values and reiterated in most international documents on human rights (Flauss 2009, 813). The court described it as constituting 'one of the essential foundations of a democratic society and one of the basic conditions for its progress and for each individual's self-fulfilment'.[7]

It is crucial to highlight at this point that ECHR case law serves as an intrinsic part of the normative structure of the Convention, forming a set of binding precedents with the status of mandatory legal norms shaping the meaning of the respective provisions as such. This allows the Convention to be adequately responsive to the dynamic developments of standards and values but lays upon the reader an additional requirement of expertise while seeking interpretation of the provisions under the present-day conditions (Bychawska-Siniarska 2017, 10).

4.2.3 *Doctrine of Margin Appreciation*

Part of the structural quality of the Convention is reflected in the established doctrine of margin appreciation[8] pursued by the ECHR, which provides for a degree of discretion for national public authorities and courts with regard to interpretation and application of the Convention (Bychawska-Siniarska 2017, 10). As such, the margin differs depending on the particularities, as it does in regard to the protection of freedom of expression, whose margin is, under the current interpretation, in principle comparatively low (Bychawska-Siniarska 2017, 10). Any state interference with the freedom must be necessitated by the fulfilment of three conditions: the action must be prescribed by law, it must be considered necessary in a democratic society, and it must be proportionate in respect to the aim pursued (Greer 2000, 10). These elements of the so-called proportionality test shall be closely inspected in a later section of this chapter.

[7] Lingens v. Austria, no. 9815/82, §41, ECHR 1986.

[8] Handyside v. the United Kingdom, no. 5493/72, §48, ECHR 1976.

4.2.4 *Components of Freedom of Expression*

The constituting element of the broader freedom of expression is the often-referenced freedom of speech. It is built upon the principle of protecting the freedom of any individual or community to voice opinions and ideas without fear of retaliation, censorship, or legal sanction. The possibility to voice one's opinions freely is a necessary precondition for the purposeful guarantee of freedom of conscience (Olteanu 2015, 261). The freedom of expression, as provided in the first paragraph of Article 10 of the Convention, is composed of three constituting components: the freedom to hold opinions (freedom of thought), the freedom to impart information and ideas (freedom of speech), and the freedom to receive information and ideas (freedom of access).

The freedom to hold opinions is a logical precondition to other aspects of free expression. Its protection is general and nearly absolute, following from the fact that it is seen from the perspective of the international community as the foundation of a democratic society (UN Human Rights Committee 2011).

In the context of disinformation, it presents the conceptual justification for the existence of disinformation. The public sector in a democratic state is not permitted to enforce one-sided information or an interpretation of an event (Bychawska-Siniarska 2017, 13). Furthermore, the difference between dissent, conspiratorial information, and disinformation is often blurry and a matter of individual perspective. The natural lack of full information and the right of each individual to a subjective perception and interpretation of events or actions provide for a democratic divergence of opinions, but they also serve as a protective shield for disseminators of disinformation. As described in Chapter 1, there is a variety of manipulative techniques to be employed and degrees of deceptiveness associated with disinformation. From the legal perspective, this fine gradation may spell the difference between the exercise of fundamental freedom and abuse of its protective framework.

Nevertheless, the dissemination of disinformation and propaganda goes by its nature beyond mere freedom of thought to its manifestation as an information shared in communication. The basic dimensions of this freedom relate to democratic governance and therefore concern primarily free political competition[9] and criticism of government[10] (Bychawska-Siniarska 2017, 14). There are many shades of freedom of speech that were considered by the ECHR in its case law, whether concerning political opinions, information on economic matters,[11] or manifestations of artistic ideas.[12] Disinformation may in essence touch upon any of these categories given that their content is not restricted to a particular context.

The individual's right to have access to information and ideas is to be interpreted in a broad sense, giving a potential basis to the right to have access to disinformation. Everyone's opinions and ideas are formed to a large degree based on external inputs. Therefore, our ability to cope with contradictory information or complex concepts is a result of repeated exposure and interaction with unstructured and conflicting pieces of information, from which each individual forms his subjective worldview and opinions on particular issues and topics. In this context, combatting disinformation or propaganda includes measures towards education and awareness (Barderi 2018, 7). If freedom of expression unlocks the potential for individuality and diversity, the right to access information is the basis for the individual development of critical thinking (McPeck 2016). Nevertheless, the scope of freedom of access is limited to the lawful sources of information and ideas available.[13] Due to the unestablished nature of fake news as expressions, it cannot be seen as a basis for their protection, but merely as a basis for the permissible dissemination of diverse opinions and content.

[9] Handyside v. the United Kingdom, no. 5493/72, §42 et seq., ECHR 1976.

[10] Lingens v. Austria, no. 9815/82, §34 et seq., ECHR 1986; Şener v. Turkey, no. 26680/95, §25 et seq., ECHR 2000; Thoma v. Luxembourg, no. 38432/97, §32 et seq, ECHR 2001; Maronek v. Slovakia, no. 32686/96, §46 et seq, ECHR 2001; Dichand and Others v. Austria, no. 29271/95, §25 et seq., ECHR 2002.

[11] Krone Verlag GmbH & Co. KG v. Austria (No. 3), no. 39069/97, §21 et seq., ECHR 2003.

[12] Muller and Others v. Switzerland, no. 10737/84, §26 et seq., ECHR 1988.

[13] Osterreichische Vereinigung zur Erhaltung, Starkung und Schaffung v. Austria, no. 39534/07, §28 et seq., ECHR 2013; Autronic AG v. Switzerland, no. 12726/87, §47, ECHR 1990.

4.2.5 *Typology of Speech*

The speech protected under the Convention is to be understood in a broad sense, encompassing various forms of idea manifestation (including e.g. pictures[14] or actions[15]) as well as their formats of expression (including e.g. radio broadcasts[16] or printed documents[17]). Consequently, various means of production, transmission, and distribution of expression are covered by the freedom, following the development of information and communication technologies (Bychawska-Siniarska 2017, 18). The internet age has not just brought new formats for expression, but also new challenges in the form of globalised information sharing platforms, which may restrict guaranteed freedoms through commercially controlled, technological means (Oozeer 2014, 348). This technological transformation can also be seen as a crucial enabler, leading to the increasing urgency of the disinformation issue.

4.2.5.1 *Hate Speech and Other Unprotected Forms of Speech*

A particular category of speech which needs to be taken into consideration while discussing disinformation consists of the established forms of unprotected speech—that is, content aimed at incitement of violence,[18] the expression of hate towards minorities,[19] or Holocaust denial or its abuse.[20] Article 10 of the Convention may not contain the explicit exclusion of these expressions; however, the Convention needs to be read as a whole, which brings into play Articles 14 and 17. Article 14 prohibits discrimination, whereas Article 17 prevents any interpretation of the Convention that would imply the right of any party to the destruction or limitation of any right or freedom under the Convention to a greater extent than it provides. This, in effect, forms the basis for the aforementioned categories of unprotected speech as established by ECHR case law (Bleich 2014, 292). In fact, hate speech may take a multitude

[14] Muller and Others v. Switzerland, no. 10737/84, ECHR 1988.

[15] Steel and Others v. the United Kingdom, no. 24838/94, §88 et seq., ECHR 1998.

[16] Groppera Radio AG and Others v. Switzerland, no. 10890/84, ECHR 1990.

[17] Handyside v. the United Kingdom, no. 5493/72, ECHR 1976.

[18] Sürek v. Turkey (No. 3), no. 24735/94, §40, ECHR 1999.

[19] Vejdeland and Others v. Sweden, no. 1813/07, §8, ECHR 2012.

[20] PETA Deutschland v. Germany, no. 43481/09, §49, ECHR 2012.

of forms beyond the originally adjudicated racial hate.[21] These include ethnic hate,[22] incitement to violence and supporting a terrorist activity,[23] negationism and revisionism,[24] religious hate,[25] or threats to the democratic order[26] (ECHR 2019c, 1–5). Such speech may contain a form of disinformation in the sense that it is fabulised or intentionally biased, but that is essentially a secondary attribute, in essence not related to the basis for exclusion from the scope of protected speech, as established above. The European approach to hate speech is, in effect, significantly more complex than the parallel system developed in the United States (Bleich 2014, 284); however, that also means that the category of hate speech is less clear-cut, and assessment under the Convention requires careful consideration of the specific circumstances of each case (Bleich 2014, 294). In consequence, hate speech can hardly be perceived as a definitive category, similar to the above established challenging classification of disinformation. Furthermore, these two categories may overlap, but given that their indicative attributes differ, the overlap is merely partial. Additionally, fake news containing expressions of hate, in particular hate against a minority, is unlikely to constitute the so-called hard cases (Dworkin 1975) in the sense of challenging the setting for guiding judicial interpretation. However, as gradually established throughout this chapter, a large portion of disinformation is likely to constitute such 'hard cases' due to a lack of clear guidelines for their adjudication.

4.2.5.2 *Conflict of Fundamental Rights or Freedoms*

The provided cases establishing the exclusion of hate speech from protection due to the excessive infringement on the expression of the rights and freedoms of others can be viewed as one extreme of a spectrum. However, most situations concerning hate speech as well as fake news do not qualify for such extremity despite presenting an obvious conflict between equally

[21] Glimmerveen and Haqenbeek v. the Netherlands, no. 8348/78,8406/78, ECHR 1979.

[22] Pavel Ivanov v. Russia, no. 35222/04, ECHR 2007.

[23] Roj TV A/S v. Denmark, no. 24683/14, ECHR 2018.

[24] Garaudy v. France, no. 65831/01, ECHR 2003.

[25] Norwood v. the United Kingdom, no. 23131/03, ECHR 2004.

[26] B.H, M.W, H.P and G.K. v. Austria, no. 12774/87, decision of the Commission 1989.

valued fundamental rights and freedoms. This is in fact the basis for most defamatory cases concerning freedom of expression in the media (ECHR 2019d). Such conflicts need to be resolved on the basis of a balancing test. This results in the proportionate restriction of the concerned rights and freedoms. This aspect shall be considered further throughout the text of this chapter.

4.2.5.3 Restrictions Permitted Under the Convention

In consequence, most expressions constituting disinformation or propaganda need to be perceived as falling under the protection of Article 10 of the Convention. This means that restriction of their dissemination by state authorities is permissible under the margin of appreciation if the conditions foreseen by the Convention are met.

4.3 Permissible Restrictions to Freedom of Speech Through State Action

Restrictions to freedom of speech must be assessed in a particular context; no general approach to the restriction of content is permissible under Article 17 of the Convention. Additionally, equality of rights protected under the Convention necessitates all restrictive authoritative actions be subject to a balancing act of permissibility (Bychawska-Siniarska 2017, 32). Following from ECHR case law, the central role in balancing the conflicting freedoms and interests falls to the three-part test for adjudicating the necessity of interference with freedom in a democratic society. Cumulative conditions for permissible interference with freedom of speech by national authorities are threefold: (i) interference is prescribed by law,[27] (ii) it is aimed at the protection of one of the interests or values enlisted in the second paragraph of Article 10,[28] and (iii) it is a necessary measure in a democratic society.[29]

The fulfilment of these conditions is to be interpreted in a strict manner in order to protect broad freedom of speech. Under this premise,

[27] The Sunday Times v. the United Kingdom, no. 6538/74, §46 et seq., ECHR 1979.

[28] Handyside v. the United Kingdom, no. 5493/72, §43–50, ECHR 1976.

[29] The Sunday Times v. the United Kingdom, no. 6538/74, §58 et seq., ECHR 1979.

a borderline case should in general be awarded in favour of the individual and his freedom rather than a state's claim to overriding interest (Rzepliński 1997, 2–3).

The restrictive approach means that no additional interests or values to those foreseen by the Convention should be used as a basis for the interference, and the content of the aforementioned three criteria should not be interpreted beyond their ordinary meaning (European Commission of Human Rights 1977, 74). This position of the ECHR towards measures limiting freedom of speech is of high relevance for possible legislative measures aimed at the systematic combating of disinformation or propaganda.

Nevertheless, apart from the criteria expressly stated in the aforementioned paragraphs, the ECHR established through its more recent case law that some regard should be given to the specific context of the expression (Bychawska-Siniarska 2017, 12). This means that consideration may be given to its particular purpose, for instance, political or commercial (Katsirea 2018, 173); its form of dissemination, such as audiovisual media or online access (Callamard 2017, 325–26); or its predominant target audience, for example, the public without restriction, including children, or just a particular interest group (Bychawska-Siniarska 2017, 12).

Furthermore, as presented early in this chapter, some of the core aspects defining disinformation, such as a provable falsity and the intention to deceive, may be considered relevant under contextual circumstances. These were mostly inferred for cases of controversial and defamatory journalistic expressions, which is close to the context of fake news. The requirements for upholding the baseline of journalistic ethics by traditional media were already mentioned; however, fake news is predominantly shared by new media in the online environment. Therefore, consideration must additionally be given to the plausibility of extending the requirement of upholding certain journalistic standards to online news dissemination as well. This issue is far from simple given that relevant online media consists of a significantly broader spectrum of subjects and structures than traditional media. There is likely little dispute over the applicability of the requirements to online news platforms of traditional media outlets. Similarly, online media with a traditional content creation process (by employees or an otherwise limited and accountable group) also likely conform with general parameters for applicability of these requirements. However, a sizable portion of the considered fake news does not originate from these structures but rather through user-generated content hosted on online platforms established for this purpose. This modern approach to the democratisation of online content creation challenges the traditional perception of journalism (Normahfuzah 2017) and also alters the consideration of applicable requirements. The source of the content is diluted among a multitude of authors who have no permanent link to the hosting provider. The hosting provider often lacks even general information about the identity of the content creators and in many cases refrains from any moderating or editing role with regards to the disseminated content.

The ECHR established in its case law that media needs to be perceived in a broad sense, including also others who engage in a public debate rather than just traditional media.[30] Katsirea infers from this interpretation that new online media should be treated similarly to traditional journalists (Katsirea 2018, 173). However, this is by no means decidedly inferable from the available case law. The position of a content creator contributing to a platform for user-generated content can vary greatly, from an occasional contributor of a comment or link to a regular blogger on par with a journalist. In any case, the multitude of creators contributing to the hosting platform fragments the roles. Therefore, the predominantly loose relationships between content creators and hosting providers cannot be compared to the structures present in traditional media for content review and editing. In consequence, the room to enforce liability for the content against the individual users is comparatively diminished. This is the basis for considerations over the (co)liability of hosting providers, which shall be discussed in the concluding section of this chapter.

4.3.1 State Interference

State interference restricting the freedom of expression is to be understood as any form of interference from any authority with public power or in public service (Bychawska-Siniarska 2017, 34). Therefore, any action of public bodies leading to the limitation of accessibility to content is to be considered as such interference. In general, censorship may take place either before or after the expression has been made available to the public.

[30] Steel and Morris v. the United Kingdom, no. 68416/01, ECHR 2005.

Censorship prior to publishing is especially perceived by the ECHR as a major intervention in the freedom of expression, which should therefore be applied with particular caution (Bychawska-Siniarska 2017, 35). For this reason, even though Article 10 of the Convention does not prohibit such a measure per se, established interpretation pursuant to ECHR case law sees only a narrow window for its permissibility.[31] Another form of interference which may come into consideration with regards to disinformation is to order the author to reveal journalistic sources and documents under sanction.[32] The ECHR did not, to the knowledge of the author, deal as of yet with a specific case concerning such measures against a disinformation disseminator, in particular with regard to the assessment of the intensity of measures taken against such expressions.

However, most suitable interference would likely constitute a post-publication censorship action or a withdrawal of a published expression from public accessibility. In such a case, the impact of the restriction concerning the denial of access and deletion of content published online seems less invasive than most interferences reproached by the ECHR in the available case law. These also encompass, aside from the abovementioned cases of prior censorship, criminal persecution for the expression as such,[33] confiscation of the means through which the information was disseminated,[34] or a prohibition of advertisement,[35] political in particular.[36]

Depending on the specific content of the disinformation or propaganda, some of these more invasive interferences may be considered relevant along with post-publication censorship, specifically criminal persecution or an advertisement prohibition of extremist political ideas. However, these would likely be extreme cases, solved under respective, specific national laws.

[31] The Sunday Times v. the United Kingdom (No. 2), no. 13166/87, §51, ECHR 1991; Observer and Guardian v. the United Kingdom, no. 13585/88, §59, ECHR 1991.

[32] Goodwin v. the United Kingdom, no. 17488/90, §27, ECHR 1996.

[33] Castells v. Spain, no. 11798/85, ECHR 1992.

[34] Muller and Others v. Switzerland, no. 10737/84, §28, ECHR 1988.

[35] Casado Coca v. Spain, no. 15450/89, §49, ECHR 1994.

[36] TV Vest AS & Rogaland Pensjonistparti v. Norway, no. 21132/05, §63, ECHR 2008.

4.3.2 *Prescribed by Law*

The first condition concerning the permissibility of state interference is its basis in national law. The measure should be enforced pursuant to national legal provisions, or, depending on the legal system of the state, in accordance with the common law, even though the parliamentary legitimacy of the measure may play a role in the justification of the restriction under the Convention (Bychawska-Siniarska 2017, 39). Therefore, as such, even the unwritten components of the common law system are perceived as a relevant basis for state interference (Ajevski 2014, 125). The court also maintains, among the relevant aspects of the legal basis, its public accessibility and foreseeability.[37] Following from these requirements, measures based on unpublished internal regulations or other sub-statutory provisions would in general not be a permissible basis for the restriction of the freedom of expression (Bychawska-Siniarska 2017, 42). Through this prism, most current national laws contain a general basis for measures against disinformation; however, most lack sufficiently specific regulatory provisions.

4.3.3 *Legitimate Aim*

Even with the respective legal framework in place, its application needs to be considered with regard to its aim. The ECHR 'has a very relaxed attitude towards the states' claims of following a legitimate aim and for not requiring a very strict connection between the state action and the legitimate aim pursued' (Ajevski 2014, 126). Aims pursued by legitimate restrictions of freedom of speech are listed under paragraph 2 of Article 10 of the Convention.

Due to the broad spectrum of content presented under disinformation or propaganda, a legitimate aim may be inferred from a multitude of available bases. However, the mere deceptive nature of the content is insufficient ground for restriction unless it can be further connected to interference with one of the protected interests. These include (i) national security, (ii) territorial integrity, (iii) public safety, (iv) prevention of disorder or crime, (v) protection of health or morals, (vi) protection of the reputation or rights of others, (vii) confidence of information, or (viii) the authority and impartiality of the judiciary.

[37] Leander v. Sweden, no. 9248/81, §50, ECHR 1987.

4.3.3.1 *National Security*

Restrictions in the interest of national security must respect the strict limits set by ECHR case law.[38] The court held that it is in general unnecessary to prevent the disclosure of certain information if it had already been made public.[39] National security information cannot be regarded en masse as confidential in order to apply restricted access to it.[40] Disinformation can certainly acquire a quality threatening the interests of national security; however, the legitimacy of its restriction needs to also take into consideration the nature of the dissemination media.[41] In this sense, fake news shared through ill-reputed portals broadly known for propaganda or conspiratorial content are unlikely to pose a serious threat to the interests of national security as such, and additional justification for the legitimacy of this aim may be required.

4.3.3.2 *Territorial Integrity*

Similar considerations apply to the interest of territorial integrity, which mostly concerns dissemination of separatist propaganda.[42] The article must be sufficiently capable of inciting violence or local dissent in order to infringe upon this interest.[43] Mere one-sidedness of political opinions or interpretation of events formulating criticism of the government do not in itself justify such interference with freedom of expression.[44] The propagandistic or deceptive nature of the expression must result in an abuse of rights or convincing promotion of conduct contrary to the spirit of the Convention so as to allow for restrictive action.[45]

[38] Observer and Guardian v. the United Kingdom, no. 13585/88, ECHR 1991.

[39] Weber v. Switzerland, no. 11034/84, §49, ECHR 1990.

[40] Vereniging Weekblad Bluf! v. the Netherlands, no. 16616/90, §38 et seq., ECHR 1995.

[41] Stoll v. Switzerland, no. 69698/01, §117 et seq., ECHR 2007.

[42] Sürek and Ozdemir v. Turkey, no. 26682/95, §49–50, ECHR 1999.

[43] Sürek v. Turkey (No. 3), no. 24735/94, §40–41, ECHR 1999.

[44] Sürek and Ozdemir v. Turkey, no. 23927/94,24277/94, §58 et seq., ECHR 1999.

[45] Kuhnen v. the Federal Republic of Germany (inadmissible), no. 12194/86, ECHR 1988.

4.3.3.3 *Public Safety, Prevention of Disorder or Crime, Authority, and Impartiality of the Judiciary*

The public safety interest may be relevant to disinformation causing panic or regarding functions and the availability of public services, such as health services, public transport, or basic utilities. Another possible basis is interference with the interest of disorder or crime prevention, previously adjudicated expressions encouraging the disobedience of armed forces,[46] or public support of violent criminal behaviour. Disinformation concerning high-profile criminal investigations or undermining the public opinion of police authorities may also be seen as conflicting with this interest. Respective case law is, however, as of yet, to the knowledge of the author, not available. Nevertheless, an analogy may be drawn from disputes concerning expressions weakening the authority and impartiality of the judiciary.[47]

4.3.3.4 *Protection of Reputation or Rights of Others*

The conflict with reputation or rights of other individuals is present primarily in cases of defamatory media content or less extreme instances of hate speech. Manifestations of hate which constitute the basis for the restriction of freedom of expression in this form include expressions supporting terrorism,[48] condoning war crimes,[49] inciting religious intolerance,[50] insulting state officials,[51] or containing hateful defamation[52] (ECHR 2019c, 13–18). The defamatory expressions were partially discussed earlier with regard to the duties and responsibilities of journalists in relation to their content and shall be further delved into in the next section.

[46] Saszmann v. Austria (inadmissible), no. 23697/94, ECHR 1997.

[47] Kudeshkina v. Russia, no. 29492/05, §81, ECHR 2009.

[48] Leroy v. France, no. 36109/03, ECHR 2008; Stomakhin v. Russia, no. 52273/07, ECHR 2018.

[49] Lehideux and Isorni v. France, no. 24662/94, ECHR 1998.

[50] İ.A. v. Turkey, no. 42571/98, ECHR 2005.

[51] Otegi Mondragon v. Spain, no. 2034/07, ECHR 2011; Stern Taulats and Roura Capellera v. Spain, no. 51168/15, 51186/15, ECHR 2018.

[52] Pihl v. Sweden (inadmissible), no. 74742/14, ECHR 2017; Savva Terentyev v. Russia, no. 10692/09, ECHR 2018.

4.3.3.5 Protection of Health or Morals, Confidence of Information

Fake news is unlikely to affect the other listed legitimate interests given that protection of morals mostly concerns obscene art expressions,[53] and confidential information is unlikely to be divulged as disinformation.

4.3.4 Necessary in a Democratic Society

Even action based on an adequate legal basis and pursuing a legitimate aim may not be deemed a permissible restriction of the freedom of expression unless found necessary. This test of proportionality in a narrow sense is perceived as the most important part of the three-part proportionality test (Ajevski 2014, 126). The assessment of proportionality reflects the principles governing a democratic society (Bychawska-Siniarska 2017, 44). The restrictive action must therefore be an appropriately strong reaction to a 'pressing social need'.[54] In essence, this is the aspect on which most ECHR cases are decided (Ajevski 2014, 126), and it was therefore partially formalised in the case law through a set of interpretative principles for the meaning of the phrase 'necessary in a democratic society'. These state the following:

> The adjective 'necessary' is not synonymous with 'indispensable', neither has it the flexibility of such expressions as 'admissible', 'ordinary', 'useful', 'reasonable' or 'desirable' … the Contracting States enjoy a certain but not unlimited margin of appreciation in the matter of the imposition of restrictions, but it is for the Court to give the final ruling on whether they are compatible with the Convention … the phrase 'necessary in a democratic society' means that, to be compatible with the Convention, the interference must, inter alia, correspond to a 'pressing social need' and be 'proportionate to the legitimate aim pursued' … [and that] those paragraphs of Articles of the Convention which provide for an exception to a right guaranteed are to be narrowly interpreted.[55]

[53] Muller and Others v. Switzerland, no. 10737/84, ECHR 1988; Vereinigung Bildender Kunstler v. Austria, no. 68354/01, ECHR 2007.

[54] The Observer and the Guardian v. the United Kingdom, no. 13585/88, §40, ECHR 1991.

[55] Silver and others v. the United Kingdom, no. 5947/72, 6205/73, 7052/75, 7061/75, 7107/75, 7113/75, 7136/75, §97, ECHR 1983.

The principles guide the ECHR in specific cases where consideration of the content of the expression, the circumstances of its dissemination, and the role of the author create the context of their application. This context then affects the available margin of appreciation for the state authorities in a way revealed throughout this chapter. Therefore, classification of the expression as political speech limits the margin for state intervention, whereas identification of the author as a journalist accentuates the duties on his or her part in order to retain the freedom of expression. In this regard, the particularities of a given set of fake news or propaganda content may justify proportionate restrictive measures, such as post-publication censorship, but the variety also provides for limits on generalised or generic restrictive measures of expressions categorised under disinformation in a broader sense.

4.4 Expressions Infringing upon the Fundamental Rights or Freedoms of Others

As mentioned above, when considering speech in conflict with the fundamental freedoms or rights of others, the case law developed an important distinction between content that constitutes verifiable facts and that which is a mere sum of an author's opinions. This distinction is highly relevant because, whereas the facts can be checked against sources and refuted, opinions include value judgements which cannot be subject to a test of truth, and their restriction would in effect infringe upon freedom of thought as such.[56] In fact, value judgements concerning political questions enjoy an even greater level of protection as they are perceived as a crucial component in a democratic society (Bychawska-Siniarska 2017, 78). This perspective stands behind some of the challenges in the qualification of fake news under the Convention as they often fall within the grey zone of speculative or manipulative pieces, which may distort facts but do so without full fabulation. Therefore, if free speech in the form of diverse personal value judgements on political matters retains a high

[56] Lingens v. Austria, no. 9815/82, §46, ECHR 1986; Oberschlick v. Austria, no. 11662/85, §63, ECHR 1991; Dichand and Others v. Austria, no. 29271/95, §42, ECHR 2002.

level of protection, the authorities in many cases lack a reliable mechanism or framework to distinguish between these categories and need to limit restrictive measures accordingly. It is mainly the risk of false positives which acts as an obstacle in legitimising some of the widely aimed measures against disinformation and propaganda. The legal framework of the Convention may provide a better setting for the restriction of fake news on a case-by-case adjudication based on conflict with the rights and freedoms of others. This is, however, unlikely to provide an adequate and timely response to the issue given its current scale.

The traditional avenue explored with regard to truthfulness of allegations concerns journalistic content deemed defamatory by the affected party. In principle, the author of a comment must in case of a dispute prove his defamatory assertions of facts are based on the truth—in other words, follow from verifiable sources. There is, however, a more nuanced balancing required. The role of media as a 'public watchdog'[57] provides it with a particularly important position with regard to issues of public concern. In such capacity, ECHR case law[58] established that the message or alternative voice may be more important than adequate fulfilment of journalistic standards, for instance, the thorough verification of sources. There is no specific definition of issues which constitute a matter of public concern; however, the case law deduced this aspect in various situations concerning issues in the public domain,[59] concerning public positions,[60] or public financing.[61]

This does not create a basis for fake news per se, but it indicates that the requirements of journalistic duties can be modified depending on the context of the expression. Based on the case law of European high courts,[62] as well as the ECHR,[63] the Venice Commission identified ten

[57] Bergens Tidende and others, no. 26132/95, §57, ECHR 2000.

[58] Thorgeirson v. Iceland, no. 13778/88, §65, ECHR 1992.

[59] Sürek v. Turkey (No. 2), no. 24122/94, ECHR 1999.

[60] Guja v. Moldova, no. 14277/04, ECHR 2008.

[61] İzzettin Dogan and others v. Turkey, no. 62649/10, ECHR 2016.

[62] Reynolds v. Times Newspapers Limited, Highest Court of the United Kingdom 1999; Böll case, Bundesverfassungsgericht 1998; no. I. US 156/99, Constitutional Court of the Czech Republic 2000; no. 1 BvR 1531/96, Federal Constitutional Court of Germany 1998; no. 2001/19, Supreme Court of Norway 2001; no. 144/1998, Constitutional Court of Spain 1998; no. 28/1996, Constitutional Court of Spain 1996.

[63] Bladet Tromsø and Stensaas V. Norway, no. 21980/93, ECHR 1999.

core factors to be considered in this balancing. These include, among others, the seriousness of the allegation, its source, attempts at its verification, urgency of the matter, the tone of the article, and circumstances of its publication (Venice Commission 2004, 4). Additionally, journalistic standards as such are not a unified set of universal principles but rather a dynamic set of best practices that is itself developing based on the transformation of the media environment (Friend and Singer 2015). There are particular efforts towards transitioning the traditional prerequisites for quality journalism into the online environment (Chapman and Oermann 2019, 3). The abovementioned aspects constitute the basis for a good faith defence, as recognised by ECHR case law.[64] As Bychawska-Siniarska summarises, 'Where a journalist or a publication has a legitimate purpose, the matter is of public concern, and reasonable efforts were made to verify the facts, the press shall not be liable even if the respective facts prove to be untrue' (Bychawska-Siniarska 2017, 78).

The measured acceptance of allegations or rumours as part of the press is established in ECHR case law.[65] There is, however, an important distinction between rumours or unfitting allegations based on good faith journalistic research and disinformation and propaganda. The intention of the author to mislead or manipulate through expression is contrary to the requirement of bona fide action and appropriate duty of care when assessing the sources (Venice Commission 2004, 4). As such, a good faith defence for disinformation as a form of journalistic expression is unlikely to hold up under judicial review. Nevertheless, as already discussed earlier in this chapter, this conclusion has only limited relevance in the context of online media, where professional standards applicable to journalists cannot be readily extended to all commentators and contributors. Furthermore, notwithstanding the conclusion that a case against particular disinformation targeting an individual is in principle likely to be strong, these legal considerations cannot be directly transposed to measures by public authorities in combatting disinformation or propaganda through measures of scale.

[64] Dalban v. Romania, no. 28114/95, §50, ECHR 1999.

[65] Bladet Tromsø and Stensaas V. Norway, no. 21980/93, §59, ECHR 1999; Dalban v. Romania, no. 28114/95, §49, ECHR 1999; Thorgeirson v. Iceland, no. 13778/88, §65, ECHR 1992.

Acknowledging these limitations, an alternative approach is being developed for the online environment. This builds on exploiting the unique position of providers of online environments where information is shared and disseminated. Platforms which host user-generated content projected themselves for a long time in the neutral role of a mere storage service provider; however, growing political and regulatory pressure (Fioretti 2018) is pushing them increasingly into the spotlight as active moderators and contributors to the dissemination and distribution of content online. It is therefore through the legal framework of (co)liability of these hosting providers that measures regulating disinformation and propaganda can be taken and expanded.

4.5 Disinformation Suppression Through Hosting Provider Liability

The regulatory benefits of enforcing restrictions on disinformation and propaganda through requirements set for hosting providers originate from their uniquely strong position in the technical sense. The hosting provider effectively creates the online environment where the information is disseminated and can be accessed by users through the facilitation of underlying data storage. Such an entity is therefore optimally positioned for the supervision of stored content, in particular when present day means of big data analysis and content recognition are taken into consideration. In the default setting, such a provider has a shared liability for the content with the user due to his contribution to facilitating the dissemination. However, efforts towards encouraging innovation and development of internet services in the European Union before the turn of the millennium led to the adoption of the Directive on electronic commerce[66] (Pearce and Platten 2000, 363 et seq.), which provided for a protective setting of exceptions from this liability on the basis of 'safe harbour' provisions.[67] One of these applies to hosting providers, that is, platforms for user-generated content, such as social media or various news portals. The directive set conditions for the application of safe harbour on hosting providers consisting of (i) no actual knowledge about the illicit content,

[66] Directive 2000/31/EC of the European Parliament and of the Council of 8 June 2000 on certain legal aspects of information society services, in particular electronic commerce, in the Internal Market (Directive on electronic commerce).

[67] Art. 12–14 of Directive on electronic commerce.

(ii) independence of the content creator from the provider, and (iii) expeditious removal of the content upon obtaining such knowledge (through a so-called 'notice and action' flagging framework).[68] The applicability of this protective provision is increasingly challenged with respect to various forms of hosting services (Friedmann 2014, 148 et seq.; Husovec 2017b, 115 et seq.) and with regard to the negative impact of newly emergent issues like disinformation.

The pressure on major hosting providers is a combination of voluntary basis cooperation with the European Commission and the gradual development of interpretation to their detriment based on relevant case law. The overview of EU joint and coordinated actions against disinformation (European Commission 2019a) indicates the increasing complexity of the cooperative network and consistently developing the basis of measures implemented by the hosting providers pursuant to impulses originating from the European Commission.

The initial signals of a turn in the tide of interpretation were provided by the CJEU through its case law[69]; however, it was mainly the ECHR which established the crucial precedents for today's approach to content moderation through platform provider activity. Notwithstanding the limited control of the platform over user-generated content as such, the ECHR held as applicable the participation of the platform in the liability for such content (Husovec 2013, 109). Authoritative here was the Grand Chamber decision in the case Delfi AS v. Estonia.[70] The court concluded that in case of an insufficiently responsive action against illegal content, the platform provider is to be held liable and adequate sanction is permissible under Article 10 of the Convention. Through this, an alternative approach to curbing disinformation was thereby opened—in other words, through the moderating role of the hosting providers (Husovec 2016, 17). Nevertheless, there are limits to the pressure which can be put on these intermediaries. Resulting from the subsequent case law,[71] it still remains essential to subject each piece of content to a balancing test assessing its impact and permissibility through the above-discussed criteria

[68] Art. 14 of Directive on electronic commerce.

[69] Google France SARL a Google, no. C-236/08, C-237/08, C-238/08, CJEU 2010; L'Oreal and others, no. C-324/09, CJEU 2011.

[70] Delfi v. Estonia, no. 64569/09, §147 et seq., ECHR 2015.

[71] Magyar Tartalomszolgaltatok Egyesulete and Index.hu Zrt v. Hungary, no. 22947/13, §78 et seq., ECHR 2016.

for conflict between fundamental rights and freedoms (Council of Europe 2018, 7 et seq.). Furthermore, the obligations of the provider need to be proportionate to its size and reach, meaning that small media platforms unknown to the wider public are allowed to have less strict management of user-generated content than those of greater renown.[72] The pressure mounted on the platforms is not limited to the dissemination of disinformation and ranges across various forms of widely persisting illicit content, be it hate speech (Heldt 2019) or unlicensed copyright content (European Commission 2019b).

All these regulatory measures signify the growing urgency for reliable classification and detection of content which should be restricted from dissemination by the hosting providers. However, the diversity of forms it may take makes such a goal tenaciously elusive. Nevertheless, unless sufficient efforts are put towards developing tools and frameworks for classification and identification of such content under independent and neutral conditions, the regulatory mechanism has a likely effect of inducing private censorship through the hosting providers (Kuczerawy 2015, 46). We can already see the negative impact of unsuitable applications of the framework in Russia through multiple cases of unjustified collateral blocking of internet content (Husovec 2017a). The issue, however, reaches beyond the scope of the ECHR's jurisdiction, necessitating an orchestrated global response (Aswad 2018).

This is a problematic outlook not just with regards to the influential role of major platforms but also due to the limited capacity of public institutions to exert necessary control over minor platforms which may play a disproportionately large role in disinformation dissemination.

4.6 Conclusions

This chapter provided an additional legal perspective on the topic of disinformation and propaganda dissemination through the prism of freedom of speech under the European Convention on Human Rights. At first, the term disinformation was confronted with this legal framework and defining characteristics were discussed. The core aspects established as relevant include the provability of its untruthfulness, qualification of its purpose, and disclosure of the author's intention. The focus was then

[72] Pihl v. Sweden (inadmissible), no. 74742/14, §31, ECHR 2017.

turned to the umbrella role of the Convention and ECHR case law in the European legal environment and its relation to the Charter of Fundamental Rights of the European Union. The reader was then introduced to the basic concepts of this framework, including the definition of freedom of expression as a fundamental right, its constituting components, and the role of the margin appreciation doctrine.

An important aspect of disinformation highlighted throughout the chapter is its versatility and varying degree of illegality. For this reason, the application of scale rather than bipolar qualification was continuously emphasised. The freedom of speech framework functions primarily as a countermeasure against censorship and the forced restriction of democratic discussion. This then demands high standards of reliability from the measures and tools aimed at labelling speech as disinformation or propaganda. From this legal perspective, there is a fine gradation in the qualification of expressions, which may spell the difference between the exercise of a fundamental freedom and abuse of its protective framework under the Convention.

The subsequent text concerned relevant features of the expression that the ECHR is taking into consideration while weighing its protection under the Convention. There are extreme forms of expression which are excluded from protection altogether, primarily represented by discriminatory hate speech, but most forms of expression considered disinformation shall fall under the protection of Article 10 of the Convention and can therefore be restricted only pursuant to interference permitted under this framework.

Such permissible restriction must pass the three-part proportionality test establishing that (i) the interference is prescribed by law, (ii) it is aimed at the protection of one of the interests or values listed in the second paragraph of Article 10, and (iii) it is a necessary measure in a democratic society. The case law generally leans towards a restrictive interpretation, allowing for broad freedom of speech.

The text of the chapter then follows these three core components and elaborates on their applicability with respect to measures of combatting speech labelled as disinformation or propaganda. The conclusion concerning state interference is that efforts against broadly or generically defined disinformation would most likely be impermissible under the Convention and case-by-case assessment of expressions is due in this regard. It is mainly the risk of false positives which acts as an obstacle in legitimising some of the widely aimed measures.

The second setting discussed is when the state provides protection to individuals against expressions infringing upon their fundamental rights or freedoms. This mostly concerns the extensively adjudicated sphere of defamatory disputes between individuals and media. Particularities of this setting are described, such as the important distinction between content that constitutes verifiable facts and that which is a mere sum of author's opinions. The disinformation phenomenon is then looked at from the perspective of political expressions; in the context of the role of media as a 'public watchdog'; as well as with acknowledgement of the modern democratisation of online content creation and the subsequent challenges to the established requirements for upholding journalistic standards. A constituting feature of disinformation, the intention of the author to mislead or manipulate, is highlighted as an important element which is removing the option of bona fide protection commonly granted to the media in this context.

The main issue with the previous setting is practical, primarily due to limited scalability. For this reason, the currently prevalently pursued venue for combatting disinformation and propaganda are actions by hosting service providers, given that they share liability for the content with the user due to their role in facilitating its dissemination. The measures currently in place are mostly the consequence of a balanced pressure from European authorities and the voluntary cooperation of the largest hosting providers as well as a recent restrictive interpretation by the European courts of the protective provisions shielding these providers from such liability within the European Union.

Nevertheless, there are limits to the pressure which can be put on these intermediaries, especially minor platforms, which may, however, play a disproportionately large role in disinformation and propaganda dissemination. The evaluation of content through the major platforms additionally creates the threat of undue private censorship. This makes the development and validation of detection and analytical tools under independent and neutral conditions an increasingly crucial issue.

Bibliography

Ajevski, M. (2014). Freedom of Speech as Related to Journalists in the ECtHR, IACtHR and the Human Rights Committee—A Study of Fragmentation. *Nordic Journal of Human Rights, 32*(2), 118–139. https://doi.org/10.1080/18918131.2014.897797.

Aswad, E. M. (2018). The Future of Freedom of Expression Online. *Duke Law & Technology Review, 17*(1), 26–70.

Barderi, D. (2018). *Antirumours Handbook*. Council of Europe.

Bleich, E. (2014). Freedom of Expression versus Racist Hate Speech: Explaining Differences Between High Court Regulations in the USA and Europe. *Journal of Ethnic and Migration Studies, 40*(2), 283–300. https://doi.org/10.1080/1369183X.2013.851476.

Bychawska-Siniarska, D. (2017). *Protecting the Right to Freedom of Expression under the European Convention on Human Rights: A Handbook for Legal Practitioners*. Strasbourg: Council of Europe. https://rm.coe.int/handbook-freedom-of-expression-eng/1680732814. Accessed 12 Dec 2019.

Callamard, A. (2017). Are Courts Re-inventing Internet Regulation? *International Review of Law, Computers & Technology, 31*(3), 323–339. https://doi.org/10.1080/13600869.2017.1304603.

Chapman, M., & Oermann, M. (2019). *Supporting Quality Journalism Through Media and Information Literacy*. MSI-JOQ. Council of Europe. https://rm.coe.int/draft-version-of-msi-joq-study-report-rev-v6-2/168098ab74. Accessed 12 Dec 2019.

Council of Europe. (2018). *Freedom of Expression, the Internet and New Technologies*. Thematic Factsheet. Strasbourg: Council of Europe. https://rm.coe.int/freedom-of-expression-internet-and-new-technologies-14june2018-docx/16808b3530. Accessed 12 Dec 2019.

Dworkin, R. (1975). Hard Cases. *Harvard Law Review, 88*(6), 1057–1109. https://doi.org/10.2307/1340249.

ECHR. (2018). Overview 1959–2018. https://www.echr.coe.int/Documents/Overview_19592018_ENG.pdf. Accessed 12 Dec 2019.

ECHR. (2019a). *European Convention on Human Rights—Official Texts, Convention and Protocols*. https://www.echr.coe.int/Pages/home.aspx?p=basictexts&c=. Accessed 12 Dec 2019.

ECHR. (2019b). *European Court of Human Rights—ECHR, CEDH, News, Information, Press Releases*. https://echr.coe.int/Pages/home.aspx?p=home. Accessed 12 Dec 2019.

ECHR. (2019c). *Factsheet—Hate Speech*. https://www.echr.coe.int/Documents/FS_Hate_speech_ENG.pdf. Accessed 12 Dec 2019.

ECHR. (2019d). *Factsheet—Protection of Reputation*. https://www.echr.coe.int/Documents/FS_Reputation_ENG.pdf. Accessed 12 Dec 2019.

Equality and Human Rights Commission. (2017). *What Is the European Convention on Human Rights?* https://www.equalityhumanrights.com/en/what-european-convention-human-rights. Accessed 12 Dec 2019.

European Commission. (2019a). *Tackling Online Disinformation.* Digital Single Market—European Commission. https://ec.europa.eu/digital-single-market/en/tackling-online-disinformation. Accessed 12 Dec 2019.

European Commission. (2019b). *Stakeholder Dialogue on the Application of Article 17 of Directive on Copyright in the Digital Single Market.* Digital Single Market—European Commission. https://ec.europa.eu/digital-single-market/en/stakeholder-dialogue-application-article-17-directive-copyright-digital-single-market. Accessed 12 Dec 2019.

European Commission of Human Rights. (1977). Application No. 6538/74—TIMES NEWSPAPERS LTD. and Others Against United Kingdom—Report of the Commission. Strasbourg: European Commission of Human Rights. https://hudoc.echr.coe.int/app/conversion/pdf?library=ECHR&id=001-73577&filename=THE%20SUNDAY%20TIMES%20v.%20THE%20UNITED%20KINGDOM%20(NO.%201).pdf. Accessed 12 Dec 2019.

European Parliament. (2019). *Completion of EU Accession to the ECHR: Legislative Train Schedule.* https://www.europarl.europa.eu/legislative-train. Accessed 12 Dec 2019.

Fioretti, J. (2018, April 26). EU Piles Pressure on Social Media over Fake News. *Reuters.* https://www.reuters.com/article/us-eu-internet-fakenews-idUSKBN1HX15D. Accessed 12 Dec 2019.

Flauss, J.-F. (2009). The European Court of Human Rights and the Freedom of Expression. *Indiana Law Journal, 84*(3). https://www.repository.law.indiana.edu/ilj/vol84/iss3/3. Accessed 12 December 2019.

Flaxman, S., Goel, S., & Rao, J. M. (2016). Filter Bubbles, Echo Chambers, and Online News Consumption. *Public Opinion Quarterly, 80*(S1), 298–320. https://doi.org/10.1093/poq/nfw006.

Friedmann, D. (2014). Sinking the Safe Harbour with the Legal Certainty of Strict Liability in Sight. *Journal of Intellectual Property Law & Practice, 9*(2), 148–155. https://doi.org/10.1093/jiplp/jpt227.

Friend, C., & Singer, J. (2015). *Online Journalism Ethics: Traditions and Transitions.* Abingdon: Routledge.

Greer, S. (2000). *The Margin of Appreciation: Interpretation and Discretion under the European Convention on Human Rights.* Council of Europe Publishing.

Heldt, A. (2019). Reading Between the Lines and the Numbers: An Analysis of the First NetzDG Reports. *Internet Policy Review, 8*(2). https://policyreview.info/articles/analysis/reading-between-lines-and-numbers-analysis-first-netzdg-reports. Accessed 12 Dec 2019.

Husovec, M. (2013). ECtHR Rules on Liability of ISPs as a Restriction of Freedom of Speech. SSRN Scholarly Paper ID 2383148. Rochester: Social Science Research Network. https://papers.ssrn.com/abstract=2383148. Accessed 12 Dec 2019.

Husovec, M. (2016). General Monitoring of Third-Party Content: Compatible with Freedom of Expression? *Journal of Intellectual Property Law & Practice, 11*, 17–20. https://doi.org/10.1093/jiplp/jpv200.

Husovec, M. (2017a). [ECtHR] Kharitonov v Russia: When Website Blocking Goes Awry. Huťko's Technology Law Blog (blog). http://www.husovec.eu/2017/07/ecthr-kharitonov-v-russia-when-website.html. Accessed 12 Dec 2019.

Husovec, M. (2017b). Holey Cap! CJEU Drills (yet) Another Hole in the e-Commerce Directive's Safe Harbours. *Journal of Intellectual Property Law & Practice, 12*(2), 115–125. https://doi.org/10.1093/jiplp/jpw203.

Katsirea, I. (2018). 'Fake News': Reconsidering the Value of Untruthful Expression in the Face of Regulatory Uncertainty. *Journal of Media Law, 10*(2), 159–188. https://doi.org/10.1080/17577632.2019.1573569.

Kuczerawy, A. (2015). Intermediary Liability & Freedom of Expression: Recent Developments in the EU Notice & Action Initiative. *Computer Law & Security Review, 31*(1), 46–56. https://doi.org/10.1016/j.clsr.2014.11.004.

Kuijer, M. (2018). The Challenging Relationship Between the European Convention on Human Rights and the EU Legal Order: Consequences of a Delayed Accession. *The International Journal of Human Rights*, 1–13. https://doi.org/10.1080/13642987.2018.1535433.

Lemmens, P. (2001). The Relation between the Charter of Fundamental Rights of the European Union and the European Convention on Human Rights—Substantive Aspects. *Maastricht Journal of European and Comparative Law, 8*(1), 49–67. https://doi.org/10.1177/1023263X0100800104.

McGonagle, T. (2017). 'Fake News': False Fears or Real Concerns? *Netherlands Quarterly of Human Rights, 35*(4), 203–209. https://doi.org/10.1177/0924051917738685.

McPeck, J. E. (2016). *Critical Thinking and Education*. Abingdon: Routledge.

Normahfuzah, A. (2017). The Decline of Conventional News Media and Challenges of Immersing in New Technology. *ESharp, 25*(1), 71–82. (University of Glasgow).

Olteanu, C. N. (2015). Some Reflections on Freedom of Expression. In *International Conference Education and Creativity for a Knowledge-Based Society* (pp. 261–264).

Oozeer, A. (2014). Internet and Social Networks: Freedom of Expression in the Digital Age. *Commonwealth Law Bulletin, 40*(2), 341–360. https://doi.org/10.1080/03050718.2014.909129.

Pearce, G., & Platten, N. (2000). Promoting the Information Society: The EU Directive on Electronic Commerce. *European Law Journal, 6*(4), 363–378. https://doi.org/10.1111/1468-0386.00113.

Regules, J. M. (2018). MCEL Master Working Paper 2018/8. Disinformation and Freedom of Expression. A Study on the Regulation of 'Fake News' in the European Union (Master Working Paper). Maastricht: Maastricht Centre for European Law. https://www.maastrichtuniversity.nl/sites/default/files/mcel_master_working_paper_regules_20188_pdf.pdf. Accessed 12 Dec 2019.

Rzepliński, A. (1997). *Restrictions to the Expression of Opinions or Disclosure of Information on Domestic or Foreign Policy of the State*. Council of Europe—Monitor/Inf 1997. http://kryminologia.ipsir.uw.edu.pl/images/stronka/Pracownicy_publikacje/A.%20Rzeplinski_Restriction%20to%20%20the%20%20expression%20of%20opinions%20or%20disclosure%20on%20information%20on%20domestic%20or%20%20foreign%20policy.pdf. Accessed 12 Dec 2019.

Sluijs, J. P. (2012). From Competition to Freedom of Expression: Introducing Article 10 ECHR in the European Network Neutrality Debate. *Human Rights Law Review, 12*(3), 509–554. https://doi.org/10.1093/hrlr/ngsO5.

UN Human Rights Committee. (2011). General Comment No. 34: Article 19: Freedoms of Opinion and Expression. United Nations. https://www2.ohchr.org/english/bodies/hrc/docs/gc34.pdf. Accessed 12 Dec 2019.

Venice Commission. (2004). Amicus Curiae Opinion on the Relationship between the Freedom of Expression and Defamation with Respect to Unproven Defamatory Allegations of Fact as Requested by the Constitutional Court of Georgia. CDL-AD(2004)011-e. Strasbourg: Council of Europe. https://www.venice.coe.int/webforms/documents/CDL-AD(2004)011-e.aspx. Accessed 12 Dec 2019.

Part II

CHAPTER 5

Technological Approaches to Detecting Online Disinformation and Manipulation

Aleš Horák, Vít Baisa, and Ondřej Herman

5.1 Introduction

The move of propaganda and disinformation to the online environment is possible thanks to the fact that within the last decade, digital information channels radically increased in popularity as a news source. The main advantage of such media lies in the speed of information creation and dissemination. This, on the other hand, inevitably adds pressure, accelerating editorial work, fact-checking, and the scrutiny of source credibility.

In this chapter, an overview of computer-supported approaches to detecting disinformation and manipulative techniques based on several

A. Horák (✉) · V. Baisa · O. Herman
Masaryk University, Brno, Czechia
e-mail: hales@fi.muni.cz

O. Herman
e-mail: xherman1@fi.muni.cz

M. Gregor and P. Mlejnková (eds.), *Challenging Online Propaganda and Disinformation in the 21st Century*, Political Campaigning and Communication,
https://doi.org/10.1007/978-3-030-58624-9_5

criteria is presented. We concentrate on the technical aspects of automatic methods which support fact-checking, topic identification, text style analysis, or message filtering on social media channels. Most of the techniques employ artificial intelligence and machine learning with feature extraction combining available information resources. The following text firstly specifies the tasks related to computer detection of manipulation and disinformation spreading. The second section presents concrete methods of solving the tasks of the analysis, and the third sections enlists current verification and benchmarking datasets published and used in this area for evaluation and comparison.

5.2 Task Specification

With the growth of digital-born and social media publishing, the origin of news distributed to the general public can be easily performed and the process of publishing a message to a wide group of readers is extremely simplified. This opens new possibilities for any pressure group to publish disinformation or purpose-modified news, which are expressed so as to be apparently accepted as objective reporting of current events (Woolley and Howard 2018). On the other hand, the predetermined availability of the texts in an online digital form opens new possibilities for the detection of such persuasive techniques through the analysis of the content, the style of the text, and its broader context.

The presented approaches usually distinguish the two main aspects of the analysed texts: (a) whether the text is intentionally truthless (disinformation, fake news), or (b) whether the text refers to an actual event or situation but the form and content is adapted from an objective description for a reason (propaganda, manipulation). Note that the first category usually does not include 'misinformation', that is, texts which are unintentionally truthless, where their author is convinced the message is faithful (see Chapter 1).

5.2.1 Fake News Detection

In general, a fully capable technical method to recognise that an input text contains truthless statement(s) would have to be implemented as an omniscient oracle. In practice, the task of fake news detection uses various second-level aspects of the text, which can be handled by a thorough analysis of the available data (Kavanagh and Rich 2018). Fake news detection approaches include:

- fact-checking,
- source credibility analysis,
- information flow analysis, and
- manipulative style recognition.

The *fact-checking* or *verification* approach implements the most logical idea of verifying whether a message is true or not, which resembles the same process executed by a human expert—a journalist when processing the input information, for example. In the automated approach, the text first needs to be analysed using natural language processing (NLP) methods, and individual objective fact statements or claims are identified. Consequently, each individual fact is verified—confirmed or refuted, usually with a confidence score—by comparing the statement to a predefined source of knowledge, for example, knowledge graphs built from Wikipedia texts (Ciampaglia et al. 2015); manual datasets of verified facts prepared by human experts, such as CNN Facts First or PolitiFact by the Poynter Institute (Hassan et al. 2017); or collaborative verification by a network of engaged specialists, such as CaptainFact or CrossCheck (Cazalens et al. 2018). Collaborative verification can be used in the broader sense of the claim verification process as the involved community can also judge the truthfulness of images and video content, which is still unrealistic with automated tools. In the process of simplifying and distributing the process of fact annotation, Duke University and Google Research (Adair et al. 2017) have published an open standard entitled ClaimReview, which details how to annotate the result of checking someone else's claims. Accessible online ClaimReviews are then aggregated and used for the continuous expansion of fact-checking databases. Since the ratio of possible errors in the fact processing chain is still rather high, practical tools for fact-checking usually offer multiple fact verification sources and offer the automated results as expert supporting tools where the final decision is left to the human specialist. Exploiting fact-supporting tools became such an important part of serious news preparation that a completely new style of editing has been defined as 'computational' or 'digital journalism' (Caswell and Anderson 2019).

Source credibility analysis exploits information about the origin of the text. This method can of course be inclined to counterfeiting or interpolating the source identification, but in cases where the text author is sufficiently documented, source credibility offers an important piece of information. The simplest case of source analysis takes the form of consulting a trustworthy database of internet IP addresses as this is the primary information about where an online text originated. An example of such a general database (and accompanying tools, e.g. web browser extensions) is the Adblock Plus tool, which allows for the management of multiple blacklisted (forbidden) and whitelisted (allowed) sources, including external community created lists, such as EasyList (Wills and Uzunoglu 2016). Intensive efforts in source certification widen the simple address-based judgement with transparency rules for best practices, covering citation and references work, reporter expertise, or other trust indicators. Even though those approaches can include analysis via automated tools, the main aspect of the credibility decisions is driven by human experts organised in an established initiative, such as Trust Project Indicators or the International Fact-Checking Network (Graves 2016).

According to Shearer (2018), more than two-thirds of US adults receive news via social media such as Facebook, YouTube, or Twitter. These networks provide detailed information about the process of sharing each message across the network and thus open the possibility of an *information flow analysis*. For example, TwitterTrails (Finn et al. 2014) uses knowledge from the Twitter network about the originator, the burst time and the whole timeline of the message, the propagators, and other actors related to the message (including the audience), and it checks whether there are any refutations of the message in the flow. Vosoughi et al. (2018) have shown that false news spreads substantially faster and reaches more people than true stories; while the most retweeted true news arrived to about a thousand people, the same category of false news found their way to tens of thousands of readers. The Hoaxy Twitter analysis system by Indiana University (Shao et al. 2016) has gathered and published the Misinformation and Fact-Checking Diffusion Network, consisting of more than 20 million retweets with timestamp and user identifiers, allowing for the observation and quantification of all message flows between Twitter users, including important statistical information about user activity and URL popularity. The data allows automated bot users to be distinguished from real humans as well as the identification of influence centres or the origins of selected fake news.

The fourth category of fake news detection tasks leans on the fact that intentional disinformation is often expressed with a specific expressive style in order to promote the intended manipulation of the reader. *Manipulative style recognition* also belongs among the detection techniques described in the next section devoted to the recognition of propagandistic texts. With fake news, the characteristic style of the news usually forms a supplemental indicator and is analysed in combination with other factors. Volkova et al. (2017) designed a neural network model processing text, social graph and stylistic markers expressing bias, subjectivity, persuasiveness, and moral foundations cues. They showed that linguistic or stylistic analysis significantly improved the results.

5.2.2 Detection of Manipulative Techniques

Within this chapter, we define propagandistic news as texts which report about (at least partially) true events or facts but use specific *manipulative techniques*, framing the content of the messages in a purposeful way to promote political, economic, or other goals (see Chapter 1). Basic algorithms to detect propaganda have been published for more than eighty years (Institute for Propaganda Analysis 1938), naturally for processing by people, not machines. The instructions presented seven stylistic techniques (propaganda devices) used by manipulators in the text, such as name-calling, transfer, or bandwagoning. In the current detection procedures, this main task remains very similar: to identify whether any specific reader manipulation technique exists in the text.[1]

Everybody has met at one point the most widespread example of simple propagandistic texts: spam email messages or web spam (Metaxas 2010). Unlike antispam techniques, which are based on the weighted occurrence scores of specific words and word combinations, the style of propaganda in news is analysed with complex metrics of *computational stylometry*. The question of whether the studied message contains a specific manipulative technique or not is here shifted to the question of whether the message is written in a specific *style* usually used with that manipulation device. Besides propaganda style detection, stylometric methods are used to recognise anonymous authorship attribution or personal information about the text author, such as his or her

[1] For detailed lists of the current analysed techniques, see Sect. 4.4 'Datasets and evaluation'.

gender, age, education, or native language (Neal et al. 2017). The input data for stylometric methods is formed by a multitude of measurable quantitative features in the input text—besides the words and word combinations themselves, the metrics exploit information about the statistics of word and sentence lengths, world class co-occurrences, syntactic (sub)structures, emoticons, typographical and grammatical errors, punctuation marks, and so on. Within the algorithms of manipulative technique recognition, these features can be supplemented with information drawn from user profile analyses or publicly available traits of a previous user's behaviour, such as ratings or registration date (Peleschyshyn et al. 2016). In detailed analyses, especially when seeking specific explanations, the identification task orients from whole documents to individual sentences where a manipulative technique should be discovered (Da San Martino et al. 2019).

5.2.3 Generating Fictive Content

Language models are probabilistic devices which can predict the probability a sequence of words is a correct phrase in a language. Besides this function, language models may be also used for *generating artificial text*, which resembles a text written by a human. Until recently, generated texts were not able to 'fool' a human reader if the generated sequence was longer than one or two sentences. However, in 2019, the OpenAI group published a new neural model named GPT-2 (Radford et al. 2019) which was able to generate coherent newspaper articles of several paragraphs which sound authentic to a reader. The main reason for this change was the growth of both the data used for training as well as the size of the underlying neural network architecture. Following this, other current neural approaches, especially BERT (Devlin et al. 2019) and Grover (Zellers et al. 2019), proved it possible to generate thematically predetermined fictive news which is very difficult to distinguish from real human-generated newspaper texts. Zellers et al. (2019) showed that propaganda texts generated by Grover were on average evaluated as better in style than human written propaganda. In such a case, the opposite question of deciding whether a news text was written by a human or generated as a fictive one by a machine becomes crucial. Fortunately, the same techniques used for generations can also be exploited for detection, and, at this task, they reach super-human performance.

5.3 Methods Specification

The amount of information posted online is very large and keeps growing as the Internet becomes more widely available and as users move from established media channels to consume and generate more content online. The immediate nature of the Internet combined with the humongous amount of content to be checked for malicious influence precludes any possibility of manual inspection of any significant part of online traffic before it is spread among more and more users. Various automated methods have been proposed to monitor and detect the actions of malicious actors online. In this section, we present a summary of these methods.

The methods can be broadly classified into four classes. (1) Fact-checking based methods inspect the information content of the articles. Automated knowledge extraction is still in its infancy, the usual approach is therefore semi-automatic, where the algorithmically extracted facts are verified by human annotators and then checked against a knowledge base. (2) Manipulative style recognition methods are based on the assumption that deception can be detected from surface features of the content. The cues include, for example, vocabulary used, sentiment, loaded language, subjectivity, and others. (3) Methods based on source credibility rely on the belief that unreliable users and sources have a higher probability of spreading deceptive information. Collaborative filtering based on crowd-sourced data, where users vote on posts or articles, can be used. Based on these noisy votes, the aim is to extract a reliable signal from which posters or the posts themselves can be classified as malicious. A closely related research stream is based on. and (4) information flow analysis. The object of the study is the flow of information between different sources and users and the interaction between them.

As the task of fake news identification is only specified very vaguely, and no objective large-scale test set of fake news currently exists, comparison between different approaches is difficult. In the following sections, we describe the most common approaches to deception detection.

5.3.1 *Fact-Checking*

Manual fact-checking by experts is a very reliable way of distinguishing fake news. However, it is very laborious and time-consuming and, therefore, expensive and not scalable with the amount of information being generated.

In addition to websites disseminating expert provided fact-checking, such as Snopes, which is one of the oldest websites debunking myths, or Hoax Slayer, dedicated mainly to combating email and social media hoaxes, websites aiming to provide crowdsourced fact-checking services have been appearing recently, for example, CrossCheck, Trive, or Fiskkit.

The fact-checking task can be split into two steps. The first step deals with the extraction of facts from the text, and, in the second step, the truthfulness of these facts is verified against a reliable knowledge base—in other words, a predefined database of (human) verified facts in a machine-readable format. A common knowledge representation format is the SPO (subject–predicate–object) triple as defined in the Resource Description Framework (Klyne et al. 2014). For example, the assertion 'The capital of France is Paris' would be represented as (Paris–capital_of–France). The knowledge can be understood as a knowledge graph, where the subjects and objects represent nodes and predicates form links between these nodes.

Approaches to knowledge base construction range from the manually built Freebase (Bollacker et al. 2008) or DBpedia (Auer et al. 2007), which extract structured facts from Wikipedia, to Knowledge Vault (Dong et al. 2014), which extracts facts from web content and also provides the probability of correctness of stored facts. These resources are mainly focused on common knowledge about the world, which changes relatively slowly, whereas fact-checking recent stories requires access to current and potentially rapidly changing knowledge.

While a knowledge base can be universal and built collaboratively from many sources, the fact-checking process is constrained to specific documents. No reliable automatic method for extracting check-worthy facts has been created yet. One possible approach towards this end has been described in Hassan et al. (2017). The authors created the ClaimBuster fact-checking platform, which contains a claim spotting model built on top of a human-labelled dataset of check-worthy claims. The system uses machine learning and natural language processing of live discourses, social media, and news to identify factual claims which are compared against a database of facts verified by professionals.

Fact confirmation or refutation based on a knowledge base requires a sophisticated search through the database. Ciampaglia et al. (2015) present a method for verifying specific claims by finding the shortest path between concept nodes in a knowledge graph of facts extracted from Wikipedia infoboxes. Published and generally known facts are often not fully covered in one specific knowledge base. Trivedi et al. (2018) describe LinkNBed, a framework able to effectively process multiple knowledge graphs and identify entity links across the databases. The linkage information then allows the resulting facts to be combined from different knowledge bases.

The fact extraction and verification (FEVER) shared task (Thorne et al. 2018) provides a comparison of 23 competing systems for automated fact-checking. The benchmark dataset consists of 185,445 human-generated claims, manually evaluated against textual evidence from Wikipedia to be true or false. The best scoring participant managed to obtain a 64.21% accuracy in correctly classified claims. The approach described in Nie et al. (2019) improves this result to obtain 66.49% accuracy.

Fact-checking is possibly the most reliable and accurate approach of detecting fake news; current automated methods serve mainly as (advanced) supporting tools. Approaches which can be deployed now must be human assisted, with annotators extracting claims from articles while fact-checking against a knowledge graph is provided automatically.

5.3.2 Manipulative Style Recognition

The assumption on which these methods are based is that the veracity of text can be assessed from its secondary characteristics and not directly from the semantics of the message itself. The mechanism has been theorised to be possibly subconscious (Zhou and Zhang 2008; Siering et al. 2016)—if the author knows that a piece of information is deceptive, or his intent is malicious, he or she will change the way the message is formulated. This theory has been confirmed in practice, and many successful methods based on this approach have been devised.

The general task is to predict, for a given article or post, whether it is deceptive or not. Older methods tend to operate on the whole investigated piece, while recent approaches are more fine-grained and also attempt to pinpoint the exact locations in the text in which deceptive techniques appear.

The methods build on the standard machinery of natural language processing and machine learning in which text classification has been studied extensively. The task is usually specified in a supervised setting. An annotated corpus consisting of representative examples of both truthful and deceptive posts is used as a training set for a machine learning classifier. The classifier attempts to find patterns in the training data, and it is then able to predict the authenticity of previously unseen articles.

In contrast to older methods which train the classifiers on various hand-crafted features extracted from the text ranging from simple measures, such as the presence of specific words or phrases, the amount of special characters, expletives, spelling errors, length of sentences, and the ratio of modal verbs, to complex ones, such as the writer's stance towards the topic discussed, its readability score, or the syntactic structure of the text, recent approaches widely employ *deep learning* methods where the classifier operates directly on the source text.

The main issue for style-based methods lies in constructing the gold standard datasets as humans have been shown to be poor at detecting deception (Rubin 2010). Nevertheless, style-based methods are a very active research area, possibly for multiple reasons: No external information is necessary, only the content itself; text classification methods are well studied in natural language processing, with many different applications; and style-based methods generalise well and can be easily applied to previously unseen data in isolation. Some interesting results of style-based deception detection are presented below.

One of the first methods is described in Burgoon et al. (2003). The authors aim to discriminate deceptive chat communications using a decision tree classifier on simple features extracted from the text. Song et al. (2012) describe their experiments in detecting deceptive reviews and essays by adding the syntactic structure of text to word sequence and part-of-speech features, and they note that syntactic features along with unigrams reach the best accuracy. Chen et al. (2015) suggest detecting misleading content by detecting *clickbait*[2] in news article headlines using support vector machines, but they do not provide a rigorous evaluation. Rubin et al. (2015) look at using features based on rhetorical structure

[2] Hyperlinks or headlines crafted to deceptively attract attention.

theory (Mann and Thompson 1987) for identifying deceptive news along with a logistic regression-based classifier. While the reported accuracy is low, the authors claim this might be due to the limited amount of training data. The work of Popoola (2017) evaluates rhetorical structure theory features against deceptive Amazon reviews and notes a significant correlation.

The experiments of Rubin et al. (2016) describe a predictive method for discriminating between satirical and truthful news articles using support vector machines based on an article's vocabulary and additional features quantifying negative affect, absurdity, humour, grammar, and punctuation. The obtained precision is 0.90, recall 0.84. Reis et al. (2019) compare multiple classifiers on a large set of features extracted from the BuzzFeed dataset and conclude that XGBoost (Chen and Guestrin 2016) and Random Forests (Breiman 2001) provide the best results in the context of fake news classification. This supports the conclusions of Fernández-Delgado et al. (2014), which compares 179 different machine learning classifiers in a more general setting. While the previously described approaches use a diverse set of classifiers, the extracted features can be used to train any of the classifiers presented. Similarly Horák et al. (2019) applied a variety of classifiers to the dataset described in Sect. 4.4.4, 'Dataset of propaganda techniques in Czech news portals (MU dataset)', achieving accuracy up to 0.96 and weighted F_1 0.85 with support vector machines trained using stochastic gradient descent.

A thorough evaluation of Mitra et al. (2017) uncovers words and phrases which correlate with a high or low credibility perception of event reports on Twitter. While this information does not directly provide a signal related to fake news, it can be used to assess how credible and, therefore, dangerous a post will appear to be.

The approaches presented so far process the input texts in a limited workflow scenario. First, each text is analysed and a set of preselected features (binary or numeric) is extracted in a table row form. All automated processing then works only with the resulting table. Such an approach reveals and summarises important aspects of the input news article, which are often sufficient and necessary for the resulting decision. However, the tabular methods are not able to distinguish subtle differences in the meaning based on the order of information (e.g. words) in the text. This is the reason why recurrent neural network (RNN) architectures, such as long short-term memory (LSTM) networks (Hochreiter and Schmidhuber 1997), have been designed to operate on word sequences instead of just extracted tabular features and are able to discriminate based on long distance meaning dependencies in the input context. The capture, score, and integrate (CSI) model (Ruchansky et al. 2017) employs a complex hybrid system which uses information about user engagement and source in addition to the article text and trains a recurrent neural network with this data. The reported accuracy on a Twitter dataset for classifying false information is 0.89.

Volkova et al. (2017) evaluate various deep neural network architectures against traditional methods and find a significant improvement in classification accuracy when including certain social network and linguistic features. The presented neural network models benefited strongly from additional inputs denoted as bias cues (e.g. expressions of tentativeness and possibility as well as assertive, factive, or implicative verbs), subjectivity cues (positive and negative subjective words and opinion words), psycholinguistic cues (persuasive and biased language), and moral foundation cues (appeals to moral foundations, such as care and harm, fairness and cheating, or loyalty and betrayal). Ajao et al. (2018) describe an RNN model for the detection of fake news on Twitter and achieve 0.82 accuracy on the PHEME dataset (Zubiaga et al. 2016), beating the previous state-of-the-art result.

The shared task described in Da San Martino et al. (2019) evaluated the performance of 25 systems for detection of 18 different deceptive techniques in news articles and the specific locations in which they appear. The most successful approaches employ the BERT (bidirectional encoder representations from transformers) language model (Devlin et al. 2019) to obtain an abstract representation of the text. The best reported F_1 for identifying deceptive techniques at the sentence level is 0.63. The best result for obtaining the locations reaches F_1 0.23. The dataset used for training and evaluation of the techniques is described in Sect. 4.4.3, 'Dataset for fine-grained propaganda detection (QCRI dataset)'.

5.3.3 Source Credibility

An article published on an unreliable website by an unreliable user is much more likely to be unreliable. From this perspective, the reliability of an article can be assessed independently of its content. In the analysis of Silverman (2016), it is shown that a vast majority of fake news comes from either hyper-partisan websites or fake news websites pretending to be regular news outlets. Therefore, identifying spam websites can assist in identifying unreliable sources. Traditional website reliability metrics which had been used by search engines, such as PageRank (Page et al. 1999), are not useful today as spammers have managed to overcome them, so new approaches are necessary.

The work of Esteves et al. (2018) provides a method of assessing the credibility of news sites by applying various machine learning methods to indicators, such as the article text content (e.g. text category, outbound links, contact information, or readability metrics) and the article metadata (e.g. the website domain, the time of the last update, or specific HTML tags). The authors exclude social-based features, such as popularity and link structure, as these rely on external data sources which can be easily manipulated and access to the information at scale is expensive.

Another approach attempts to identify automated malicious users and bots that spread misleading information. Mehta et al. (2007) characterise the behaviour of spam users and the patterns of their operations and propose a statistical method of identifying these users based on outlier detection.

Abbasi and Liu (2013) describe the CredRank algorithm which quantifies user credibility. The main idea is that malicious users cooperate and form larger and more coherent clusters compared to regular users, who are likely to form smaller clusters. Shu et al. (2017) devise a framework for evaluating news credibility based on the relationship between the publisher, the news piece, user engagement, and social links among the users. These metrics are obtained from different sources and then the resulting score is extracted using optimisation methods.

5.3.4 Information Flow Analysis

This approach is based on the patterns in which fake news propagates—how users and other sources interact with it, and how it is shared. As actual empirical information on the prevalence of fake news is sparse, studies in this field also commonly investigate rumours or unconfirmed news which can be identified more easily.

A central concept for this approach is a *propagation tree* or *propagation cascade* (Wu et al. 2015; Vosoughi et al. 2018). The tree consists of nodes, representing posts, and edges, which connect pairs of posts. The edges represent the relationship between the posts—commonly *is a share of* or *is a response to*. The root of the propagation tree is the original post.

The propagation patterns of fake news and those of regular news differ. Vosoughi et al. (2018) analyse the diffusion of verified true and false news stories on Twitter and report that falsehoods diffuse significantly farther, faster, and broader than truth. This effect was even more pronounced for political news. The authors report that they did not observe any acceleration in the propagation of false news due to the effect of bots, which suggests that humans, not bots, are the cause of the faster spread of false news.

The inherent weakness of these methods is their need to first observe the behaviour of a significant amount of users in order to make any judgements, so their predictive power is low in the early diffusion stages; reliable predictions can be obtained only after most of the damage had already been done.

5.4 Datasets and Evaluation

Despite the importance of the task, there are only a few existing datasets suitable to evaluate automatic methods for the analysis and detection of propaganda. In this section, we describe them in detail.

In general, the datasets are rather small, which is due to the often complex annotation process. Annotators need to go through specific training and the annotation itself is also very tedious. Annotation schemes differ, so the datasets are hard to compare as each of them serves a different purpose and is suitable for different tasks. The datasets are also heterogenous and not all are in English.

5.4.1 *Trusted, Satire, Hoax, and Propaganda (TSHP) 2017 Corpus*

For the purpose of language analysis of fake news, Rashkin et al. (2017) have prepared a dataset comprising articles from eleven sources and labelled with four classes: trusted (articles from Gigaword News–see Graff and Cieri 2003), satire (The Onion, The Borowitz Report, Clickhole), hoax (American News, DC Gazette) and propaganda (The Natural News, Activist Report), together 22,580 news articles fairly balanced between the classes. The data is available for download (Rashkin n.d.; Rashkin et al. 2017). The accompanied linguistic analysis showed that the level of news reliability can be predicted using the detection of certain language devices, such as subjectives (brilliant), superlatives, or action adverbs (foolishly).

5.4.2 *QProp Corpus*

Barrón-Cedeño et al. (2019) have built a dataset containing 52 thousand articles from over one hundred news sources. The articles are annotated on the document-level with either 'propagandistic' (positive) or 'non-propagandistic' (negative) labels. If an article comes from a source considered 'propagandistic' by Media Bias Fact Check (Media Bias/Fact Check n.d.), then it is labelled as positive. Authors also added meta-information from the GDELT project (Global Database of Events, Language, and Tone, see Leetaru and Schrodt 2013). The corpus is available for download (Barrón-Cedeño et al. 2019).

5.4.3 *Dataset for Fine-Grained Propaganda Detection (QCRI Dataset)*

The dataset has been used in the shared task on fine-grained propaganda detection, organised in 2019 as a part of the 'Conference on Empirical Methods in Natural Language Processing' and the '9th International Joint Conference on Natural Language Processing'. It has also been used for 'Hack the News Datathon Case—Propaganda Detection' held in January 2019 and in 'Semeval 2020' for Task 11. It has been provided by researchers from the Qatar Computing Research Institute (QCRI).

The authors worked with propaganda defined as 'whenever information is purposefully shaped to foster a predetermined agenda'. The propaganda in the dataset is classified into the following 18 types of manipulative techniques:

1. loaded language (strongly positive and negative, emotionally loaded vocabulary);
2. name-calling or labelling (linking subjects with words of fear, hate, desire, and other emotions);
3. repetition (i.e. 'a lie that is repeated a thousand times becomes truth');
4. exaggeration or minimisation;
5. doubt;
6. appeal to fear/prejudice;
7. flag-waving (playing on a strong national, ethnic, racial, cultural, or political feeling);

8. causal oversimplification (replacing a complex issue with one cause);
9. slogans;
10. appeal to authority;
11. black-and-white fallacy, dictatorship[3] (eliminating many options with only two alternatives or even with only a single right choice);
12. thought-terminating cliché (e.g. 'stop thinking so much' or 'the Lord works in mysterious ways');
13. whataboutism (do not argue but charge opponents with hypocrisy);
14. *reductio ad Hitlerum* (Hitler hated chocolate, X hates chocolate, therefore X is a Nazi);
15. red herring (divert attention away by introducing something irrelevant);
16. bandwagoning (a form of *argumentum ad populum*);
17. obfuscation, intentional vagueness, and confusion (deliberately unclear language); and
18. straw man (arguing with a false and superficially similar proposition as if an argument against the proposition were an argument against the original proposition).

A more detailed explanation of the techniques is described in Da San Martino et al. (2019). The dataset has been created by a private company named A Data Pro and contains 451 articles gathered from 48 news outlets (372 from propagandistic and 79 from non-propagandistic sources). The dataset contains 21,230 sentences (350,000 words) with 7485 instances of propaganda technique used. The most common are *loaded language* and *name–calling/labelling*.

The inter-annotator agreement has been assessed with a gamma measure (Mathet et al. 2015) suitable for tasks with annotations containing potentially overlapping spans. For an independent annotation of four annotators and six articles = 0.31. To improve this rather low agreement, the annotation schema was changed, and pairs of annotators came up with a final annotation together with a consolidator. This yielded a significantly higher (up to 0.76) when measured between an individual annotator and the appropriate consolidated annotation.

[3] This manipulative technique is sometimes referred as a *false dilemma*.

Below is a sentence example with an annotation:

In a glaring sign of just how [400]stupid and petty[416] things have become in Washington these days, Manchin was invited on Fox News Tuesday morning to discuss how he was one of the only Democrats in the chamber for the State of the Union speech [607]not looking as though Trump [635]killed his grandma[653].

The three fragments are labelled as follows:

1. 400–416 loaded language;
2. 607–653 exaggeration or minimisation; and
3. 635–653 loaded language.

5.4.4 *Dataset of Propaganda Techniques in Czech News Portals (MU Dataset)*

Since 2016, researchers from the Department of Political Science at the Faculty of Social Studies, Masaryk University (MU) have been collecting and manually annotating propaganda techniques at document-level in articles from four Czech media outlets[4] with a frequent pro-Russian bias and/or manipulative content as the original research focus has been mainly on pro-Russian propaganda. Since 2017, the annotation has been made more fine-grained, and techniques have also been annotated at the phrase-level. This was accomplished by using a dedicated editor built by researchers from the Natural Language Processing Centre at the Faculty of Informatics, MU.

The dataset contains binary and multi-value attributes with the phrase-level attributes capturing the presence of a certain kind of manipulation and the document-level attributes framing the broader context of the news article.

Phrase-level attributes (with possible values) include:

1. blaming (yes/no/not sure; accusing someone of something);
2. labelling (yes/no/not sure);

[4] www.sputnik.cz, www.parlamentnilisty.cz, www.ac24.cz, and www.svetkolemnas.info.

3. argumentation (yes/no/not sure; does the text contains arguments for or against a proposition?);
4. emotions (outrage/compassion/fear/hatred/other/not sure);
5. demonising (yes/no/not sure; extreme form of negative labelling);
6. relativising (yes/no/not sure);
7. fearmongering (yes/no/not sure; appeal to fear, uncertainty, or threat);
8. fabulation (yes/no/not sure; rumouring and fabrication);
9. opinion (yes/no/not sure; does the text contain the clearly stated opinion of the author?);
10. location (EU/Czech Republic/USA/other country/Russia /Slovakia/not sure);
11. source (yes/no/not sure; is the proposition backed up with a reference?);
12. Russia (positive example/neutral/victim/negative example/hero /not sure; how is Russia portrayed?);
13. expert (yes/no/not sure; is the fact corroborated by an expert?); and
14. attitude towards a politician (positive/neutral/negative/ acclaiming/not sure).

Document-level attributes include:

15. topic (migration crisis/domestic policy/foreign policy [diplomacy]/society [social situation]/energy/social policy/conflict in Ukraine/culture/conflict in Syria/arms policy/economy [finance]/conspiracy/other);
16. genre (news/interview/commentary);
17. focus (foreign/domestic/both/not sure); and
18. overall sentiment (positive/neutral/negative).

The dataset was described in detail in Horák et al. (2019) but was later enlarged with annotated data from 2018. It contains 5500 documents from 2016, 1994 documents from 2017, and 2200 documents from 2018. The documents from 2016 are annotated one annotator per article, but before annotating there was a pilot phase in which the annotators were trained and tested including multiple-round control of the inter-annotator agreement.[5] The other documents have been annotated by three annotators, so the inter-annotator agreement can be measured. If at least two annotators agreed upon a value of an attribute, it was included in the final dataset. The overall percentage agreement has been around 80%; however, as attributes differ in value sets, the average Cohen's kappa (Cohen 1960) ranges from 0.2 (relativisation) to 0.7 (location), clearly showing the difficulty of the annotation task.

An example of annotated data[6]:

> Film director Nvotová: ((Slovakia)[location=Slovakia] is rotten)[labelling=yes], (its politics has its brutal roots in corruption.)[argumentation=yes] President of the (Czech Republic)[location=Czech republic] Miloš Zeman said during his inaugural speech that there were no voters in the better and worse category. ('The president should not grade political parties because there are no better and worse category parties',)[argumentation=yes] (said)[source=yes] President Zeman.

5.4.5 *Dataset to Study Fake News in Portuguese*

Moreno and Bressan (2019) introduced corpus FACTCK.BR, a dataset to study fake news. It contains 1309 claims in paragraph form (a short text) which have been fact-checked by one of nine Brazilian fact-checking initiatives. Each claim consists of the following items:

1. URL of origin;
2. fact-checking author;
3. publishing date;
4. date the claim was reviewed;

[5] Inter-coder reliability was tested using Cohen's kappa. In total, five rounds of pilot coding were conducted before the results for each variable were satisfactory. The most difficult was to find the annotators ability to identify the presence of the author's opinion in the text (0.63), and the manipulative technique of relativisation (0.65) was moderate, while the level of agreement on the presence of the manipulative technique of labelling (0.89) was strong (with other variables' scoring in between).

[6] The dataset is in Czech. The example was translated in English by authors. The Czech original is: Režisérka Nvotová: Slovensko je prohnilé, tamní politika má brutální kořeny korupce. Prezident České republiky Miloš Zeman během svého inauguračního projevu prohlásil, že neexistují voliči první a druhé kategorie. 'Prezident by neměl známkovat politické strany, protože nejsou strany první a druhé kategorie', řekl president Zeman.

5. the claim itself;
6. title of the article;
7. rating of the veracity;
8. best rating (based on various ratings); and
9. text label (various fact-checking agencies use different labels—false, true, impossible to prove, exaggerated, controversial, inaccurate, etc.).

The data items in this dataset are short texts but, in fact, the annotation is document-level. This makes this resource similar to the Proppy corpus.

5.4.6 *Topics and Emotions in the Russian Propaganda Dataset*

The study from Miller (2019) has used a dataset consisting of roughly two hundred thousand tweets from 3814 Twitter accounts associated by Twitter with the Russia-based Internet Research Agency (Popken 2018). The same dataset was used in the special counsel's investigation (2017–2019) of Russian interference in the 2016 United States elections. The dataset does not contain manual annotation but is useful for the analysis of topics, keywords, and emotions in Russian propaganda on social media.

5.4.7 *The BuzzFeed-Webis Fake News Corpus 2016*

This dataset, introduced in Potthast et al. (2017), contains a sample of posts published on Facebook from nine news agencies close to the 2016 United States election. Posts and linked articles from mainstream, left-wing, and right-wing publishers have been fact-checked by five journalists. It contains 1627 articles—826 mainstream, 356 left-wing, and 545 right-wing articles. Posts have been labelled as mostly true, mixture of true and false, mostly false, and no factual content if the post lacked a factual claim.

5.4.8 *Liar*

Wang (2017) gathered 12,836 short statements labelled by fact-checkers from PolitiFact. The statements come from news releases, television or radio interviews, and campaign speeches. The labels represent a range of fact-checked truthfulness including 'pants on fire' (utterly false), false, barely true, half true, mostly true, and true.

5.4.9 *Detector Dataset*

This dataset (Risdal 2016) has been collected from 244 websites classified by a browser extension B.S. Detector[7] developed for checking (and notifying users of) news truthfulness. It comprises the texts and metadata of 12,999 posts.

5.4.10 *Credbank*

Mitra and Gilbert (2015) crowdsourced a dataset of approximately 60 million tweets covering the end of 2015. The tweets have been linked to over a thousand news events and each event has been assessed for credibility by 30 annotators from Amazon Mechanical Turk (Table 5.1).

Table 5.1 Overview of datasets and corpora

Name	*Data + annotation*	*Approx. size*	*Lang*
TSHP	web articles in four classes	22,000 articles	En
Qprop	news articles in two classes	52,000 articles	En
QCRI dataset	news articles labelled with manipulation techniques	451 articles	En
MU dataset	news articles labelled with manipulation techniques	9500 articles	Cs
FACTCT.BR	statements rated by veracity	1300 paragraphs	Pt
IRA twitter	unclassified tweets	3800 tweets	En
BuzzFeed	Facebook posts	1600 articles	En
LIAR	statements labelled with truthfulness	13,000 statements	En
BS detector	web pages in a few classes	13,000 posts	En
CREDBANK	tweets linked to events classified by credibility	60 M tweets	En

Source Authors

[7] B.S. here stands for bullshit.

5.5 Summary

In this chapter, we have summarised the latest approaches to the automatic recognition and generation of fake news, disinformation, and manipulative texts in general. The technological progress in this area accelerates the dispersal of fictive texts, images, and videos at such a rate and quality that human forces cease to be sufficient. The importance of high-quality propaganda detection techniques thus increases significantly. Computer analyses allow the identification of many aspects of such information misuse based on the text style of the message, the information flow characteristics, the source credibility, or exact fact-checking. Nevertheless, final precautions always remain with the human readers themselves.

References

Abbasi, M.-A., & Liu, H. (2013). Measuring User Credibility in Social Media. In A. M. Greenberg, W. G. Kennedy, & N. D. Nathan (Eds.), *Social Computing, Behavioral-Cultural Modeling and Prediction* (pp. 441–448). Lecture Notes in Computer Science. Berlin, Heidelberg: Springer Berlin Heidelberg. https://doi.org/10.1007/978-3-642-37210-0_48.

Adair, B., Li, C., Yang, J., & Yu, C. (2017). *Progress Toward 'the Holy Grail': The Continued Quest to Automate Fact-Checking*. Evanston: Northwestern University.

Ajao, O., Bhowmik, D., & Zargari, S. (2018). *Fake News Identification on Twitter with Hybrid CNN and RNN Models*. Proceedings of the 9th International Conference on Social Media and Society—SMSociety '18. New York: ACM Press. https://doi.org/10.1145/3217804.3217917.

Auer, S., Bizer, C., Kobilarov, G., Lehmann, J., Cyganiak, R., & Ives, Z. (2007). DBpedia: A Nucleus for a Web of Open Data. *The Semantic Web, 4825*, 722–735. Lecture Notes in Computer Science. Berlin, Heidelberg: Springer Berlin Heidelberg. https://doi.org/10.1007/978-3-540-76298-0_52.

Barrón-Cedeño, A., Jaradat, I., Da San Martino, G., & Nakov, P. (2019). Proppy: Organizing the News Based on Their Propagandistic Content. *Information Processing and Management, 56*(5), 1849–1864. https://doi.org/10.1016/j.ipm.2019.03.005.

Bollacker, K., Evans, C., Paritosh, P., Sturge, T., & Taylor, J. (2008). *Freebase: A Collaboratively Created Graph Database for Structuring Human Knowledge*. Proceedings of the 2008 ACM SIGMOD International Conference on Management of Data—SIGMOD '08, 1247. New York: ACM Press. https://doi.org/10.1145/1376616.1376746.

Breiman, L. (2001). Random Forests. *Machine Learning, 45*, 3–32. https://doi.org/10.1023/a:1010933404324.

Burgoon, J. K., Blair, J. P., Qin, T., & Nunamaker, J. F. (2003). Detecting Deception Through Linguistic Analysis. In C. Hsinchun, R. Miranda, D. R. Zeng, C. Demchak, J. Schroeder, & T. Madhusudan (Eds.), *Intelligence and Security Informatics, 2665*, 91–101. Lecture Notes in Computer Science. Berlin, Heidelberg: Springer Berlin Heidelberg. https://doi.org/10.1007/3-540-44853-5_7.

Caswell, D., & Anderson, C. W. (2019). Computational Journalism. In T. P. Vos, F. Hanusch, D. Dimitrakopoulou, M. Geertsema-Sligh, & A. Sehl (Eds.), *The International Encyclopedia of Journalism Studies* (pp. 1–8). Wiley. https://doi.org/10.1002/9781118841570.iejs0046.

Cazalens, S., Lamarre, P., Leblay, J., Manolescu, I., & Tannier, X. (2018). *A Content Management Perspective on Fact-Checking*. Companion of the The Web Conference 2018 on The Web Conference 2018—WWW '18, 565–574. New York: ACM Press. https://doi.org/10.1145/3184558.3188727.

Chen, T., & Guestrin, C. (2016). *XGBoost: A Scalable Tree Boosting System*. Proceedings of the 22nd ACM SIGKDD International Conference on Knowledge Discovery and Data Mining—KDD '16, 785–794. New York: ACM Press. https://doi.org/10.1145/2939672.2939785.

Chen, Y., Conroy, N. J., & Rubin, V. L. (2015). *Misleading Online Content: Recognizing Clickbait as 'False News'*. Proceedings of the 2015 ACM on Workshop on Multimodal Deception Detection—WMDD '15, 15–19. New York: ACM Press. https://doi.org/10.1145/2823465.2823467.

Ciampaglia, G. L., Shiralkar, P., Rocha, L. M., Bollen, J., Menczer, F., & Flammini, A. (2015). Computational Fact Checking from Knowledge Networks. *PLoS ONE, 10*(6), e0128193. https://doi.org/10.1371/journal.pone.0128193.

Cohen, J. (1960). A Coefficient of Agreement for Nominal Scales. *Educational and Psychological Measurement, 20*(1), 37–46. https://doi.org/10.1177/001316446002000104.

Da San Martino, G., Barrón-Cedeño, A., & Nakov, P. (2019). *Findings of the NLP4IF-2019 Shared Task on Fine-Grained Propaganda Detection*. Proceedings of the Second Workshop on Natural Language Processing for Internet Freedom: Censorship, Disinformation, and Propaganda, 162–170. Stroudsburg: Association for Computational Linguistics. https://doi.org/10.18653/v1/D19-5024.

Da San Martino, G., Yu, S., Barrón-Cedeño, A., Petrov, R., & Nakov, P. (2019). *Fine-Grained Analysis of Propaganda in News Article*. Proceedings of the 2019 Conference on Empirical Methods in Natural Language Processing and the 9th International Joint Conference on Natural Language Processing (EMNLP-IJCNLP), 5640–5650. Stroudsburg: Association for Computational Linguistics. https://doi.org/10.18653/v1/D19-1565.

Devlin, J., Chang, M.-W., Lee, K., & Toutanova, K. (2019). BERT: Pre-Training of Deep Bidirectional Transformers for Language Understanding. Proceedings of the 2019 Annual Conference of the North American Chapter of the Association for Computational Linguistics (NAACL 2019). Association for Computational Linguistics.

Dong, X., Gabrilovich, E., Heitz, G., Horn, W., Lao, N., & Murphy, K., et al. (2014). *Knowledge Vault: A Web-Scale Approach to Probabilistic Knowledge Fusion*. Proceedings of the 20th ACM SIGKDD International Conference on Knowledge Discovery and Data Mining—KDD '14, 601–10. New York: ACM Press. https://doi.org/10.1145/2623330.2623623.

Esteves, D., Reddy, A. J., Chawla, P., & Lehmann, J. (2018). *Belittling the Source: Trustworthiness Indicators to Obfuscate Fake News on the Web*. Proceedings of the First Workshop on Fact Extraction and VERification (FEVER), 50–59. Stroudsburg: Association for Computational Linguistics. https://doi.org/10.18653/v1/W18-5508.

Fernández-Delgado, M., Cernadas, E., Barro, S., & Amorim, D. (2014). Do We Need Hundreds of Classifiers to Solve Real World Classification Problems? *The Journal of Machine Learning Research, 15*(1), 3133–3181.

Finn, S., Metaxas, P. T., & Mustafaraj, E. (2014). Investigating Rumor Propagation with TwitterTrails. ArXiv.

Graff, D., & Cieri C. (2003). English Gigaword. *LDC2003T05. Web Download*. Philadelphia: Linguistic Data Consortium. https://doi.org/10.35111/0z6y-q265.

Graves, L. (2016). Boundaries Not Drawn. *Journalism Studies*, June, 1–19. https://doi.org/10.1080/1461670X.2016.1196602.

Hassan, N., Arslan, F., Li, C., & Tremayne, M. (2017). *Toward Automated Fact-Checking: Detecting Check-Worthy Factual Claims by ClaimBuster*. Proceedings of the 23rd ACM SIGKDD International Conference on Knowledge Discovery and Data Mining—KDD '17, 1803–1812. New York: ACM Press. https://doi.org/10.1145/3097983.3098131.

Hochreiter, S., & Schmidhuber, J. (1997). Long Short-Term Memory. *Neural Computation, 9*(8), 1735–1780. https://doi.org/10.1162/neco.1997.9.8.1735.

Horák, A., Baisa, V., & Herman, O. (2019). *Benchmark Dataset for Propaganda Detection in Czech Newspaper Texts*. Proceedings of Recent Advances in Natural Language Processing, RANLP 2019, 77–83. Varna: INCOMA Ltd.

Institute for Propaganda Analysis. (1938). How to Detect Propaganda. *Bulletin of the American Association of University Professors, 24*(1), 49–55.

Kavanagh, J., & Rich, M. (2018). Truth Decay: An Initial Exploration of the Diminishing Role of Facts and Analysis in American Public Life. *RAND Corporation*. https://doi.org/10.7249/RR2314.

Klyne, G., Carroll, J. J., & McBride, B. (2014, February 25). *RDF 1.1 Concepts and Abstract Syntax*. https://www.w3.org/TR/rdf11-concepts/. Accessed 1 Dec 2019.

Leetaru, K., & Schrodt, P. A. (2013). GDELT: Global Data on Events, Location, and Tone, 1979–2012. *ISA Annual Convention, 2,* 1–49.

Mann, W. C., & Thompson, S. A. (1987). Rhetorical Structure Theory: A Theory of Text Organization. University of Southern California, Information Sciences Institute.

Mathet, Y., Widlöcher, A., & Métivier, J.-P. (2015). The Unified and Holistic Method Gamma (γ) for Inter-Annotator Agreement Measure and Alignment. *Computational Linguistics, 41*(3), 437–479. https://doi.org/10.1162/COLI_a_00227.

Mehta, B., Hofmann, T., & Fankhauser, P. (2007). *Lies and Propaganda: Detecting Spam Users in Collaborative Filtering*. Proceedings of the 12th International Conference on Intelligent User Interfaces—IUI '07, 14. New York: ACM Press. https://doi.org/10.1145/1216295.1216307.

Metaxas, P. T. (2010). Web Spam, Social Propaganda and the Evolution of Search Engine Rankings. In J. Cordeiro & J. Filipe (Eds.), *Web Information Systems and Technologies, 45,* 170–182. Lecture Notes in Business Information Processing. Berlin, Heidelberg: Springer Berlin Heidelberg. https://doi.org/10.1007/978-3-642-12436-5_13.

Miller, D. T. (2019). Topics and Emotions in Russian Twitter Propaganda. *First Monday, 24*(5). https://doi.org/10.5210/fm.v24i5.9638.

Mitra, T., & Gilbert, E. (2015). *Credbank: A Large-Scale Social Media Corpus with Associated Credibility Annotations*. Proceedings of the Ninth International AAAI Conference on Web and Social Media. AAAI Press.

Mitra, T., Wright, G. P., & Gilbert, E. (2017). *A Parsimonious Language Model of Social Media Credibility Across Disparate Events*. Proceedings of the 2017 ACM Conference on Computer Supported Cooperative Work and Social Computing—CSCW '17, 126–145. New York: ACM Press. https://doi.org/10.1145/2998181.2998351.

Moreno, J., & Bressan, G. (2019). *FACTCK.BR: A New Dataset to Study Fake News*. Proceedings of the 25th Brazillian Symposium on Multimedia and the Web—WebMedia '19, 525–527. New York: ACM Press. https://doi.org/10.1145/3323503.3361698.

Neal, T., Sundararajan, K., Fatima, A., Yan, Y., Xiang, Y., & Woodard, D. (2017). Surveying Stylometry Techniques and Applications. *ACM Computing Surveys, 50*(6), 1–36. https://doi.org/10.1145/3132039.

Nie, Y., Chen, H., & Bansal, M. (2019). Combining Fact Extraction and Verification with Neural Semantic Matching Networks. *Proceedings of the AAAI Conference on Artificial Intelligence, 33*(July), 6859–6866. https://doi.org/10.1609/aaai.v33i01.33016859.

Page, L., Brin, S., Motwani, R., & Winograd, T. (1999). *The PageRank Citation Ranking: Bringing Order to the Web*. The PageRank Citation Ranking: Bringing Order to the Web.

Peleschyshyn, A., Holub, Z., & Holub, I. (2016). Methods of Real-Time Detecting Manipulation in Online Communities. *XIth International Scientific and Technical Conference Computer Sciences and Information Technologies (CSIT 2016)*, 15–17. IEEE. https://doi.org/10.1109/STC-CSIT.2016.7589857.

Popken, B. (2018). *Twitter deleted 200,000 Russian troll tweets*. Read them here. NBC News, 14. https://www.nbcnews.com/tech/social-media/now-available-more-200-000-deleted-russian-troll-tweets-n844731.

Popoola, O. (2017). *Using Rhetorical Structure Theory for Detection of Fake Online Reviews*. Proceedings of the 6th Workshop on Recent Advances in RST and Related Formalisms, 58–63. Stroudsburg: Association for Computational Linguistics. https://doi.org/10.18653/v1/W17-3608.

Potthast, M., Kiesel, J., Reinartz, K., Bevendorff, J., & Stein, B. (2017). *A Stylometric Inquiry into Hyperpartisan and Fake News*. ArXiv Preprint. ArXiv:1702.05638.

Radford, A., Wu, J., Child, R., Luan, D., Amodei, D., & Sutskever, I. (2019). Language Models are Unsupervised Multitask Learners. Technical Report. OpenAi.

Rashkin, H., Choi, E., Jang, J. Y., Volkova, S., & Choi, Y. (2017). *Truth of Varying Shades: Analyzing Language in Fake News and Political Fact-Checking*. Proceedings of the 2017 Conference on Empirical Methods in Natural Language Processing, 2931–2937. Stroudsburg: Association for Computational Linguistics. https://doi.org/10.18653/v1/D17-1317.

Reis, J. C. S., Correia, A., Murai, F., Veloso, A., Benevenuto, F., & Cambria, E. (2019). Supervised Learning for Fake News Detection. *IEEE Intelligent Systems, 34*(2), 76–81. https://doi.org/10.1109/MIS.2019.2899143.

Risdal, M. (2016). *Getting Real about Fake News*. Text & metadata from fake & biased news sources around the web. Web Download. Kaggle Inc. https://www.kaggle.com/mrisdal/fake-news

Rubin, V. L. (2010). On Deception and Deception Detection: Content Analysis of Computer-Mediated Stated Beliefs. *Proceedings of the American Society for Information Science and Technology, 47*(1), 1–10. https://doi.org/10.1002/meet.14504701124.

Rubin, V. L., Conroy, N. J., & Chen, Y. (2015). Towards News Verification: Deception Detection Methods for News Discourse. Hawaii International Conference on System Sciences.

Rubin, V., Conroy, N., Chen, Y., & Cornwell, S. (2016). *Fake News or Truth? Using Satirical Cues to Detect Potentially Misleading News*. Proceedings of the

Second Workshop on Computational Approaches to Deception Detection, 7–17. Stroudsburg: Association for Computational Linguistics. https://doi.org/10.18653/v1/W16-0802.

Ruchansky, N., Seo, S., & Liu, Y. (2017). *CSI: A Hybrid Deep Model for Fake News Detection*. Proceedings of the 2017 ACM on Conference on Information and Knowledge Management—CIKM '17, 797–806. New York: ACM Press. https://doi.org/10.1145/3132847.3132877.

Shao, C., Ciampaglia, G. L., Flammini, A., & Menczer, F. (2016). *Hoaxy: A Platform for Tracking Online Misinformation*. Proceedings of the 25th International Conference Companion on World Wide Web—WWW '16 Companion, 745–750. New York: ACM Press. https://doi.org/10.1145/2872518.2890098.

Shearer, E. (2018). News Use Across Social Media Platforms 2018. Pew Research Center.

Shu, K., Wang, S., & Liu, H. (2017). Exploiting Tri-Relationship for Fake News Detection. ArXiv Preprint ArXiv:1712.07709.

Siering, M., Koch, J.-A., & Deokar, A. V. (2016). Detecting Fraudulent Behavior on Crowdfunding Platforms: The Role of Linguistic and Content-Based Cues in Static and Dynamic Contexts. *Journal of Management Information Systems, 33*(2), 421–455. https://doi.org/10.1080/07421222.2016.1205930.

Silverman, C. (2016, November 16). This Analysis Shows How Viral Fake Election News Stories Outperformed Real News on Facebook. *BuzzFeed News*. https://www.buzzfeednews.com/article/craigsilverman/viral-fake-election-news-outperformed-real-news-on-facebook. Accessed 1 Dec 2019.

Song, F., Ritwik, B., & Yejin, C. (2012). *Syntactic Stylometry for Deception Detection*. Proceedings of the 50th Annual Meeting of the Association for Computational Linguistics (Volume 2: Short Papers), 171–175. Jeju Island: Association for Computational Linguistics.

Thorne, J., Vlachos, A., Cocarascu, O., Christodoulopoulos, C., & Mittal, A. (2018). *The Fact Extraction and Verification (FEVER) Shared Task*. Proceedings of the First Workshop on Fact Extraction and VERification (FEVER), 1–9. Stroudsburg: Association for Computational Linguistics. https://doi.org/10.18653/v1/W18-5501.

Trivedi, R., Sisman, B., Dong, X. L., Faloutsos, C., Ma, J., & Zha, H. (2018). *LinkNBed: Multi-Graph Representation Learning with Entity Linkage*. Proceedings of the 56th Annual Meeting of the Association for Computational Linguistics (Volume 1: Long Papers), 252–262. Stroudsburg: Association for Computational Linguistics. https://doi.org/10.18653/v1/P18-1024.

Volkova, S., Shaffer, K., Jang, J. Y., & Hodas, N. (2017). *Separating Facts from Fiction: Linguistic Models to Classify Suspicious and Trusted News Posts on Twitter*. Proceedings of the 55th Annual Meeting of the Association for Computational Linguistics (Volume 2: Short Papers), 647–653. Stroudsburg:

Association for Computational Linguistics. https://doi.org/10.18653/v1/P17-2102.

Vosoughi, S., Roy, D., & Aral, S. (2018). The Spread of True and False News Online. *Science, 359*(6380), 1146–1151. https://doi.org/10.1126/science.aap9559.

Wang, W. Y. (2017). *'Liar, Liar Pants on Fire': A New Benchmark Dataset for Fake News Detection.* Proceedings of the 55th Annual Meeting of the Association for Computational Linguistics (Volume 2: Short Papers), 422–426. Stroudsburg: Association for Computational Linguistics. https://doi.org/10.18653/v1/P17-2067.

Wills, C. E., & Uzunoglu, D. C. (2016). *What Ad Blockers are (and are Not) Doing.* 2016 Fourth IEEE Workshop on Hot Topics in Web Systems and Technologies (HotWeb), 72–77. IEEE. https://doi.org/10.1109/HotWeb.2016.21.

Woolley, S. C., & Howard, P. N. (Eds.). (2018). *Computational Propaganda: Political Parties, Politicians, and Political Manipulation on Social Media.* Oxford: Oxford University Press.

Wu, K., Yang, S., & Zhu, K. Q. (2015). *False Rumors Detection on Sina Weibo by Propagation Structures.* 2015 IEEE 31st International Conference on Data Engineering, 651–662. IEEE. https://doi.org/10.1109/ICDE.2015.7113322.

Zellers, R., Holtzman, A., Rashkin, H., Bisk, Y., Farhadi, A., & Roesner, F., et al. (2019, May). Defending Against Neural Fake News. ArXiv.

Zhou, L., & Zhang, D. (2008). Following Linguistic Footprints. *Communications of the ACM, 51*(9), 119. https://doi.org/10.1145/1378727.1389972.

Zubiaga, A., Liakata, M., & Procter, R. (2016). Learning Reporting Dynamics during Breaking News for Rumour Detection in Social Media. arXiv preprint arXiv:1610.07363.

CHAPTER 6

Proportionate Forensics of Disinformation and Manipulation

Radim Polčák and František Kasl

6.1 Introduction

The development of technological capacities for online disinformation and manipulation detection described in the previous chapter opens new possibilities for the deployment of these techniques. Adoption of these tools for authoritative action, however, further requires its adequate incorporation into existing regulatory frameworks. In order to pursue and

R. Polčák · F. Kasl (✉)
Institute of Law and Technology, Faculty of Law, Masaryk University, Brno, Czechia
e-mail: frantisek.kasl@law.muni.cz
URL: https://www.muni.cz/en/people/462266-frantisek-kasl

R. Polčák
e-mail: polcak@muni.cz
URL: https://www.muni.cz/en/people/21177-radim-polcak

M. Gregor and P. Mlejnková (eds.), *Challenging Online Propaganda and Disinformation in the 21st Century*, Political Campaigning and Communication,
https://doi.org/10.1007/978-3-030-58624-9_6

suppress the spread of online disinformation and propaganda, permissible electronic evidence must be gathered from the available data and its content assessed. This can be achieved only if the particularities of the virtual online environment are taken into consideration, as well as distinguishing the characteristics of data, information, and electronic evidence.

6.2 Data, Information, and Evidence

6.2.1 Online Discovery

The term *virtual* is used in everyday language as the opposite of *real*. As noted by Lévy (1998), such use is quite problematic. When a phenomenon becomes virtualised, it means that it still exists but now in another possible form. Virtualisation thus means changing the form while preserving the existence and core properties of the respective phenomenon.

In this edited volume, we deal with online disinformation and manipulation. These phenomena appear only to be virtualised forms of offline disinformation or manipulation already known under different names as propaganda and scaremongering, among other terms. While online manipulation is still the same as its offline counterpart, by its nature, the virtualised form makes it a relatively new societal threat to tackle (Royster 2017). It is not only the immaterialised nature of online manipulation but also the efficiency of its respective means, the scale of impact, or the availability and range of harmful options (Waldman 2018) which make the virtualised form of this phenomenon a relatively new and specific object of scientific attention.

In law, virtualisation often does not bring immediate needs to change the substance of the respective legal rules. Substantive laws are made primarily to cover the core of the problematic societal phenomena, and new forms of such phenomena do not necessarily make existing laws obsolete (Easterbrook 1996). That is also the case with substantive legal rules regulating manipulation or hate speech, which are in essence still able to cope with online forms of such misbehaviour (Vojak 2017).

Substance, however, is only a part of the essence of the legal coverage of problematic societal phenomena. The other essential element is procedure. It is even considered an undisputed requirement of morality (and legality) of law that substantive rights are backed with procedures which are fit to effectively enforce them (Fuller 1969).

Discovery and forensic analysis of evidence represents the basis of each legal procedure. The main purpose of evidentiary proceedings is to provide facts for consequent legal consideration. While discovery tools and mechanisms provide for identification and gathering of procedurally relevant facts, consequent forensic analysis leads to the final procedural product—evidence.

The scope of individuals whose rights might be at stake in discovery and the further processing of evidence is often much broader than only the parties of a respective case and might include even multiple individuals with no connection at all to the parties or the case as such. In that regards, internet-related cases are often far more complex than similar offline matters as they might involve users of information society services which operate on unprecedented scales. Consequently, the scope of individuals whose rights might be touched upon by an investigation, discovery, or further use of evidence represents one of the key reasons why electronic discovery represents a relatively separate procedural discipline (Browning 2011).

The second, and even more obvious, reason for tackling electronic discovery (or electronic evidence) as a specific discipline is the technical nature of evidence and of its carriers. There is no difference or specialty in the way electronic evidence represents information which serves the court in the discovery of facts. Rather, what is fundamentally different is the representation of procedurally relevant factual information in combination with the matter (or rather the measure) on which this information is fixed. Evidence is in this case represented by data which is either fixed to physical carriers or (far more often) to various information society services (Wortzman and Nickle 2009).

The third reason why electronic evidence is considered specific results from the above two. The multitude of stakeholders whose rights might be touched upon in discovery and subsequent use of electronic evidence might, thanks to the nature of the Internet, include nationals or residents from multiple jurisdictions. Similarly, a multi-jurisdictional situation in discovery might also arise (and irrespective of the nationality or location of stakeholders) due to the fact that relevant data is being processed within an information society service which is operated from abroad. Specifically, in the case of online manipulation or disinformation, it is quite common that perpetrators and/or the affected audience might reside in the European Union, while the providers of services which process and store respective data are located offshore—mostly in the United States. Discovery and processing of electronic evidence might, in these cases, be not only technically difficult but also legally cumbersome, as general standards of privacy protection, freedom of speech, or fair trials may substantially differ among jurisdictions (Svantesson 2015).

In any case, not all specific features of electronic discovery are, compared to offline discovery, utterly problematic. The nature of secondary networking effects causes the user-generated content (UGC) market for information society services currently used for mass communication, such as Twitter, Facebook, and so on, to have a strong tendency towards monopolisation. The result is relatively few market players whose services are used for the coordinated manipulation or disinformation, shall such conduct arise (Yoo 2012).

At the same time, any form of online acting, despite its aims, scope, or means-used, is technically relatively complex and leaves a rather substantial amount of data behind as a trace. Even a simple Twitter post generates a considerable amount of metadata at various service providers, which, even if not identifying a particular user, can be further forensically processed. If available and analysed properly, this metadata can generate a much richer picture of respective behaviour and its context than anything we know from the offline world.

6.2.2 *The Game of Proportionality*

European states provide protection of fundamental rights unprecedented anywhere else in the world. The fundamental person-centred teleology of the Council of Europe's laws and the laws of the European Union means that all laws and legal institutions are fundamentally built and function on the basis of human rights.

As noted by most influential law academics and ruled by constitutional and similar instances across the European Union, fundamental rights differ from standard legal norms (Alexy 1996). They do provide, similarly to norms, for deontic orders, but their scope of application is not properly defined.

Norms apply if their hypotheses are fulfilled, whereas, on the contrary, when their hypotheses are not fulfilled, they do not apply. Norms thus have two simple states, depending on the factual fulfilment of their hypotheses—apply (in full) or do not apply (Alexy 2000).

In that sense, fundamental rights do not work as norms but rather as legal principles. They all apply permanently and simultaneously, so it is not possible to state that some fundamental right does apply in full or does not apply at all. They all apply all the time, but with varying intensity.

The basic ontological dilemma in the case of legal norms is as regards the fulfilment of their hypotheses. To the contrary, principles, including fundamental rights, are ontologically dependent on their relative intensity in relation to other principles. It is then common for top courts to measure the intensity of colliding principles and choose the one with the most intense relevance.

While the collision of norms is being resolved by empirical and logical posteriority and speciality, colliding principles are sorted according to various doctrines of proportionality. Whereas constitutional or similar instances in different states use slightly different doctrinal approaches, the proportionate assessment of principles always depends on how intense respective ad hoc principles are and whether all principles at stake have been protected to the maximum possible extent (Alexy 2000).

It implies that there is no a priori hierarchy of legal principles and so there is no general hierarchy of fundamental rights. It also implies that while one principle is preferred over another in one case (e.g. privacy over freedom of speech), it does not constitute a precedent for future cases.

Furthermore, it indicates that principles which have not been considered of the utmost relevance (intensity) still apply ad hoc, but they are not dominant. That is very important for electronic discovery and subsequent forensic practice because it limits the scope and use of data collection and processing. In cases where electronic discovery is legally possible—that is, when it is possible to intrude upon privacy, property, or other rights by gathering or processing data—it is still necessary to protect these rights to the maximum possible extent. Thus, procedural instruments which enable electronic discovery are always accompanied by legal, institutional, and technical safeguards providing for the minimum possible intrusion of respective rights.

6.2.3 Data and Information

The biggest challenge in the discovery of online manipulation or disinformation is based on the general distinction between data and information. The methodological understanding of this difference goes back to the roots of cybernetics and to the work of Norbert Wiener (1965). His investigation of the mechanism which organises life led to the understanding of the true nature of information, which is, quite simply, the opposite of entropy.

The scientifically correct understanding of information is thus an induced process of reducing entropy in a respective system. Consequently, information is to be understood as a process rather than a static element. The presence or level of information can therefore be discovered in a given system only over time because information is a positive change in the organisational level of such a system. The absence of information or presence of disinformation or noise can also be detected only over time, as they mean, to the contrary, a rise in entropy.

It implies that using information as a synonym to data is not entirely correct. There is no such thing as wrongful information, harmful information, or even information overload, because information can only have a positive impact on its target system.

Data, to the contrary, has no informational value per se. Data can become information or disinformation, depending on its quality, the quality of the target system, and many other variables.

It is, of course, possible to guess with some degree of probability the informational potential of certain data, mostly on the basis of previous experience. Even the laws against disinformation or hate speech emerged from previous experience with such conduct (McGoldrick and O'Donnell 1998). Given past implications, society has learned that these forms of public communications cause chaos, and so they are not welcome. However, there is no way of guessing one hundred per cent how particular data will affect a target system unless it actually enters it.

The general inability to exactly guess the informational entropic potential of data is obviously important, namely for the substance of legal measures against manipulation or disinformation being discussed throughout this book. Procedurally, this difficulty mostly affects the accuracy of the assessment as to which data and how one might demonstrate and prove illegal conduct. If stripped to the bones, investigators and all consequent actors in legal procedures stand in front of zillions of zeroes and ones of highly variable availability and must guess whether and how they might inform (or organise) the respective procedure (Polcak and Svantesson 2017).

The broader and the less understandable the data is, the more we rely on advanced technologies in terms of its interpretation. Making data into information fit to serve the purpose of evidence in legal procedures was traditionally a task mostly for interpretive algorithms which made such data comprehensible to humans. Electronic discovery was, besides finding relevant data, mostly about reading and showing respective meanings by simply logically transforming all those zeroes and ones into a human-readable output. If we put aside very specific tools, like steganography, this process was mostly relatively simple and empirically verifiable.

With the growing semantic and subjective complexity of the substrate of electronic discovery, existing, purely logical, and verifiable algorithms need to be supplemented with tools which are significantly more powerful, yet less accurate and explainable. If we assume that a typical case of intentional online manipulation or disinformation might consist of a number of actions which use a multitude of communication modes and dissemination channels, it is obvious that the data available to investigators is extremely broad and incoherent. In addition, we also must assume that the picture of the respective actions can never be complete due to technical and legal difficulties in obtaining all the relevant data and metadata. As a result, we need not only highly sophisticated tools to properly interpret broad and inconsistent data structures but also means to adequately fill possible gaps or inaccuracies (Polcak 2019).

The shift from relatively simple and verifiable algorithms, which turn data into procedurally relevant information, to highly complex, sophisticated, and naturally inexplainable tools is inevitable. If legal procedures should serve their purpose in backing substantive legal rules, there is no other way than to accept this inevitable level of uncertainty and lack of ability to explain respective forensic and analytical tools simply because there is no other way to discover and analyse the data in question.

In any case, the main constraint in implementing inexplainable (or less explainable) forensic tools based typically on deep learning is, at least in continental Europe, mostly psychological. European procedural laws give courts very broad possibilities in choosing and processing means of evidence. So it is possible, without need for any significant updates to procedural law, to work in courts with evidence generated by autonomous forensic systems. The courts are, however, still used to relying on the interpretation of computer-based facts mostly through algorithms which can be fully, logically explained and empirically verified. It is still not common for a court to work with evidence generated by an algorithm whose functioning is incomprehensible not only for the court itself but for any human.

6.3 Electronic Evidence of Disinformation and Manipulation

The above-described challenges, bound as they are to the complexity of working with electronic evidence, are further exacerbated by legal obstacles ensuing from the fact that online conduct is not limited by jurisdiction. Cross-border cooperation in the procurement of electronic evidence is therefore often unavoidable.

6.3.1 *Legal Framework for Collecting and Evaluating Electronic Evidence in the European Union*

Issues concerning online disinformation and propaganda are predominantly created in a multi-jurisdictional context and necessitate international cooperation in the pursuit of electronic evidence. The digital footprints of the manipulative actions in question are likely to originate from a source located abroad and disseminated through a service or platform falling yet to another jurisdiction. Moreover, the particular evidence in a form of data recorded on a server is likely to be stored on cloud service servers distributed throughout the world. It is this extraterritorial feature of online conduct which poses a major obstacle to authorities struggling to curb criminal activities in cyberspace, be it issues of illegal trading on the dark web, cybersecurity incidents, or the dissemination of disinformation.

Two major approaches can be seen in the instruments available to the public authorities for combatting manipulative techniques. The first is directly aimed towards penalising the conduct and prosecuting the perpetrator of the offence under criminal law. The second concerns the indirect limitation of the impact of the disseminated content through enforcing the (co)liability of the internet service provider (see Chapter 4). These two directions are largely intertwined in a network of specific procedures determined by the conduct in question and the structure of the subjects concerned. As such, combatting disinformation or hate speech on major social media platforms like Facebook, Twitter, and YouTube differs in suitable procedural measures to restricting the propaganda distribution of minor online news outlets, either local (e.g. aeronet.cz) or international (e.g. nwoo.org).

The investigation and pursuit of illegal online conduct largely depends on mutual legal assistance (hereinafter referred to as MLA) provided by courts and law enforcement authorities in the country in question. This persistently formalised mechanism for requesting and obtaining evidence for criminal investigation and prosecution is, however, ill-suited for the kind of electronic evidence pursued by authorities regarding disinformation or propaganda.

6.3.1.1 Mutual Legal Assistance

Cooperation between the authorities of the involved countries under MLA is in principle communicated and coordinated through the respective ministries of justice, without direct contact or communication between the involved courts or departments on lower levels. This often leads to a fragile and cumbersome process, which may significantly prolong the investigation or prosecution. In order to expedite the processes of MLA and increase the efficiency of cross-border investigations and prosecutions, numerous countries have entered into bilateral or multilateral agreements concerning the framework of MLA. These, on the one hand, establish a mutual obligation to provide assistance if requested and, on the other hand, set procedural rules which standardise the communication and steps in the process. The cooperation throughout Europe in this regard was and remains at the forefront, initiated through ratification of the European Convention on Mutual Assistance in Criminal Matters (further referred to as the 'European Convention') by Council of Europe member states (Council of Europe 2019a). The treaty has been in force since 1962 and is currently ratified by 50 countries, including non-member countries Chile, Israel, and South Korea (Council of Europe 2019b). The framework of the European Convention underwent gradual revitalisation, first through the 1978 Additional Protocol (Council of Europe 1978) and, later, through the Second Additional Protocol at the turn of the millennium (Council of Europe 2001b). The development of the procedural cooperative mechanisms was further supported by unification of qualifications which constitute a crime in the online environment (Council of Europe 2019c). This was provided through the Convention on Cybercrime (Council of Europe 2001a), which entered into force in 2004, and its subsequent protocol concerning expressions of online racism and xenophobia (Council of Europe 2003), which entered into force in 2006.

For context concerning this publication, it is relevant that European Convention has represented since March 2000 the main instrument for cooperation with law enforcement authorities of the Russian

Federation (Council of the European Union 2012). This relationship is on many levels challenging, which also impacts mutual cooperation in legal matters (Committee on Foreign Affairs 2019). Previous efforts towards closer judicial cooperation in civil, criminal, and commercial matters were suspended following Russia's illegal annexation of Crimea (European Union External Action Service 2019). Nevertheless, a positive development can be seen in the fact that the Russian Federation ratified the Second Additional Protocol to the European Convention, which entered into force on 1 January 2020 (Council of Europe 2019d).

Within the European Union, the legal framework for judicial and police cooperation was significantly strengthened among most member states through the Schengen Acquis (European Communities 2000). The next major development in establishing an efficient environment for MLA within the European Union was then the establishment of the Convention of 29 May 2000 on Mutual Assistance in Criminal Matters between the Member States of the European Union (further referred to as the EU Convention) (European Judicial Network 2011a). The progress seen in this treaty also concerns newly agreed terms for cooperation in the interception of telecommunications, as set out by Articles 17–22 of the treaty (European Judicial Network 2011b, 2). The EU Convention remains the foundation of MLA within the European Union, allowing for comparatively broad and agile cross-border cooperation between law enforcement authorities of the member states. However, increasing demands for speedy collection of evidence, in particular electronic evidence, has led to the prioritisation of mutual recognition instruments (e.g. the European Investigation Order), which has been gradually replacing the need to apply an MLA framework among EU member states (European Commission 2019a).

Nevertheless, the international nature of globalised affairs, as well as the borderless nature of cyberspace, increasingly necessitate efficient frameworks for cooperation with non-EU countries, in particular with the United States, where most of the major tech industry players are incorporated. From the efforts for updated and harmonised cooperation between the United States and EU member states, which would not be subject to diverse bilateral treaties, ensued the 2003 Agreement on Mutual Legal Assistance between the European Union and the United States of America (further referred to as the 'EU-US MLA Agreement') (European Union 2003), which entered into force on 1 February 2010 (European Commission 2019a). The agreement was in many ways a harmonised formalisation of bilaterally agreed frameworks as well as established cooperative actions in the form of joint investigative teams (Council of the European Union 2011, 24–25). One of the outcomes of this closer cooperation is that the United States is today one of the main recipients of MLA requests for access to electronic evidence from EU member states (European Commission 2019b).

However, due to the increasing accent on electronic evidence, the EU-US MLA Agreement framework has become increasingly inadequate as it does not elaborate on this issue in particular (Tosza 2019, 271). For this reason, new efforts by EU representatives aim towards closer cooperation directly with internet service providers (European Commission 2019b). Currently, obtaining electronic evidence from an internet service provider based in the United States takes on average ten months, whereas the aim of the current negotiations is to develop a cooperative mechanism which would allow this period to decrease to ten days (European Commission 2019b). As of now, voluntary cooperation with US based internet service providers exists; however, this covers only non-content data and is subject to case-by-case decisions of compliance on the part of the internet service provider (European Commission 2019b).

These efforts are unfolding parallel to the establishment of new mutual recognition instruments for electronic evidence currently applicable or developed within the European Union, namely, the European Investigation Order and, in particular, the proposed European Production and Preservation Orders.

6.3.1.2 European Investigation Order

Cooperation within the European Union has gradually risen far beyond the MLA framework. A multitude of practical tools continue being developed, either under the European Judicial Network (European Judicial Network 2019a) or through other European harmonisation or recognition mechanisms (Council of the European Union 2017). These concern numerous specific areas of criminal activity (European Judicial Network 2019b) including combatting hate speech (Council of European Union 2008).

The central element of the existing mechanisms for collecting and accessing electronic evidence within the European Union is the European Investigation Order (EIO) framework established through the Directive 2014/41/EU of the European Parliament and of the Council of 3 April 2014 regarding the European Investigation Order in criminal matters (further referred to as the 'EIO Directive') (European Union 2014), which the member states were to implement by May 2017. As stated on the Eurojust[1] (European Union 2016) website, 'Since 15 September 2018, all Member States take part in the EIO with the exception of Denmark and Ireland' (Eurojust 2019). Nevertheless, the implementation and realisation of the framework under the national laws of the member states face diverse and persistent challenges (Papucharova 2019, 174). A particular example of such a challenge is the absence of a harmonising effect in the framework regarding the admissibility of evidence (Siracusano 2019, 85 et seq.). The subsequent challenge is a tension between the efficiency of such a transnational cooperation instrument and inherent procedural variations in national laws (Daniele and Calvanese 2018, 353 et seq.).

As further summarised in the overview of key features of the framework, it provides a single comprehensive instrument, which replaced the previously used letters of request and simplified and accelerated cross-border criminal investigation, as it allows for direct communication between judicial authorities in the involved member states and sets strict deadlines for gathering the requested evidence (Eurojust 2018).

The primary simplification provided through the EIO framework is in recognition of the request. Pursuant to Article 9 of the EIO Directive, 'the executing authority shall recognise an EIO, transmitted in accordance with this Directive, without any further formality being required, and ensure its execution in the same way and under the same modalities as if the investigative measure concerned had been ordered by an authority of the executing State, unless that authority decides to invoke one of the grounds for non-recognition or non-execution or one of the grounds for postponement provided for in this Directive'. This in itself presents a significant improvement of the procedure and provides a boost to the speed of the investigation. Nevertheless, the implementation of direct contact among the judicial authorities does not eliminate the relevance of the facilitating role provided by Eurojust, in particular when coordinating complex multilateral cases (Guerra and Janssens 2019, 46 et seq.).

Additionally, the celerity and priority assigned to the investigative measure shall be equal to that of a domestic case and within time limits

[1] European Union Agency for Cybersecurity.

set in Article 12 of the EIO Directive. The decision on the recognition or execution of the EIO shall be taken no later than 30 days after reception. Subsequent investigative measures shall be carried out within 90 days, unless grounds for postponement under Article 15 are present. The instrument covers the whole process of investigation, starting with the quick-freezing of evidence and ending with the final transfer to the requesting authorities (Papucharova 2019, 170). Article 12 para. 2 provides for respecting of urgent circumstances, which would substantiate a shorter procedural deadline; however, even so, the usability of the EIO for dynamic or transitory electronic evidence remains limited in practice.

Ramos rightly emphasised that the EIO represents 'a significant step forward in judicial cooperation when it comes to the trans-border gathering of evidence' (Ramos 2019, 53). However, it also serves as an example of the obstacles which still remain in place for cross-border investigation dependent on electronic evidence. The framework simplifies access to cross-border electronic evidence; however, it was not designed with applicability to such evidence per se (Tosza 2019, 273). The European legislators are aware of these limits and have pursued since 2017 the adoption of a regulation providing for specific mechanisms aimed at speedy gathering and access to electronic evidence (European Union 2018a).

6.3.1.3 Proposal for European Production and Preservation Orders

An optimal procedure towards gathering electronic evidence requires a minimal number of nodes between the investigating authority and the entity in possession of the respective data. Progress in the cooperative frameworks through MLA to EIO was signalled by a reduction of entities in both concerned countries which had to participate in the procedure. The newest concept within EU legislation, which should eliminate barriers of multiple jurisdiction to effective investigation based on electronic evidence, envisages direct access of the investigative authority in one member state to private internet service providers in another member state. This would mean a fully new dimension of online criminal conduct investigation; however, the instruments for close cross-border public–private cooperation remain challenged on multiple levels (Robinson 2018, 347 et seq.).

The proposal for a regulation on European production and preservation orders for electronic evidence in criminal matters (European Union

2018b) was introduced through ordinary legislative procedure on 18 April 2018 and remains ongoing, currently in the Council of the European Union (European Union 2019). Despite an urgent need for this new generation of legislative instruments responding to the continuous digitalisation of modern society, there currently persists disunity with regard to some of the constituting elements of the framework. During the legislative deliberations, requests for numerous amendments of the original proposal emerged. Therefore, as of now, there is no certainty about the final wording of the provisions establishing these mechanisms. As such, the latest outcome of the legislative proceedings from 11 June 2019 (Council of the European Union 2019) shall serve as the basis for the following short description and commentary.

The basic contours of the framework are that a court, prosecutor, or other competent authority in criminal proceedings may issue an order to preserve or produce specified electronic evidence directly to an internet service provider in another member state if the conditions under the regulation are fulfilled (Chankova and Voynova 2018, 121 et seq.). These include the severity of the criminal offence, the nature of the data, necessity, or proportionality. The core progressive aspect of the production order is its speed since it currently expects the addressee to transmit the requested electronic evidence within ten days upon receipt of a valid order; in emergency situations, even as quickly as six hours (Council of the European Union 2019, 36). This would spell a gargantuan improvement over the currently applicable timeframe of 120 days under the EIO. The preservation order is then aimed at retention of the requested data without undue delay for 60 days unless validly prolonged by the requesting authority (Council of the European Union 2019, 38). This would then help solve the issue of the temporality of certain types of electronic evidence, which is otherwise in principle unattainable by investigating authorities.

The first aspect still developing under the proposal is the scope of internet service providers to whom it shall apply. Under the current wording, should this scope be broadly understood, it would cover all forms of hosting services, including cloud computing (Council of the European Union 2019, 6). The scope of the regulation covers services provided in the European Union (Council of the European Union 2019, 8). There is special consideration to be given to the limitation of criminal liability due to freedom of press and freedom of expression in other media (Council of the European Union 2019, 11–12). Relevant to the speed of the procedure is the newly introduced requirement to have necessary judicial validation provided before the order is issued (Council of the European Union 2019, 14). The authenticity and validity of the order shall be established through a certificate (Council of the European Union 2019, 15); however, the specification of issuance and transmission of the certificates still remains a matter of debate (Council of the European Union 2019, 29). The core issue which still requires most consensus is, nonetheless, the approach to reimbursement of costs resulting from the order (Council of the European Union 2019, 40).

6.3.2 *Proportionate Approach to Digital Forensic Analysis of Disinformation and Propaganda*

Functional mechanisms for the collection and preservation of electronic evidence provide the necessary basis for investigation and adjudication of online activities. However, as aptly expressed by Boddington, 'Evidence is blind and cannot speak for itself, so it needs an interpreter to explain what it does or might mean' (Boddington 2016, 14).

6.3.2.1 *The Role of Digital Forensic Practitioners*

This role falls to practitioners of digital forensic analysis (DFA), who combine in their expertise (a) the abilities of an analyst knowledgeable in technical aspects of data processes run by computer devices and networks with (b) an investigatory approach to identify evidence of criminal behaviour, and (c) the necessary awareness of the legal prerequisites for due procedures and admissible evidence in court (Boddington 2016, 20). As an interpreter, the forensic expert provides the court with a scientific opinion, which must abide by strict standards, including impartiality of the assessment, avoiding a judgemental conclusion; the presentation of the full range of reasonable explanations; and appropriate probative bases for their presented view (Boddington 2016, 15). Through this, digital forensic practitioners fulfil a crucial role in the transformation of collected data into electronic evidence utilisable in a court of law. Due to their increasing significance in this regard, close attention is given to the formulation of DFA principles. These are then the basis for the development of best practices, which enshrine sound and well-established processes, leading to forensic examination that satisfies the legal requirements and provides accurate and reliable interpretation (Boddington 2016, 20; Daniel and Daniel 2011, 26).

6.3.2.2 *Fundamental Principles of Digital Forensic Analysis*

DFA best practices are constantly developing as they need to reflect the dynamic nature of the respective technological environment. However, the fundamental principles are of a more permanent nature, providing general tenets for due procedures. At the core of all forensic investigation stands Lockard's Exchange Principle: 'Every contact leaves trace' (Watson and Jones 2013, 10). This axiom is then reflected in pervasive emphasis on cautious interaction with the evidence.

Broadly recognised in the European context (ENISA 2015, 5) as a body of reference is the *Good Practice Guide for Computer-Based Electronic Evidence* issued and updated by the UK Association of Chief Police Officers (ACPO; Association of Chief Police Officers 2014). The principles of DFA contained therein are as follows:

- Principle 1: No action taken by law enforcement agencies or their agents should change data held on a computer or storage media which may subsequently be relied upon in court.
- Principle 2: In circumstances where a person finds it necessary to access original data held on a computer or on storage media, that person must be competent to do so and be able to give evidence explaining the relevance and the implications of their actions.
- Principle 3: An audit trail or other record of all processes applied to computer-based electronic evidence should be created and preserved. An independent third party should be able to examine those processes and achieve the same result.
- Principle 4: The person in charge of the investigation (the case officer) has overall responsibility for ensuring that the law and these principles are adhered to (Association of Chief Police Officers 2014, 4).

These four principles summarise the essence of the lawful and permissible handling of electronic evidence. Nevertheless, the dynamic nature of the online environment should be kept in mind as the application to new technological contexts may prove challenging. An example of such a setting may be seen in the investigation of cloud-based electronic evidence or the real-time investigation of evidence transmitted through a network (Watson and Jones 2013, 10).

The aforementioned tenets are expanded upon in other broadly observed best practices, such as the 2015 *Electronic evidence—a basic guide for First Responders*, issued by ENISA (2015). The five principles formulated under this framework reiterate and deepen the requirements set in the ACPO guide. They highlight the centrality of data integrity preservation at all stages of the process. Due to the volatile nature of digital data, chain of custody is essential in establishing the authenticity of the evidence. With regard to this audit trail, the need for detail is crucial (ENISA 2015, 7). Given the risks of modification connected with any manipulation of the electronic evidence, the data should be handled only by a specialist with the right equipment as early in the investigatory process as possible (ENISA 2015, 7–8). The interpretative role assigned to these specialists then requires their appropriate and constant training, which remains a prerequisite for successfully tackling the continuously emerging challenges connected to the investigation of new forms of electronic evidence. Nevertheless, the technical expertise of the forensic expert is inadequate unless supplemented by clear legal guidance, ensuring the legality of the process and admissibility of the evidence (ENISA 2015, 8).

Other examples of materials providing insight into applicable best practices include the 2015 *Best Practice Manual for the Forensic Examination of Digital Technology* by ENFSI[2] (2015) or the 2016 *Guidelines on Digital Forensics for OLAF[3] Staff* (OLAF 2016).

6.3.2.3 Challenges to the Digital Forensic Analysis of Disinformation and Propaganda

Despite the convergence of principles and best practices in the field of DFA, fragmentation and a lack of standardisation persist as a challenge. This remains true particularly with regard to standardisation of the analytical tools and unification of the terminology and analytical processes (Boddington 2016, 17).

Certification is broadly used, whether for forensic software or for the skills of the forensic practitioners. However, in both cases the true authority of the certification is often lacking. As summarised by Huber, ‘It’s important to understand that certification does not mean mastery.

[2] European Network of Forensic Science Institutes.

[3] European Anti-Fraud Office.

It just means that an outside organization has validated that an individual has met the ***minimum*** standards as defined by the organization. In fact, certification doesn't necessarily even mean professional ***competency***' (Huber 2010). This is similarly true of the forensic tools. Boddington stresses that 'forensic software certification to confirm forensic soundness is not widely and formally tested' (Boddington 2016, 18). Vincze adds that 'proprietary hardware and software manufacturers offer training and certifications for their individual products. Yet, despite a rapid increase in the number of digital forensic examinations and the scrutiny experienced by other forensic disciplines, there remains no standard for digital forensic examiner certifications. Thus, the investigators working with digital evidence have varied and uncertain qualifications' (Vincze 2016, 187). This then leads to a versatility in the approaches taken by digital forensic practitioners, including the use of non-validated or open source digital forensic tools, whose limits are often obscured from the recipients of the expert's opinion (Boddington 2016, 18). This obscurity regarding the foundations of DFA is further strengthened by the often unavoidable technical complexity of the interpreted data and processes. Under such conditions, providing fully reliable analysis remains a largely unattainable standard for digital forensic practitioners (Boddington 2016, 19).

Digital forensic analysis of disinformation and propaganda is mostly plagued by ills similar to other specialised areas of this discipline—in some regards, even more acutely. The electronic evidence stored as data on internet service provider network servers is fragile and susceptible to alternation or loss. More than in the case of standard electronic evidence stored on computer storage media, cloud-based server storage may be threatened by the temporally limited availability of data records (Karie and Venter 2015, 888). This then leads to a limited window of opportunity for the collection of electronic evidence, delineated by the technical availability of the data and the time it takes for the cross-border cooperative processes to unfold (Karie and Venter 2015, 888). The legal obstacles can be further seen not just with regard to procedural aspects but also in the increasing misalignment between the legal framework for cybercrime and available digital forensics models and investigatory procedures (Karie and Venter 2015, 889). This disparity is likely to be further widened by fragmentation in the practice of forensic practitioners due to frequent incompatibility among heterogeneous DFA tools (Karie and Venter 2015, 888). These tools are often designed to serve a limited purpose (Arthur and Venter 2004, 3), which means they are able to provide only a part of the analysis. With increasing complexity of the analysed issues, incompatibilities among the selected tools present an increasing challenge. This therefore puts a growing importance on proper processes of standardisation and validation of forensic tools (Craiger et al. 2006, 91 et seq.). Unless the processes and techniques employed meet proven scientific standards, they should not be acceptable as a basis for evidence in criminal proceedings (Karie and Venter 2015, 889).

6.3.2.4 Detecting Online Disinformation and Propaganda Using Automated Analytical Tools

An automated analytical tool for tagging certain content through qualitative metadata could prove an efficient instrument in combatting online disinformation and propaganda. However, as presented throughout this publication, the development of such a tool must tackle challenges on multiple levels, ranging from the qualification and identification of relevant manipulative techniques and their manifestation across a dataset, to the reliable development of such a tool on the basis of machine learning which provides sufficiently convincing results in order to minimise false results to an acceptably low level. In addition to these challenges, the limits to the utilisation of a tool ensuing from the legal requirements must be recognised. This chapter provided an overview of the perception of data as electronic evidence, focusing on its unique conceptual attributes, challenging procedural frameworks for international collection, and the specific role of DFA specialists in translating its qualities into a language recognisable in the court of law. Any implementation of an automated analytical tool into these processes needs to be compliably inserted into these frameworks and shall be in principle limited in its impact by their structure. If an automated analytical tool provides an assessment of the content with regard to the recognised expressions of manipulative techniques, the limits of the informative value of such an assessment must be taken into consideration.

The main challenge then that needs to be embraced is the potential susceptibility of the algorithm to bias. Notwithstanding the measures taken during the data set curation, the assessment of content is interpretative and thereby affected by the subjective perception of the individual. This provides for an unavoidable balance between the neutralisation of prejudice introduced through the learning dataset and the informative value, which can be derived from the manipulative techniques utilised in the content piece (Caliskan et al. 2017, 183). Aside from this issue, there are other potential deficiencies of the dataset which may impact the objectivity of the assessment, 'such as confirmation bias, outcome bias, blind-spot bias, the availability heuristic, clustering illusions and bandwagon effects' (Završnik 2019, 11).

These can be partially eliminated through the intermediary role of a DFA specialist with sufficient expert knowledge of the data and the algorithm in order to soberly interpret the provided assessment and help the decision-making authority avoid the fallacy of the algorithmic aura of objectivity (Završnik 2019, 13). In this sense, any automated analytical tool must be viewed merely as such, which means merely as an informational input for assessment and adjudication of the situation based on a wholesome picture and not as a preformulated objective suggestion for qualification of the case.

6.4 Conclusions

This chapter presented a set of components in the regulatory framework aimed at the collection and use of electronic evidence. The focus was therefore on the legal prerequisites for the utilisation of outputs provided by online disinformation and manipulation detection tools, which were described in the previous chapter, in a court of law.

At first, the particularity of the virtual form of the core phenomena was highlighted, distinguishing data from information and formulating what constitutes electronic evidence. The next section reflected the fact that authoritative actions taken against the dissemination of disinformation or propaganda need to follow respective procedural requirements, which poses a particular challenge for national enforcement entities due to the borderless quality of the online environment. The progress towards overcoming these obstacles was briefly presented. Particular attention was dedicated to the efforts aimed at effective and timely procedures for cross-border cooperation in the collection of electronic evidence, exemplified by the latest efforts in the European Union towards the adoption of the Regulation on European Production and Preservation Orders for electronic evidence in criminal matters. The third and final perspective introduced to this context was the role of digital forensic practitioners in mediating the informative value of collected data and the outputs of online disinformation and manipulation detection tools.

There are several conclusions drawn throughout the chapter with respect to particular aspects of this topic. Firstly, the complexity of phenomena like disinformation or propaganda requires the development and application of detection and analytical tools which operate with incomplete data and must unavoidably operate with a non-negligible level of uncertainty and lack of explainability. These tools can in principle be utilised in a court of law under current European procedural laws; however, their adoption can likely be successfully facilitated only with the help of expert witnesses—the digital forensic practitioners.

Additionally, the effective combat of online disinformation and propaganda dissemination requires fast and straightforward procedures for cross-border electronic evidence collection. These need to link the investigating authority with the internet service provider in possession of the data with as minimal delay and intermediation as possible. It was shown that such instruments are currently discussed within the European Union. However, not only are these not yet in place but cooperation with other states, in particular with the United States and the Russian Federation, remains procedurally cumbersome and time-consuming, limiting the potential for the pursuit of the illegal online activities in question by public authorities.

The final conclusion concerns challenges to the validation of the outputs of disinformation and propaganda detection tools as part of a digital forensic analysis. Despite broadly acknowledged general principles being in place, the specifics of standardisation and certification of digital forensic tools are often fragmented. Given that the outputs of these tools are likely to require mediation and interpretation by the digital forensic practitioners in order to reach a court of law, transparent and reliable approaches to testing and assessment of these detection and analytical tools should be further developed.

Bibilography

Alexy, R. (1996). Discourse Theory and Human Rights. *Ratio Juris, 9*(3), 209–235.

Alexy, R. (2000). On the Structure of Legal Principles. *Ratio Juris, 13*(3), 294–304.

Arthur, K. K., & Venter, H. S. (2004). An Investigation into Computer Forensic Tools. In *ISSA 2004 Proceedings* (pp. 1–11). IEEE Computer Society

Publishers. https://digifors.cs.up.ac.za/issa/2004/Proceedings/Full/060.pdf. Accessed 30 Nov 2019.

Association of Chief Police Officers. (2014). *Good Practice Guide for Computer-Based Electronic Evidence*. Official release version 4.0. Association of Chief Police Officers. https://www.7safe.com/docs/default-source/default-document-library/acpo_guidelines_computer_evidence_v4_web.pdf. Accessed 30 Nov 2019.

Boddington, R. (2016). *Practical Digital Forensics*. Birmingham: Packt Publishing—ebooks Account.

Browning, J. G. (2011). Digging for the Digital Dirt: Discovery and use of Evidence from Social Media Sites. *SMU Science and Technology Law Review, 14*(3), 465–496.

Caliskan, A., Bryson, J. J., & Narayanan, A. (2017). Semantics Derived Automatically from Language Corpora Contain Human-like Biases. *Science, 356*(6334), 183–186. https://doi.org/10.1126/science.aal4230.

Chankova, D., Voynova, R. (2018). Towards New European Regulation for Handling Electronic Evidence. *US-China Law Review*, 15(3), 121–129.

Committee on Foreign Affairs. (2019). *Report on the State of EU-Russia Political Relations*. Brussels: European Parliament. http://www.europarl.europa.eu/doceo/document/A-8-2019-0073_EN.html. Accessed 30 Nov 2019.

Council of Europe. (1978). *Additional Protocol to the European Convention on Mutual Assistance in Criminal Matters: European Treaty Series No. 99*. Strasbourg: Council of Europe. https://rm.coe.int/1680077975. Accessed 30 Nov 2019.

Council of Europe. (2001a). *Details of Treaty No.185: Convention on Cybercrime*. https://www.coe.int/en/web/conventions/full-list. Accessed 30 Nov 2019.

Council of Europe. (2001b). *Second Additional Protocol to the European Convention on Mutual Assistance in Criminal Matters*. https://www.coe.int/fr/web/conventions/full-list. Accessed 30 Nov 2019.

Council of Europe. (2003). *Details of Treaty No.189: Additional Protocol to the Convention on Cybercrime, Concerning the Criminalisation of Acts of a Racist and Xenophobic Nature Committed through Computer Systems*. https://www.coe.int/en/web/conventions/full-list. Accessed 30 Nov 2019.

Council of Europe. (2019a). *Budapest Convention and Related Standards*. https://www.coe.int/en/web/cybercrime/the-budapest-convention. Accessed 30 Nov 2019.

Council of Europe. (2019b). *Details of Treaty No.030: European Convention on Mutual Assistance in Criminal Matters*. https://www.coe.int/en/web/conventions/full-list/-/conventions/treaty/030. Accessed 30 Nov 2019.

Council of Europe. (2019c). Russian Federation Ratifies the Second Additional Protocol to the European Convention on Mutual Assistance in Criminal Matters. *Committee of Experts on the Operation of European Conventions on Co-Operation in Criminal Matters (PC-OC)* (blog). https://www.coe.int/en/web/transnational-criminal-justice-pcoc/home/-/asset_publisher/1f469eJfgY9m/content/russian-federation-ratifies-the-second-additional-protocol-to-the-european-convention-on-mutual-assistance-in-criminal-matters. Accessed 30 Nov 2019.

Council of Europe. (2019d). *Chart of Signatures and Ratifications of Treaty 030: European Convention on Mutual Assistance in Criminal Matters*. https://www.coe.int/en/web/conventions/full-list/-/conventions/treaty/030/signatures?p_auth=uJ11NBHx. Accessed 30 Nov 2019.

Council of European Union. (2008). *Council Framework Decision 2008/913/JHA of 28 November 2008 on Combating Certain Forms and Expressions of Racism and Xenophobia by Means of Criminal Law*. Official Journal of the European Union, *328*. http://data.europa.eu/eli/dec_framw/2008/913/oj/eng. Accessed 30 November 2019.

Council of the European Union. (2011). *Handbook on the Practical Application of the EU-U.S. Mutual Legal Assistance and Extradition Agreements 8024/11*. Brussels: Council of the European Union. https://www.statewatch.org/news/2011/mar/eu-council-eu-usa-mla-handbook-8024-11.pdf. Accessed 30 Nov 2019.

Council of the European Union. (2012). *EU-Russia Cooperation in Criminal Matters 14316/1/12 REV 1*. Brussels: Council of the European Union. https://www.statewatch.org/news/2012/oct/eu-council-russia-criminal-matters-14316-rev1-12.pdf. Accessed 30 Nov 2019.

Council of the European Union. (2017). *European Union Instruments in the Field of Criminal Law and Related Texts*. Brussels: Council of the European Union. https://www.consilium.europa.eu/media/32557/eu-instrumentsdecember2017.pdf. Accessed 30 Nov 2019.

Council of the European Union. (2019). *Regulation of the European Parliament and of the Council on European Production and Preservation Orders for Electronic Evidence in Criminal Matters—General Approach 10206/19*. Brussels: Council of the European Union. https://eur-lex.europa.eu/legal-content/EN/TXT/PDF/?uri=CONSIL:ST_10206_2019_INIT&from=EN. Accessed 30 November 2019.

Craiger, P., Swauger, J., Marberry, C., Hendricks, C. (2006). Validation of Digital Forensic Tools. In P. Kanellis, E. Kiountouzis, N. Kolokotronis, D. Martakos (Eds.), *Digital Crime and Forensic Science in Cyberspace* (pp. 91–105). Hershey, PA: Idea Group. https://doi.org/10.4018/978-1-59140-872-7.ch005.

Daniel, L., & Daniel, L. (2011). *Digital Forensics for Legal Professionals: Understanding Digital Evidence from the Warrant to the Courtroom*. Waltham, MA: Syngress.

Daniele, M., & Calvanese, E. (2018). Evidence Gathering. In R. Kostoris (Ed.), *Handbook of European Criminal Procedure* (pp. 353–391). Cham: Springer.
Easterbrook, F. H. (1996). *Cyberspace and the Law of the Horse*. Chicago, IL: University of Chicago Legal Forum.
ENFSI. (2015). *Best Practice Manual for the Forensic Examination of Digital Technology*. ENFSI-BPM-FIT-01. http://enfsi.eu/wp-content/uploads/2016/09/1._forensic_examination_of_digital_technology_0.pdf. Accessed 30 Nov 2019.
ENISA. (2015). *Electronic Evidence—a Basic Guide for First Responders*. https://www.enisa.europa.eu/publications/electronic-evidence-a-basic-guide-for-first-responders. Accessed 30 Nov 2019.
Eurojust. (2018). *European Investigation Order*. http://www.eurojust.europa.eu/doclibrary/corporate/Infographics/European%20Investigation%20Order/2018-European-Investigation-Order.pdf. Accessed 30 Nov 2019.
Eurojust. (2019). *European Investigation Order*. http://www.eurojust.europa.eu/Practitioners/operational/EIO/Pages/EIO.aspx. Accessed 30 Nov 2019.
European Commission. (2019a). *Mutual Legal Assistance and Extradition*. https://ec.europa.eu/info/law/cross-border-cases/judicial-cooperation/types-judicial-cooperation/mutual-legal-assistance-and-extradition_en. Accessed 30 Nov 2019.
European Commission. (2019b). Questions and Answers: Mandate for the EU-U.S. Cooperation on Electronic Evidence. *Press Releases*. https://europa.eu/rapid/press-release_MEMO-19-863_en.htm. Accessed 30 Nov 2019.
European Communities. (2000). The Schengen Acquis—Convention Implementing the Schengen Agreement of 14 June 1985 between the Governments of the States of the Benelux Economic Union, the Federal Republic of Germany and the French Republic on the Gradual Abolition of Checks at Their Common Borders. *Official Journal of the European Union 239*, 19–62. https://eur-lex.europa.eu/LexUriServ/LexUriServ.do?uri=CELEX%3A42000A0922%2802%29%3AEN%3AHTML. Accessed 30 Nov 2019.
European Judicial Network. (2011a). Full Text of Convention of 29 May 2000 on Mutual Assistance in Criminal Matters between the Member States of the European Union. *Judicial Library*. https://www.ejn-crimjust.europa.eu/ejn/libdocumentproperties/EN/16. Accessed 30 Nov 2019.
European Judicial Network. (2011b). Explanatory Report on the Convention MLA 2000. *Judicial Library*. https://www.ejn-crimjust.europa.eu/ejn/libdocumentproperties/EN/575. Accessed 30 Nov 2019.
European Judicial Network. (2019a). *Practical Tools for Judicial Cooperation*. https://www.ejn-crimjust.europa.eu/ejn/EJN_Home.aspx. Accessed 30 Nov 2019.

European Judicial Network. (2019b). Specific Areas of Crime Legal Instruments (Adopted by the EU). *Judicial Library*. https://www.ejn-crimjust.europa.eu/ejn/libcategories/EN/170/-1/-1/-1. Accessed 30 Nov 2019.

European Union. (2003). Agreement on Mutual Legal Assistance between the European Union and the United States of America. *Official Journal of the European Union L, 181/34*. https://eur-lex.europa.eu/LexUriServ/LexUriServ.do?uri=OJ:L:2003:181:0034:0042:en:PDF. Accessed 30 Nov 2019.

European Union. (2014). *Directive 2014/41/EU of the European Parliament and of the Council of 3 April 2014 Regarding the European Investigation Order in Criminal Matters*. https://eur-lex.europa.eu/legal-content/EN/TXT/?uri=celex%3A32014L0041. Accessed 30 Nov 2019.

European Union. (2016). *Eurojust*. https://europa.eu/european-union/about-eu/agencies/eurojust_en. Accessed 30 Nov 2019.

European Union. (2018a). Internal Procedure: Proposal for a Regulation on European Production Orders for Electronic Evidence and a Directive on Legal Representation. *Eur-Lex*. https://eur-lex.europa.eu/legal-content/EN/PIN/?uri=COM:2018:225:FIN. Accessed 30 Nov 2019.

European Union. (2018b). *Proposal for a Regulation of the European Parliament and of the Council on European Production and Preservation Orders for Electronic Evidence in Criminal Matters*. COM/2018/225 final-2018/0108 (COD). https://eur-lex.europa.eu/legal-content/EN/TXT/?uri=COM%3A2018%3A225%3AFIN. Accessed 30 Nov 2019.

European Union. (2019). Procedure: COM (2018) 225: Proposal for a Regulation of the European Parliament and of the Council on European Production and Preservation Orders for Electronic Evidence in Criminal Matters. *Eur-Lex*. https://eur-lex.europa.eu/legal-content/EN/HIS/?uri=COM:2018:225:FIN. Accessed 30 Nov 2019.

European Union External Action Service. (2019). *The European Union and the Russian Federation*. Brussels: EEAS. https://eeas.europa.eu/headquarters/headquarters-homepage/35939/european-union-and-russian-federation_en. Accessed 30 Nov 2019.

Fuller, L. L. (1969). *The Morality of Law*. London: Yale University Press.

Guerra, J. E., & Janssens, M.-C. (2019). Legal and Practical Challenges in the Application of the European Investigation Order: Summary of the Eurojust Meeting of 19–20 September 2018. *Eucrim: The European Criminal Law Associations' Forum, 1*, 46–53.

Huber, E. (2010, November 13). Certification, Licensing, and Accreditation in Digital Forensics. *A Fistful of Dongles: Eric Huber's Cybercrime and Digital Forensics Blog* (blog). https://www.afodblog.com/2010/11/certification-licensing-and.html. Accessed 30 Nov 2019.

Karie, N. M., & Venter, H. S. (2015). Taxonomy of Challenges for Digital Forensics. *Journal of Forensic Sciences*, *60*, 885–893. https://doi.org/10.1111/1556-4029.12809.
Lévy, P. (1998). *Becoming Virtual: Reality in the Digital Age*. New York, NY: Plenum Trade.
McGoldrick, D., & O'Donnell, T. (1988). Hate-Speech Laws: Consistency with National and International Human Rights Law. *Legal Studies*, *18*(4), 453–485.
OLAF. (2016). *Guidelines on Digital Forensic Procedures for OLAF Staff*. https://ec.europa.eu/anti-fraud/sites/antifraud/files/guidelines_en.pdf. Accessed 30 Nov 2019.
Papucharova, G. (2019). Short Profiles of Different European Investigation Order Domestic Regulations in the European Union. *International Conference Knowledge-Based Organization*, *25*(2), 169–175. https://doi.org/10.2478/kbo-2019-0075.
Polcak, R., & Svantesson, D. (2017). *Information Sovereignty*. Cheltenham: Edward Elgar.
Polcak, R. (2019). Procedural and Institutional Backing of Transparency in Algorithmic Processing of Rights. *Masaryk University Journal of Law and Technology*, *13*(2), 401–414.
Ramos, J. A. E. (2019). The European Investigation Order and its Relationship with Other Judicial Cooperation Instruments. *The European Criminal Law Association's Forum 2019*(1), 53–60. https://doi.org/10.30709/eucrim-2019-004.
Robinson, G. (2018). The European Commission's e-Evidence Proposal. *European Data Protection Law Review (EDPL)*, *4*(3), 347–352.
Royster, L. K. (2017). Fake News: Political Solutions to the Online Epidemic. *North Carolina Law Review*, *96*(1), 270–[vi].
Siracusano, F. (2019). The European Investigation Order for Evidence Gathering Abroad. In T. Rafaraci & R. Belfiore (Eds.), *EU Criminal Justice: Fundamental Rights, Transnational Proceedings and the European Public Prosecutor's Office* (pp. 85–101). Cham: Springer.
Svantesson, D. (2015). The Holy Trinity of Legal Fictions Undermining the Application of Law to the Global Internet. *International Journal of Law and Information Technology*, *23*(3), 219–234.
Tosza, S. T. (2019). Cross-Border Gathering of Electronic Evidence: Mutual Legal Assistance, Its Shortcomings and Remedies. In D. Flore & V. Franssen (Eds.), *Société Numérique et Droit Pénal*. Belgique, France, and Europe: Bruylant. http://dspace.library.uu.nl/handle/1874/384506. Accessed 30 Nov 2019.

Vincze, E. A. (2016). Challenges in Digital Forensics. *Police Practice and Research, 17*(2), 183–194. https://doi.org/10.1080/15614263.2015.1128163.

Vojak, B. (2017). Fake News: The Commoditization of Internet Speech. *California Western International Law Journal, 48*(1), 123–158.

Waldman, A. E. (2018). The Marketplace of Fake News. *University of Pennsylvania Journal of Constitutional Law, 20*(4), 845–870.

Watson, D. L., & Jones, A. (2013). *Digital Forensics Processing and Procedures: Meeting the Requirements of ISO 17020, ISO 17025, ISO 27001 and Best Practice Requirements*. Waltham, MA: Syngress.

Wiener, N. (1965). *Cybernetics: Or Control and Communication in the Animal and the Machine*. Cambridge, MA: Massachusetts Institute of Technology Press.

Wortzman, S., & Nickle, S. (2009). Obtaining Relevant Electronic Evidence. *Advocates' Quarterly*, *36*(2), 226–268.

Yoo, C. S. (2012). When Antitrust met Facebook. *George Mason Law Review, 19*(5), 1147–1162.

Završnik, A. (2019). Algorithmic Justice: Algorithms and Big Data in Criminal Justice Settings. *European Journal of Criminology*. https://doi.org/10.1177/1477370819876762.

CHAPTER 7

Institutional Responses of European Countries

Jan Hanzelka and Miroslava Pavlíková

7.1 Introduction

After the Ukrainian conflict began in 2014, disinformation campaigns were identified in various European countries. Occurrences like the Brexit campaign '#leave' influence operations during parliamentary elections in Europe (in Germany or France, for example) or domestic active measures scandals, such as Austria's Freedom Party of Austria (FPÖ) stressed the need to counteract such tactics and protect targets—nation states as well as supranational structures. The dynamics of influence operations and forms of disinformation dissemination are very fast, flexible, and even harder to maintain.

In reaction to the latest disruptive propaganda campaigns in Europe, the institutions of some countries have focused on countermeasures. Some include the establishment of special governmental bodies, the installation of special task force groups, new laws, and active cooperation

J. Hanzelka · M. Pavlíková (✉)
Department of Political Science, Faculty of Social Studies, Masaryk University, Brno, Czechia

M. Gregor and P. Mlejnková (eds.), *Challenging Online Propaganda and Disinformation in the 21st Century*, Political Campaigning and Communication,
https://doi.org/10.1007/978-3-030-58624-9_7

between governments, political parties, media, non-governmental organisations, and academia. However, particular counter steps, the willingness of authorities, and the adequacy of measures differ. This chapter analyses how European countries deal with malicious online disinformation and propaganda. We will assess the European state authorities' and institutions' countermeasures against information warfare, especially the good examples and specific approaches of particular countries. The text focuses on lessons from election interference and the preparedness of particular countries, taking into consideration long-term measures as well. According to the mentioned approaches, we have formulated a categorical framework for the analysis of institutional countermeasures, which we then use to analyse the cases of several European countries.

Actors who aim to defend themselves against propaganda and disinformation campaigns need to study the newest cases, technologies, and tactics to counter these hostile activities effectively. Although we can perceive coordination efforts on the international level, there are still many differences between European states in their approaches to countermeasures. There are good examples of preparation, active responses, as well as coordination and the sharing of good practices among states. On the other hand, some actors still have a lot to learn. In this chapter, we will focus on three examples from across Europe: The case of Denmark demonstrates a country which has a leading position in countermeasure formulation; in central Europe, Czech Republic is an example of a country which is 'half-way'; and the south-eastern European country of Bulgaria reveals a country with barely noticeable measures. All three countries are members of the European Union and NATO. However, all three have different approaches to challenging propaganda and disinformation, and they thus make evident how different political attitudes, different histories, and different starting positions can affect the approach towards countermeasures.

7.2 Framework for Analysis: Institutional Countermeasures Against Influence Operations

In the following section, a framework with types of institutional responses for the complex analysis of case studies is proposed. In this chapter, influence operations instead of disinformation and propaganda are often mentioned, even though this concept is more complex and also covers other activities (see Chapter 1). The reason is European states' usage of influence operations in its proclamations and documents. Countermeasures against disinformation and propaganda are often part of the bigger package covered under the influence operations' umbrella.

The particular categories are derived from the most viable countermeasure examples found in different European countries and existing frameworks, which have been evaluated as relevant and actual. The framework proposal by Brattberg and Maurer (2018) of the Carnegie Endowment for International Peace serves as inspiration in its consideration of good examples from chosen European countries (Germany, Sweden, France, and Netherlands). It focuses on resilience and legal measures, public statements, and the education of voters as it concerns disinformation campaigns. They also suggest training and educating political parties, conducting government-media dialogue, engaging media companies to mitigate threats, and, finally, sharing lessons learned as well as best practices to support international cooperation. Moreover, the authors suggest clearly warning citizens about possible interference, promoting citizen fact-checking and investigative journalism, and urging political parties to assert that they will not use social media bots. This might generally cover avoidance of negative campaigns and usage of disinformation, as well as placing stress on transparency (see Flamini and Tardáguila 2019). The analysis is secondly inspired by the categorisation of the Ministry of Foreign Affairs of Denmark, which presented 11 initiatives to counter hostile influence operations. Besides the abovementioned responses, Denmark suggests the establishment of an intergovernmental task force to strengthen the monitoring of disinformation, train communication officers, and reinforce intelligence services activities (Ministry of Foreign Affairs of Denmark 2018).

The following section will introduce particular categories and their measures. Furthermore, examples of real countermeasure usage will be explained with a focus on European countries. These examples have been chosen based on the availability of information and the possible effectivity of the countermeasures. The aim is to focus on good or even best practices. However, it is obvious, that some countermeasures are unique and evaluation on effectivity needs historical distance. In accordance with an index from the European Policy Initiative of the Open Society Institute (2018, In: Mackintosh and Kiernan 2019) measuring the post-truth phenomenon in countries, the Scandinavian countries, Estonia, and the Netherlands rank first. If possible and available, good examples from these countries are described in more depth. Besides European countries, we also focus on the supranational level. Countermeasures from the European Union and NATO will also be assessed, including the actions of particular European countries in regard to these supranational entities. We consider this one of the categories for analysis, and it is listed in Table 7.1.

7.2.1 Actions with the Public

The institution of *clear warning* resonates especially with the secret services or other governmental bodies in terms of its impact on security. Secret services might occasionally present warnings about serious security issues or present actual threats in their annual public reports. Warning by secret services might have greater value for the public than the proclamations of other authorities. In the Netherlands, for example, the 2018 annual public report of the General Intelligence and Security Service (Algemene Inlichtingen- en Veiligheidsdienst in Dutch) mentioned covert

Table 7.1 Categorisation of institutional countermeasures against influence operations

Category	*Activities*
Actions with the public	Clear warnings Public statements Voter education Education of parties
State measures	Establishment of special ministerial bodies or other state institutions Employee education
Legal measures	Implementation of legal measures Cooperation with business
Actions with the media	Train communication officers Strengthen disinformation monitoring Support investigative journalism
Actions with political parties	Urge parties into political culture compliance Organise training for political parties and campaigners
Direct countermeasures	Information operations against hostile actors Diplomatic pressure
Actions with supranational entities	Cooperation Join task forces Join discussions Accept recommendations

Source Authors

influence and manipulation of the public perception by Russia and China (General Intelligence and Security Service 2018). It also informed about surveillance by the Russian hacking group Cozy Bear, after which they publicly attributed an attack to Russia (Brattberg and Maurer 2018). In a public report from March 2019, the Estonian Foreign Intelligence Service (Valisluuveramet) warned about the Russian threat before the European parliamentary election, revealing that France, Germany, and Italy were the main targets (Estonian Foreign Intelligence Service 2019; EU Observer 2019). The report considers cyber threats by Russian secret services especially, in addition to mention of troll activities, to be an integral part. A recent Estonian report also stresses that 'China is more and more active in influence operations and propaganda'. Islamic State propaganda in Europe is also highlighted. In May 2019, the Federal Office for the Protection of the Constitution (Bundesamt für Verfassungsschutz) in Germany, warned against the Austrian government (saying it could not be trusted) because of its ties to Russia and a possible information flow between them (Stone 2019). The whole warning derives from the activities of the then governing party FPÖ, the Russians, and negotiations about the production of favourable media coverage.

Naturally, a lot of clear warnings or public attributions were made by governments, politicians, and other high state authorities. French President Emmanuel Macron, the British foreign secretary at the time, Boris Johnson, as well as German chancellor Angela Merkel warned against Russian interference into election processes (Brattberg and Maurer 2018). This might be connected to *public statements* and *voter education*, which is often utilised by governments or authorities. An interesting example can be found in the French government's clear labelling of Sputnik and RT as pro-Kremlin outlets, and their subsequent exclusion from press conferences in Élysée Palace as well as regular refusal in covering official events (EUvsDisinfo 2019). The Swedish Civil Contingencies Agency, under the Ministry of Defence, launched an awareness campaign for *public education* about propaganda (Robinson et al. 2019). In a 20-page-long document called *If Crisis or War Comes*, a chapter about false information has its place with easily written advice and interactive questions (Swedish Civil Contingencies Agency 2018). The government also planned to teach children in primary schools how to recognise fake news (Roden 2017). A similar governmental approach appeared in Finland as well (Charlton 2019). CNN labelled Finland a country which is winning the war on fake news (Mackintosh and Kiernan 2019). The government's anti-fake news programme is based on cross-departmental engagement, learning best practices from around the world, and a bottom-up approach starting with country's education system[1] (KennyBirch 2019). Public governmental campaigns in the United Kingdom have intensified after the Skripal case. Shortly after the attack, the UK government established communication teams which informed the public about Russian manipulative tactics. Currently, the British government is starting a public campaign focused on empowering citizens in disinformation recognition and awareness of its malicious effects. The campaign started with the issue of measles and vaccination against it.

7.2.2 State Measures

State measures is mostly meant as the formation of special governmental or state bodies, strengthening the role of institutions in the influence operations fight, and other intragovernmental provisions. In some countries, *special task forces* or other ministerial bodies have been established to counter-influence operations. In 2017, as a reaction to Russian activities, the Danish government established an inter-ministerial task force for countering these campaigns. This special body coordinates efforts across government as well as Danish national intelligence and security services (EUvsDisinfo 2018). In Sweden, for example, a psychological defence authority (psykologiskt försvar) has been launched. This authority focuses on countering disinformation and boosting the population's resistance to influence operations. In the Netherlands, the National Coordinator for Security and Counterterrorism received in 2019 responsibilities related to the detection of influence operations run by foreign state powers. In Czech Republic, the Ministry of the Interior established the Centre Against Terrorism and Hybrid Threats for expert and analytical activities, including disinformation campaigns (Ministry of the Interior of the Czech Republic 2017). Its activities remain mostly classified. In Ukraine, meanwhile, a whole ministry focusing on information policy was founded. The ministry was established to fight against information attacks (Interfax-Ukraine 2014). In 2019, it presented a white book on information operations against Ukraine (*Bila kniga specialnih informacijnih operacij proti Ukraïni*, see Ministry of Information Policy of Ukraine

[1] For example, the project for schools called 'Facts, please!'.

2018) considering Russia's influence operations in the country between 2014 and 2018 (Ukrainian Independent Information Agency of News 2019).

As regards *state employee education*, Finland launched a programme on countering propaganda for government officials. The programme emphasises the importance of creating a new narrative which highlights Finnish values and a 'Finnish story' (KennyBirch 2019). In Sweden, the Civil Contingencies Agency produced a manual countering information operations which might target public service workers (Klingová and Milo 2018). *Countering Information Influence Activities: A Handbook for Communicators* (Swedish Civil Contingencies Agency 2019) provides techniques and advice on how to counter information influence operations, including preparing organisations for a quick and effective response.

7.2.3 Legal Measures

Focusing on legal measures would take an entire chapter or even book (see Chapters 4 and 6 for European level of legal measures), thus we will cover only special laws reacting to disinformation. In Italy, for example, citizens can use a special online service where it is possible to report fake news to the police (Robinson et al. 2019). After abandonment of this measure, a bill proposing sentences for spreading fake news was tabled in 2017. In 2017, Germany passed a law called NetzDG which is meant to combat fake news and hate speech on the Internet. Under this law, social media platforms have 24 hours after receiving a report to remove a post which violates German law. It furthermore forces networks to reveal the identities of those behind posts. The law has become a subject of discussion about freedom of speech violations (Bleiker and Brady 2017).

In 2018, the French parliament passed a law related to election campaigns, according to which the electoral jurisdiction has a responsibility to decide on the withdrawal of manipulative materials from the Internet. However, there must be evidence that such material was intentionally spread on a wide scale with the intention of interfering and disrupting the elections (Rozgonyi 2018).

Nevertheless, these legal measures have a few weaknesses. First of all, they mix together terrorist content, hate speech, and acts that are part of influence operations. However, influence operations may demand different counter approaches than terrorist propaganda. Secondly, the legal measures focus on content and do not deal with the tools and techniques of influencing, for example, the use of fake accounts, bots, and algorithms.

Currently, we can see a trend in the efforts of European governments to engage the cooperation of Facebook and Google in the case of negative social issues.[2] General efforts, such as systematic work towards 'stopping of misinformation and false news' can be seen. In Facebook's 'Community Standards' there is a paragraph which reads, 'There is also a fine line between false news and satire or opinion. For these reasons, we do not remove false news from Facebook, but instead significantly reduce its distribution by showing it lower in the News Feed'. The article is part of a broader Facebook strategy to handle fake news (Facebook 2019). This solution is dependent on the problematic identification of fake news without deep research and fact-checking. They are trying to avoid accusations of political persecution from certain opinion groups, which would otherwise be faced with the deletion of content. In certain countries (Facebook 2020), Facebook has third-party fact-checking partners. There, partners are trained to assess the truth of a post and, in the case of fake news, use predefined tools to limit the available contributions or prohibit monetisation (Facebook 2020). Google has a similar initiative, which is described in the white paper *How Google Fights Disinformation* (Google 2019). The Google initiative is based on ranking and labelling content, and the results are reflected in the search algorithm. Less credible news is less relevant in a search. Google declares that they 'welcome a constructive dialogue with governments, civil society, academia, and newsrooms' (Google 2019).

7.2.4 Actions with the Media

Cooperation with media might play a key role in controlling the disinformation flow as well as promoting media literacy. Belgium provides an example of an active approach from government to media. The Flemish Ministry of Education and Training sponsors Média Animation ASBL, a media education resource which focuses on media literacy in schools as well as for politicians and other decision-makers (Kremlin Watch 2020;

[2] An example is the problem of hate speech and current German legislation, which is trying to delegate responsibility for this issue to social media providers (Hanzelka and Kasl 2018).

Media Animation ASBL 2020). The Swedish government also expressed the will to cooperation with media when the government, together with the Swedish national television broadcaster, invested in a digital platform providing automatic fact-checking and news in a way which crosses the borders of filter bubbles. In Latvia, we can find an example supporting investigative journalism since 2017. The new programme was launched under the auspices of the Ministry of Culture, and it has financially supported about 20 projects (Robinson et al. 2019). Another interesting example of an approach to media can be found in Estonia. Its politicians and administration officers claim they never give interviews to Russian state-controlled media (Sternstein 2017). Some countries must also deal with its Russian minorities and the need for Russian-language media; this is mostly relevant in the Baltic countries. Estonia started its own Russian-language channel in 2015. This repression of Russian-language sources with connections to the Russian government is also a strategy some countries deploy to protect minorities. In Lithuania, for example, the government pulled RTR-Planeta, run by the Russian government, off the air (PressTV 2017; Sternstein 2017).

7.2.5 Actions with Political Parties

There are many discussions over voter education about disinformation, but little is said about the education of political parties. Moreover, as for example the Brexit referendum has shown,[3] political parties might have a strong role in the spread of disinformation. However, only a few examples of this kind of political culture improvement can be found. German political parties entered into a 'gentlemen's agreement' before the 2017 election. They stated they would not use leaked information for political purposes, nor use social media bots (Brattberg and Maurer 2018). In Finland, the *education of political parties* is part of a cross-department strategy.[4] The electoral administration under the Ministry

[3] For example, the connection between the far-right United Kingdom Independent Party (UKIP) and the company Cambridge Analytica using big data from Facebook to produce a micro-targeted campaign (see Chapter 2) (Scott 2018).

[4] A so called *whole-of-government approach* also covers the coordination of monitoring, evaluation, and management of hybrid threats. A special government ambassador ensures cooperation between institutions as well as the private sector, and an inter-ministerial group deals with influence operations (Klingová and Milo 2018).

of Justice organised anti-disinformation training for political parties and candidates. Trainings are conducted in various regions so as to be available to everyone. Training should help candidates to recognise and report suspected disinformation and improve their cybersecurity (France 24 2019; KennyBirch 2019).

7.2.6 Direct Countermeasures

We found it necessary to also mention *real time counter-propaganda* as a governmental response. After the poisoning of double agent Sergei Skripal, many European countries expelled their Russian diplomats. This represents a typical example of a direct countermeasure on the state level. No action like this was taken in connection with a hostile propaganda campaign. However, other forms of direct reactions can be identified. French President Macron's IT support, in response to a leaked documents and conversations affair inside his campaign team, fed attackers with bogus information to degrade the value of the leaked content (Brattberg and Maurer 2018; Mohan 2017). This reaction was prepared in advance with campaign staff having anticipated the hacking of their computers; different scenarios were formulated as campaigners realised the threat of interference (EUvsDisinfo 2019).

7.3 Actions of the European Union and NATO

7.3.1 European Union

This is an evolution of the joint approach against disinformation on the EU level; examples of task forces, special bodies countering influence operations, new laws as well as media cooperation can be found. There is a joint task force on the European Union level which was established in 2015. The East StratCom Task Force addresses Russian information campaigns and submits plans for strategic communication. The team consists of staff recruited from EU institutions, or it is seconded by EU member states. The task force's budget exists within the EU budget and those of its member states. (European Union External Action 2018). One of the most visible activities of the task force is the project 'EUvs-Disinfo', which 'identifies, compiles, and exposes disinformation cases originating in pro-Kremlin media that are spread across the EU and

Eastern Partnership countries'. The project's current monitoring capabilities 'also uncover disinformation spread in the Western Balkans and the EU's Southern neighbourhood'. The project publishes in 15 languages, updates every week, and distributes a weekly newsletter (EUvsDisinfo, n.d.). In addition to the East StratCom Task Force, the High-Level Expert Group (HLEG) on Fake News and Online Disinformation was established.

An embodiment of these direct countermeasures is one of the Action Plan against Disinformation's pillars: the Rapid Alert System (RAS; European Commission 2019a; European Union External Action 2019). In practice, the RAS should function like an online platform where member states and institutions share their experience and knowledge and prepare common actions. It also aims to cooperate with NATO, the G7, and other partners (European Commission 2019a) The first meeting took place on 18 March 2019, and the RAS has been operational ever since. All member states have designated contact points and institutions (European Parliament 2019a). However, the system needs to be better implemented and tested. There are some critiques about its functioning. For example, Emmott et al. (2019) cites an EU official who stresses that the system is barely used. Kalenský (2019) stresses the problem might be that the RAS is not available to journalists and researchers, so it is not transparent.

When it comes to actions with the media, there is an increasing effort to take the cooperation seriously. Under the Action Plan against Disinformation, the European Union External Action (2018) mobilised an alliance of journalists and fact-checkers with governments, civil society, and academics. The European Union invests in new technologies for content verification (Horizon 2020 programme) and supports the Social Observatory for Disinformation and Social Media Analysis (SOMA), which enables the sharing of best practices among fact-checkers (European Commission 2019a; Emmott et al. 2019). From 18–22 March 2019, the European Commission held Media Literacy Week aiming to 'raise awareness of the importance of media literacy across the EU'. One of the activities was a high-level conference where best practices were presented (European Commission 2019b). Cooperation between the European Union and media companies has occurred with networks such as Facebook, Twitter, and YouTube, including the Code of Practice on Disinformation agreement, published in September 2018 to combat disinformation and fake accounts on their platforms (Emmott et al. 2019). In accordance with the code, Facebook, for example, reported over 1.2 million actions in the European Union for violation of policies in ads and content. The Code of Practice on Disinformation was built within the context of previous EU initiatives at fighting illegal content, hate speech, and terrorism in the online environment. In May 2016, Facebook, Microsoft, Twitter, and YouTube agreed with the Commission to an EU Code of Conduct on Countering Illegal Hate Speech Online, which set the rules of cooperation and the methodology of content evaluation for countering the spread of illegal hate speech online. In September 2017, the Communication on Tackling Illegal Content Online set other guidelines and principles for collaboration between online platforms, national authorities, member states, and other relevant stakeholders in the fight against illegal content online. In March 2018, the Recommendation on Measures to Effectively Tackle Illegal Online Content focused on calls for proactive measures from providers but also mentioned the importance of human verification. In September 2018, the European Commission proposed the Regulation on the Prevention of the Dissemination of Terrorist Content Online, which contains more restrictive tightening measures against terrorist content, for example, the 'one hour rule' to take terrorist content offline after an order from responsible national authorities (European Parliamentary Research Service 2019).

7.3.2 Nato

On the NATO level, a special initiative called the Strategic Communications Centre of Excellence (Stratcom CoE) has the most visible activities in countering disinformation. Within the NATO structure, it has a specific position and is a NATO-accredited international military organisation. The Centres of Excellence are 'international military organisations that train and educate leaders and specialists from NATO member and partner countries' (NATO Strategic Communications Centre of Excellence 2020a). The institution is not a part of the NATO command structure, nor is it subordinate to another NATO entity. The centre was established after the 2014 Wales Summit, and it aims mostly to contribute to the alliance's strategic communication where research on influence operations and disinformation are included. It also organises conferences and seminars, publishes strategies, and supports NATO exercises (NATO Strategic Communications Centre of Excellence 2020b). As it concerns the cooperation of national governments, 'the decision to join a centre is up to each NATO country. The NATO StratCom Center of Excellence has fourteen Alliance members, plus the non-NATO countries Sweden and Finland' (Foster 2019). The centre's senior employees consist of Latvian, Estonian, and Polish nationals; other staff hail from the United Kingdom, Belgium, and Germany.

Another significant NATO organisation operating within the topic of cyber and information defence is the NATO Cooperative Cyber Defence Centre of Excellence (The NATO Cooperative Cyber Defence Centre of Excellence 2020). Even though it is more focused on cyber defence, operations in cyberspace, given its complexity, could not be considered without the wider context, where influence operations have irreplaceable positions.

In 2016, the European Centre of Excellence for Countering Hybrid Threats, a joint initiative of the European Union as well as NATO, was established. The centre consists of European Union and NATO member states. The centre aims to be 'an international hub for practitioners and experts' which will assist member states and institutions with hybrid threats defence. It also wants to share practices between states and be a neutral facilitator between the European Union and NATO (The European Centre of Excellence for Countering Hybrid Threats 2019).

7.4 Case Studies

Focused through the analytical framework mentioned above, this chapter illustrates three different approaches to dealing with disinformation and propaganda via three case studies geographically spaced from the western to eastern Europe. This fact is important in the context of the pro-Russian information campaign, which is responsible for one of the biggest shares in spreading disinformation and propaganda in all three countries.

The western case of Denmark reveals a country with a leading position in countermeasures. In central Europe's case, Czech Republic is an example of a country which is 'half-way', with established institutions, international cooperation, and the political will to fight disinformation and propaganda. The last case, from the south-eastern European country of Bulgaria, represents a country which does not have efficient measures.

Of course, this is not an exhaustive list of countries and possible countermeasures. Many other cases could be covered. Nevertheless, we believe these case studies show a wide range of approaches present even in culturally and politically somehow similar countries (at least from a global perspective)—all three countries are members of the European Union and NATO. However, all three have different approaches to challenging propaganda and disinformation, and it can be seen how different political attitudes, different histories, and different starting positions can affect the approach to countermeasures.

7.4.1 Denmark: Ambitiously Fighting Disinformation

7.4.1.1 Current Situation

Among the threats within the cyber domain, the Danish Defence Intelligence Service (2019) considers Russia, China, Iran, and North Korea as the most active. In comparison to other European states, Denmark is in strong opposition to Russian influence operations. It expelled Russian diplomats after the Skripal affair, and the country was also strongly against the incidents in the Kerch Strait (Scarsi 2019). In hostile disinformation campaigns, Denmark is often framed as a typical Western country in moral decay, especially because of its liberal state model.

In 2018, the Danish government presented 11 initiatives focused on their elections to counter hostile foreign influence. These include a task force, training for communication officers, strengthening the work of intelligence services, emergency preparedness, advising political parties and leaders, dialogue with the media, and updates to its legislation (Ministry of Foreign Affairs of Denmark 2018).

7.4.1.2 Institutional Responses

The Danish Defence Intelligence Service clearly mentioned in its recent annual report, *DDIS Intelligence Risk Assessment 2019*, the threat of Russian cyber and influence operations, which are deployed against well-defined targets. The report also describes China and its cyber and espionage activities with efforts to gather information on an adversary as a threat to Denmark. Clear warning form other state bodies or authorities can also be found (see EUvsDisinfo 2018).

As the European Parliament (2019b) notes, the Ministry of Foreign Affairs is the main safeguard of Danish democracy from foreign influence. In 2019, the ministry launched a strengthened disinformation monitoring programme as a part of the government's new action plan (Ministry of Foreign Affairs of Denmark 2020).

As part of its 11 initiatives, the Danish government launched an inter-ministerial task force to coordinate efforts against disinformation. The ministries are to coordinate together their responses and recognition of threats (Baumann and Hansen 2017). Denmark considers cyber threats not only disruptions by hostile codes but also influence operations with stress on disinformation and propaganda. The Danish Centre for Cyber Security is a national IT security authority, a network security service, and a national centre for excellence, with a mission 'to advise Danish public authorities and private companies that support functions vital to society on how to prevent, counter and protect against cyber attacks' (Cyber Security Intelligence 2020a; Baumann and Hansen 2017). The centre also considers the role of fake news and social media and covers it in its news analysis (Cyber Security Intelligence 2020b).

Concerning the education of employees, Denmark plans to train communication officers from government authorities on the ongoing handling of disinformation (Ministry of Foreign Affairs of Denmark 2020). An interesting example of this state employee education is the training of Danish soldiers in how to combat disinformation. The plan was a part of NATO's military exercise in Estonia in 2017 (EUvsDisinfo 2017a; Just and Degn 2017). The country intends, in regard to the media, to initiate a dialogue to find models of cooperation (European Parliament 2019b). It is also worth mentioning the documentary *Factory of Lies*, which was aired by the Danish Broadcasting Corporation, exploring the so-called troll farms run by the Kremlin (EUvsDisinfo 2018).

Denmark does not take a strict approach with regard to the regulation of propaganda. The country instead considers it better to strengthen civil society (European Parliament 2019b). When it comes to direct countermeasures, Danish embassy employees are urged to monitor media and mock manipulative stories about Denmark. They were given a great degree of freedom to work offensively at the local and social media level, without the need of coordination from Copenhagen.

Denmark is an active member of the NATO Strategic Communications Centre of Excellence. Cooperation on the supranational level is considered part of its strategy against foreign influence campaigns (The Danish Government 2018). Denmark was one of the actors participating in criticism of the activities of the East StratCom Task Force, especially because of its media categorisation. This event also contributed to questioning Danish membership (for more, see Kulager 2017).

7.4.1.3 Conclusion

Denmark outlined 11 initiatives to fight influence operations covering all aspects. Its approach is aimed more at the role of civil society rather than repressive tools. However, Denmark is very straightforward in naming and warning about adversarial activities. The country has established its own task force and works on inter-ministerial cooperation. It also has a centre focused on cyber threats; however, its approach is more complex and also considers influence operations. Denmark has a great framework as well as plan to deal with hostile propaganda, which could be an inspiration for other European countries. Its implementation is still in its infancy, so the forthcoming years will show its effectivity.

7.4.2 Czech Republic: On the Halfway Mark

7.4.2.1 Current Situation

Czech Republic is currently threatened most by Russian and Chinese intelligence operations, including information warfare (see Security Information Service 2019). There is a large amount of so-called disinformation media with pro-Kremlin sentiments which take information from Russian state sources as well as other disinformation media. Most of these Czech-based platforms, therefore, have no link to the Russian state and instead play the role of sympathisers. Czech Republic, as well as other European states, has become a target of a sophisticated cyber espionage campaign by a hacker group believed to belong to the Russian GRU. In 2019, a cyberattack on the Czech Ministry of Foreign Affairs was revealed to have indicators leading to this group (Lipská 2019). There is also the active role of 'the Castle' in Russian as well as Chinese influence operations, embodied by President Miloš Zeman. He publicly undermines warnings about Russian activities by the Czech Security Information Service (BIS) and plays an important role in disinformation campaigns himself (see Dolejší 2019; Procházková 2018).

7.4.2.2 Institutional Responses

In March 2019, the director of the civil domestic intelligence service BIS, Michal Koudelka, stressed that Russia might interfere, also via a disinformation campaign, in the EU parliamentary election (Kundra 2019; Brolík 2019). Recent annual reports from this service have warned against

Russian secret services and its hybrid strategy to influence decision-making processes as well as Chinese influence actions (Security Information Service 2019). Warnings and statements appear across the political sphere. Minister of the Interior Jan Hamáček (of the Czech Social Democratic Party) warned against disinformation, stressing its importance to Russian President Vladimir Putin, and he recommended citizens check information and discuss it with their relatives (Dragoun 2019). Some opposition parties are also participating in the warning process, albeit with a different discourse. The Civic Democratic Party, for example, emphasised the role of Russia in President Zeman's election and the future threat[5] (see ODS 2018).

The Czech Ministry of Defence also participates in warnings to the public—mostly through individuals though, which is sometimes criticised by the Czech Army itself. General Petr Pavel highlighted the threat from Russia for Czech Republic (iRozhlas 2018). Brigadier General Karel Řehka (2017) wrote a book called *Informační válka* (Information warfare) for academics, the public, and military professionals which is, for example, part of the recommended literature for military courses at the University of Defence.

In 2019, the National Cyber and Information Security Agency (NÚKIB; Národní úřad pro kybernetickou a informační bezpečnost in Czech) published a warning against the use of technologies from Chinese companies Huawei and ZTE (2019a). This warning is also linked to the threat of Chinese influence operations in Czech Republic. The most visible state measure is the Ministry of the Interior's establishment of the Centre Against Terrorism and Hybrid Threats for expert and analytical activities, including disinformation campaigns. The centre is active on Twitter, where it focuses on actual disinformation on the Czech internet (Ministry of the Interior of the Czech Republic 2017). As the centre's head, Benedikt Vangeli, stressed, disproving disinformation includes only about 5–9 per cent of its activities (Janáková 2018). Therefore, we suppose that many of its activities are of a secret nature for a reason. Even though its activities are still not disclosed to public, the centre still functions today.

[5] Contrarywise, the Communist Party is debunking any Russian interference (see KSČM 2017).

The education of employees is manifested through courses for military personnel at the University of Defence, where courses on cyber and information warfare are conducted. NÚKIB organises educational activities for students at universities where it also can recruit its future employees (especially Masaryk University). The agency also organises exercises on cyber and information warfare (11 in 2018), for example, for Czech military personnel, the Czech Integrated Rescue System, and the Czech Statistical Office. NÚKIB describes its activities as an example of whole-of-government, stressing the importance of close cooperation between institutions (National Cyber and Information Security Agency 2019b).

Considering direct countermeasures, it is hard to analyse whether this predominantly covers secret service activities. It is not publicly known if these services are participating in direct information operation activities. However, in 2019, the Cyber and Information Operations Command was established under the Army of the Czech Republic. On its official website, it states that the command will also conduct operations in the information space (Army of the Czech Republic 2019). Even if the description is mostly focused on defensive activities, offensive ones are also relevant to consider.

From interviews with authorities, we can ascertain that Czech Republic is very sensitive to anything concerning free speech and disinformation labelling and may be the reason why the country is careful with content regulation.

On a supranational level, Czech Republic can be considered active and responsible. The country is participating in the East StratCom Task Force. The task force cooperates with the country but also directly with ministries as well as the business sphere. Czech Republic has been a member of the NATO Cooperative Cyber Defence Centre of Excellence since joining in 2018. It actively participates in the centre's activities, achieving, for example, excellent results in cybersecurity exercises. Since 2019, the re-elected EU commissar Věra Jourová gained the values and transparency portfolio also dealing with disinformation. As part of her new mandate, she is working on a new EU action plan where Russia is openly labelled as a threat.[6]

[6] Interview with EU officials.

7.4.2.3 *Conclusion*

Czech Republic holds a wide spectrum of counter-influence operations activities. Secret services and military officials as well as state authorities emphasise these threats. It is done especially in regard to hostile Russian actions. The country has also established a special body which deals with hybrid threats, unique in the context of central Europe. On the education front, NÚKIB has a role in the education of citizens; however, its focus is mostly on cybersecurity issues. There is no close cooperation or approach with regard to the media and social network providers. Czech Republic actively participates in international cooperation and takes threats from influence operations seriously. Interested state officials often mention an underestimation of strategic communication on the state level as well as its coordination with supranational entities. Together with better implementation into the state education system and amendments to its legal framework, these are the challenges facing the country in the years to come.

7.4.3 *Bulgaria: Internal Disunity Through External Influences*

7.4.3.1 *Current Situation*

When speaking about disinformation and propaganda in today's Bulgaria, it is mostly connected with Russian information strategies which try to influence the political orientation of the country from the West to the East, most frequently displayed via disinformation about EU bureaucrats and 'EU bans' on popular food and beverage products (Cheresheva 2017). Bulgaria also suspects Russia of supporting anti-migrant vigilantes with equipment and anti-Muslim rhetoric (Fiott and Parkes 2019). One of the most significant connections to the problem of disinformation was the case of leaked documents from the Bulgarian Socialist Party (BSP) (the successor of the Bulgarian Communist Party, see Mavrodieva 2019) which described its strategy for the 2016 presidential election. During the presidential elections, Leonid Reshetnikov, director of the Russian Institute for Strategic Studies, had a meeting with BSP representatives, about the optimisation of their election strategy, where he supposedly instructed BSP on the distribution of fake news and the misinterpretation of election surveys (EUvsDisinfo 2017b). The presidential election was then actually won by BSP candidate Rumen Radev, who is known for his pro-Russian stance (Tsolova 2016). The following section describes the context of the creation of disinformation and propaganda and the active measures applied against it.

Bulgaria is a specific actor in the question of disinformation and propaganda. On the one hand, it is a member of the European Union and NATO, but it is also, on the other hand, linked to Russia. Disunity in Bulgarian relations to Russia was present in the past and is still present today. You can find here strong pro-Russian tendencies from prominent politicians as well as the presence of anti-Russian discourse. This applies to both the political sphere and to ordinary citizens. One of the latest cases which exacerbated relations between Russia and Europe was the poisoning of the double agent Sergei Skripal and his daughter. Bulgaria was one of the countries which did not expel Russian diplomats as a reaction; the Bulgarian government considered the evidence of Russian involvement in the attack insufficient (de Carbonnel and Tsolova 2018). Citizens also acknowledged this decision. According to a poll, 88 per cent of respondents were against expulsion (Mediapool.bg 2018).

The pro-Russian propaganda channels and instruments are similar to those we know from other European countries, which means using social networks and spreading fake news but also troll farms (Colborne 2018). The main pro-Russian propaganda discourse in Bulgaria concerns European cultural decline under the weight of EU immigration and puppet politics. The European Union is seen as a US-NATO construct, and it is perceived as slowly dying. In contrast, Russia is growing stronger despite Western aggression, especially through adherence to traditional values. Bulgarian civic organisations, non-profit organisations, and the media are then only puppets or foreign agents of the West (Milo et al. 2017). The name George Soros is presented in the country as a sponsor of organisations promoting Western political sentiment in Bulgaria.

7.4.3.2 Institutional Responses

In the category of action with the public and state measures, it is difficult to create countermeasures focused on disinformation coming out of the Russian disinformation strategy because of the division among political elites in relation to the Russian position. The parliament adopted a 2015 report on national security which mentions Russia in the context of its growing military capabilities and the destabilisation of Eastern Ukraine and the countries of the Caucasus, but there is no direct information about a pro-Russian disinformation campaign (BTA 2015). The risk of propaganda and disinformation is not mentioned either in the annual public reports (SANS 2020) of the State Agency for National Security (SANS) for the years 2016, 2017, and 2018. But in all reports from 2016, there is an unspecified risk for Bulgaria as 'an object of a serious intelligence interest from countries, which view the Union and the Alliance as threats to their own security' (SANS 2016).

There are no specific legal measures, procedures, or laws which were specifically directed against disinformation and propaganda. However, there are law articles connected to the election (see Bayer et al. 2019) which could be potentially used to counter fake news, propaganda, and disinformation as well as regulations concerning the use of campaign finance in electoral codes/acts. For example, Articles 165, 166, and 167 of the 2014 Election Code of Bulgaria define and restrict the amount and sources of money which can be spent on financing election campaigns. Article 168, for its part, states that a party, a coalition, or a nomination committee shall not receive donations from certain sources, such as anonymous donors, legal entities, and religious institutions (Election Code of Bulgaria 2014).

It is additionally difficult to find a direct contribution from Bulgaria on the supranational level. Bulgaria as an EU member state has both information available and the possibility to cooperate in the European External Action Service as well as in the East StratCom Task Force, but there is no evidence that it takes these opportunities. The East StratCom Task Force had pointed out the situation in Bulgaria in several cases. Bulgaria also does not participate in the European Centre of Excellence for Countering Hybrid Threats (2019).

Unfortunately, there are no signs of state activity with the media, political parties, or in direct countermeasures.

7.4.3.3 Conclusion

Bulgaria is an example of a country which, despite having international cooperation with the European Union and NATO and their member states, has very limited active measures against propaganda and disinformation. The key element of this is the relationship of some Bulgarian political actors to Russia. This example shows that disinformation and propaganda are highly politicised issues, and, without the support of local political elites, efforts from the international level are inefficient. In this case, all measures targeting pro-Russian disinformation are problematic, but there is still a place for measures focused more broadly—on election campaigns in general, corruption, and so forth.

It is possible that with stronger pressure from the Russian side, it will be easier to find the political will for a clear stance against disinformation. Expelling Russian diplomats in January 2020 over espionage allegations in October 2019 and declining to grant a visa to an incoming Russian defence attaché may possibly cause the situation to reverse. The relationship between Bulgaria and Russia may be worsened by the fact that Bulgarian prosecutors charged three Russians with the attempted murder of an arms trader and two other Bulgarians whose poisoning is being investigated by Sofia for possible links with the 2018 nerve-agent attack on Skripal (Reuters 2020).

7.5 Conclusion

The approach of European national institutions to disinformation and propaganda covers a wide spectrum of countermeasures. Together, it is possible to formulate a joint framework and apply it to specific actors to evaluate its capabilities. Denmark, Czech Republic, and Bulgaria were chosen because of their different states of countermeasure development to disinformation and propaganda. This approach should help to better understand the issues in the fight against disinformation and present the application of the proposed framework in practice.

Seven categories of state institutional responses against disinformation and propaganda have been formulated. The first group of countermeasures are *actions with the public* and *state measures*, which cover the most common countermeasures in Europe, and it is possible to identify them in all our cases. The second group of countermeasures are *legal measures*, *actions with the media*, and *actions with political parties*. These are more complex and demand processed legislation and a long-term coherent strategy. For these reasons, we can see these countermeasures in countries which are leading the development of measures against disinformation, such as in Finland or Denmark. The final categories are *direct countermeasures* and *actions with supranational entities*. They are the most problematic due to a lack of public information concerning them. These categories are closely connected with security services and diplomacy, and we can only identify public acts, such as the expulsion of diplomats or public initiatives in international organisations like NATO or the European Union.

All in all, this chapter introduces an analytical framework in which to analyse a set of countermeasures against disinformation as part of influence operations, and it has given the researcher the opportunity to depict the issue in its complexity and, therefore, to study the strengths and weaknesses of the system. The analytical framework and its usage were demonstrated on a limited scale. More detailed research is recommended, specifically in the collection of data through the use of interviews with political campaign managers, specialists, high-level state authorities, and experts.

Bibliography

Algemene Inlichtingen- en Veuligheidsdiest. Ministerie Binnenlandse Zaken en Koninkrijksrelaties. (2018). Spionage en ongewenste inmenging. *Report*. https://www.aivd.nl/onderwerpen/jaarverslagen/jaarverslag-2018/spionage. Accessed 15 Nov 2019.

Army of the Czech Republic. (2019). *Velitelství kybernetických sil a informačních operací* [Chief of Cyber and Information Operations]. http://www.acr.army.cz/struktura/generalni/kyb/velitelstvi-kybernetickych-sil-a-informacnich-operaci-214169/. Accessed 15 Nov 2019.

Baumann, A., & Hansen, A. R. (2017, September 10). *Danmark får ny kommandocentral mod misinformation*. https://www.mm.dk/tjekdet/artikel/danmark-faar-ny-kommandocentral-mod-misinformation. Accessed 15 Nov 2019.

Bayer, J., et al. (2019). *Disinformation and Propaganda—Impact on the Functioning of the Rule of Law in the EU and Its Member States*. Policy Department for Citizens' Rights and Constitutional Affairs. http://www.europarl.europa.eu/RegData/etudes/STUD/2019/608864/IPOL_STU(2019)608864_EN.pdf. Accessed 15 Nov 2019.

Bleiker, C., & Brady, K. (2017, June 30). Bundestag Passes Law to Fine Social Media Companies for Not Deleting Hate Speech. *Deutsche Welle*. https://www.dw.com/en/bundestag-passes-law-to-fine-social-media-companies-for-not-deleting-hate-speech/a-39486694. Accessed 15 Nov 2019.

Brattberg, E., & Maurer, T. (2018). *Russian Election Interference: Europe's Counter to Fake News and Cyber Attacks*. Carnegie Endowment for International Peace. https://carnegieendowment.org/2018/05/23/russian-election-interference-europe-s-counter-to-fake-news-and-cyber-attacks-pub-76435. Accessed 15 Nov 2019.

Brolík, T. (2019, May 3). Šéf BIS: Rusko se nám pokusí vměšovat do voleb [Director of Security Intelligence Service: Russia Will Try to Meddle into

Our Elections]. *Respekt*. https://www.respekt.cz/politika/sef-bis-rusko-se-u-nas-pokusi-vmesovat-do-eurovoleb. Accessed 15 Nov 2019.

BTA. (2015, September 1). Parliament Adopts Report on National Security in 2015. *Bulgarian News Agency*. http://www.bta.bg/en/c/DF/id/1408996. Accessed 15 Nov 2019.

Charlton, E. (2019, May 21). How Finland Is Fighting Fake News—In the Classroom. *World Economic Forum*. https://www.weforum.org/agenda/2019/05/how-finland-is-fighting-fake-news-in-the-classroom. Accessed 15 Nov 2019.

Cheresheva, M. (2017, December 12). False Reports of EU Bans InflameBulgarians. *Balkan Insight*. https://balkaninsight.com/2017/12/12/myths-about-tough-eu-bans-scare-bulgarians-12-11-2017/. Accessed 15 Nov 2019.

Colborne, M. (2018, May 9). Made in Bulgaria: Pro-Russian Propaganda. *Coda Story*. https://codastory.com/disinformation-crisis/foreign-proxies/made-in-bulgaria-pro-russian-propaganda. Accessed 15 Nov 2019.

Cyber Security Intelligence. (2020a). https://www.cybersecurityintelligence.com/centre-for-cyber-security-cfcs-3071.html. Accessed 4 Mar 2020.

Cyber Security Intelligence. (2020b). *Publishers Spread Fake News*. https://www.cybersecurityintelligence.com/blog/publishers-spread-fake-news–4756.html. Accessed 4 Mar 2020.

Danish Defence Intelligence Service. (2019). Intelligence Risk Assessment 2019. *An Assessment of Developments Abroad Impacting on Danish Security*. https://fe-ddis.dk/SiteCollectionDocuments/FE/EfterretningsmaessigeRisikovurderinger/Intelligence%20Risk%20Assessment%202019.pdf. Accessed 15 Nov 2019.

de Carbonnel, A., & Tsolova, T. (2018, March 29). Old Ties with Russia Weigh on Bulgarian Decision in Spy Poisoning Case. *Reuters*. https://www.reuters.com/article/us-britain-russia-bulgaria/old-ties-with-russia-weigh-on-bulgarian-decision-in-spy-poisoning-case-idUSKBN1H52BR. Accessed 15 Nov 2019.

Denmark Ministry of Foreign Affairs. (2018, September 7). The Danish Government Presents a Plan with 11 Initiatives Aimed at Strengthening Danish Resilience Against Influence Campaigns. *Twitter*. https://bit.ly/2HV3ja1. Accessed 15 Nov 2019.

Dolejší, V. (2019, May 8). CIA mu dala cenu, Zeman označil za „čučkaře“. Proč šéfa BIS už potřetí nejmenuje prezident generálem [He Was Awarded by CIA, Zeman Labelled Him as Amateur. Why the Director of the Security and Information Service Will Not Be Promoted for the Third Time to General]. *Seznam zprávy*. https://www.seznamzpravy.cz/clanek/cia-mu-dala-cenu-zeman-oznacil-za-cuckare-proc-sefa-bis-uz-potreti-nejmenuje-prezident-generalem-71687. Accessed 15 Nov 2019.

Dragoun, R. (2019, May 3). Hamáček varoval před dezinformacemi. Eurovolby jsou pro Putina klíčové, říká analytic [Hamáček Warned Against Disinformation. Analyst Says That European Elections Are Crucial for Putin]. *Aktualne.cz*. https://zpravy.aktualne.cz/zahranici/evropsky-parlament/volby-budou-cilem-dezinformatoru-varoval-hamacek/r~5dd9119e6d8e11e9b2a00cc47ab5f122/. Accessed 15 Nov 2019.

Election Code of Bulgaria. (2014). https://www.venice.coe.int/webforms/documents/default.aspx?pdffile=CDL-REF(2014)025-e. Accessed 15 Nov 2019.

Emmott, R., Carbonnel, A., & Humphries, C. (2019, March 16). Who Burnt Notre Dame? Brussels Goes After Fake News as EU Election Nears. *Reuters*. https://ru.reuters.com/article/worldNews/idUKKCN1SM0LA. Accessed 15 Nov 2019.

Estonian Foreign Intelligence Service. (2019). *International Security and Estonia 2019*. https://www.valisluureamet.ee/pdf/raport-2019-ENG-web.pdf. Accessed 15 Nov 2019.

EU Observer. (2019, March 13). *Estonian Spies Warn EU on Russian Security Threat*. https://euobserver.com/foreign/144389. Accessed 15 Nov 2019.

European Commission. (2019a). Action Plan Against Disinformation. *Report on Progress*. https://ec.europa.eu/commission/sites/beta-political/files/factsheet_disinfo_elex_140619_final.pdf. Accessed 15 Nov 2019.

European Commission. (2019b). *European Media Literacy Week*. https://ec.europa.eu/digital-single-market/en/news/european-media-literacy-week. Accessed 15 Nov 2019.

European Parliament. (2019a). *Answer Given by Vice-President Mogherini on Behalf of the European Commission*. http://www.europarl.europa.eu/doceo/document/P-8-2019-001705-ASW_EN.html. Accessed 15 Nov 2019.

European Parliament. (2019b). Automated Tackling of Disinformation. Panel for the Future of Science and Technology European Science-Media Hub. European Parliamentary Research Service. https://www.europarl.europa.eu/RegData/etudes/STUD/2019/624278/EPRS_STU(2019)624278_EN.pdf. Accessed 15 Nov 2019.

European Parliamentary Research Service. (2019). *Regulating Disinformation with Artificial Intelligence*. https://www.europarl.europa.eu/RegData/etudes/STUD/2019/624279/EPRS_STU(2019)624279_EN.pdf. Accessed 15 Nov 2019.

European Union External Action. (2018). *Questions and Answers About the East StratCom Task Force*. https://eeas.europa.eu/headquarters/headquarters-homepage/2116/-questions-and-answers-about-the-east-stratcom-task-force_en. Accessed 15 Nov 2019.

European Union External Action. (2019). *Factsheet: Rapid Alert System*. https://eeas.europa.eu/headquarters/headquarters-Homepage_en/59644/Factsheet:%20Rapid%20Alert%20System. Accessed 15 Nov 2019.

EUvsDisinfo. (2017a, July 25). *Denmark to Educate Soldiers in Combatting Disinformation*. https://euvsdisinfo.eu/denmark-to-educate-soldiers-in-combatting-disinformation/. Accessed 15 Nov 2019.

EuvsDisinfo. (2017b, March 28). *Fake News and Elections in Bulgaria*. https://euvsdisinfo.eu/fake-news-and-elections/. Accessed 15 Nov 2019.

EUvsDisinfo. (2018, September 10). *Denmark's Defence Against Disinformation*. https://euvsdisinfo.eu/denmarks-defence-against-disinformation/. Accessed 15 Nov 2019.

EUvsDisinfo. (2019, May 6). *Tackling disinformation à la française*. https://euvsdisinfo.eu/tackling-disinformation-a-la-francaise/. Accessed 15 Nov 2019.

EUvsDisinfo. (n.d.). *About*. https://euvsdisinfo.eu/about/. Accessed 15 Nov 2019.

Facebook. (2019). *Community Standards: False News*. https://www.facebook.com/communitystandards/false_news. Accessed 15 Nov 2019.

Facebook. (2020). *Fact-Checking on Facebook: What Publishers Should Know*. https://www.facebook.com/help/publisher/182222309230722. Accessed 15 Nov 2019.

Fiott, D., & Parkes, R. (2019). *Protecting Europe: The EUs Response to Hybrid Threats*. Paris: European Union Institute for Security Studies. https://www.iss.europa.eu/sites/default/files/EUISSFiles/CP_151.pdf. Accessed 15 Nov 2019.

Flamini, D., & Tardáguila, C. (2019). *A First Look at the OAS's Recommendations for Best Practices Against Electoral Misinformation, Part 2*. https://www.poynter.org/fact-checking/2019/a-first-look-at-the-oass-recommendations-for-best-practices-against-electoral-misinformation-part-2/. Accessed 15 Nov 2019.

Foster, H. (2019). *#StrongerWithAllies: Meet the Latvian Who Leads NATO's Fight Against Fake News*. Washington: Atlantic Council. https://www.atlanticcouncil.org/blogs/new-atlanticist/strongerwithallies-latvian-leads-nato-s-fight-against-fake-news/. Accessed 15 Nov 2019.

France 24. (2019, April 13). *Election Ads Urge Finns 'Think for Yourself' Amid Fake News Fears*. https://www.france24.com/en/20190413-election-ads-urge-finns-think-yourself-amid-fake-news-fears. Accessed 15 Nov 2019.

Google. (2019). *How Google Fights Disinformation*. https://kstatic.googleusercontent.com/files/388aa7d18189665e5f5579aef18e181c2d4283fb7b0d4691689dfd1bf92f7ac2ea6816e09c02eb98d5501b8e5705ead65af653cdf94071c47361821e362da55b. Accessed 15 Nov 2019.

Hanzelka, J., & Kasl, F. (2018). Sekuritizace a právní nástroje pro boj s projevy nenávisti na internetu v Německu [Securitization and Legal Instruments for Countering Cyber Hate in Germany]. *Acta Politologica, 10*(3), 20–46. https://doi.org/10.14712/1803-8220/15_2018.

Interfax-Ukraine. (2014). *Poroshenko: Information Ministry's Main Task Is to Repel Information Attacks Against Ukraine*. https://en.interfax.com.ua/news/economic/238615.html. Accessed 15 Nov 2019.

iRozhlas. (2018, November 8). *Petr Pavel: Aktivity Ruska jsou pro Česko větší hrozba než terorismus* [Petr Pavel: Russian Activities Are for the Czech Republic More Serious Threat Than Terrorism]. https://www.irozhlas.cz/zpravy-domov/petr-pavel-rusko-hrozba-nato_1811081818_cen. Accessed 15 Nov 2019.

Janáková, B. (2018, March 23). Centrum proti terorismu vyvrátilo za rok 22 dezinformací. Má i jiné úkoly [Centre Against Terrorism Debunked 22 Disinformation in the Las Year. It Has Also Other Tasks]. *Idnes*. https://www.idnes.cz/zpravy/domaci/dezinformace-hoaxy-fake-news-centrum-proti-terorismu-a-hybridnim-hrozbam-cthh-ministerstvo-vnitra-lu.A180314_105400_domaci_bja. Accessed 15 Nov 2019.

Just, A. N., & Degn, S. F. (2017, July 17). Danske soldater skal beskyttes mod fake news fra Rusland. *DR*. https://www.dr.dk/nyheder/politik/danske-soldater-skal-beskyttes-mod-fake-news-fra-rusland. Accessed 15 Nov 2019.

Kalenský, J. (2019). *Evaluation of the EU Elections: Many Gaps Still Remain. Disinfo Portal*. https://disinfoportal.org/evaluation-of-the-eu-elections-many-gaps-still-remain/. Accessed 15 Nov 2019.

KennyBirch, R. (2019, December 3). How Finland Shuts Down Fake News. *Apolitical*. https://apolitical.co/en/solution_article/how-finland-shuts-down-fake-news. Accessed 15 Nov 2019.

Klingová, K., & Milo, D. (2018). *Boj proti hybridným hrozbám v krajinách EÚ: príklady dobrej praxe* [Fight Against Hybrid Threats in EU Countries: Good Practice Examples]. Bratislava: GLOBSEC. Accessed 15 Nov 2019.

Kremlin Watch. (2020). Belgium. *Counties Compared*. https://www.kremlinwatch.eu/countries-compared-states/belgium/. Accessed 15 Nov 2019.

KSČM. (2017). *Ovlivnila hybridní válka o lithiové baterie volby? Konspirační teorie versus fakta* [Did Hybrid War on Lithium Batteries Affected Elections? Conspiracy Theory Versus Facts]. https://www.kscm.cz/cs/aktualne/medialni-vystupy/komentare/ovlivnila-hybridni-valka-o-lithiove-baterie-volby-konspiracni. Accessed 15 Nov 2019.

Kulager, F. (2017, April 17). Informationskrigen under lup: Sådan spreder Ruslands dagsorden sig i Danmark. *Zetland*. https://www.zetland.dk/historie/sOXVEKv3-aOZj67pz-3bd93. Accessed 15 Nov 2019.

Kundra, O. (2019, March 13). Ředitel BIS: Rusko má zájem ovlivnit evropské volby [Director of the Security and Information Service: Russia Has Interest to Influence European Elections]. *Respekt*. https://www.respekt.cz/politika/bis-evropske-volby. Accessed 15 Nov 2019.

Lipská, J. (2019, August 13). Byl to útok cizí státní moci, uvedl NÚKIB k napadení serverů ministerstva zahraničí [National Cyber Authority Says About

Cyber Attack on Ministry of Foreign Affairs: It Was Attack of Foreign State Actor]. *Seznam zprávy*. https://www.seznamzpravy.cz/clanek/byl-to-utok-cizi-statni-moci-rekl-nukib-k-napadeni-serveru-ministerstva-zahranici-77215. Accessed 15 Nov 2019.

Mackintosh, E., & Kiernan, E. (2019, May 18). Finland Is Winning the War on Fake News. What It's Learned May Be Crucial to Western Democracy. *CNN*. shorturl.at/clFX4. Accessed 15 Nov 2019.

Marsden, C., & Meyer, T. (2019). *Regulating Disinformation with Artificial Intelligence*. https://www.europarl.europa.eu/RegData/etudes/STUD/2019/624279/EPRS_STU(2019)624279_EN.pdf. Accessed 15 Nov 2019.

Mavrodieva, I. (2019). Bulgaria. In O. Eibl & M. Gregor (Eds.), *Thirty Years of Political Campaigning in Central and Eastern Europe*. London: Palgrave.

Media Animation ASBl. (2020). https://media-animation.be/. Accessed 3 Mar 2020.

Mediapool.bg (2018, April 6). Проучване: Българите са солидарни с Русия по случая "Скрипал". *Mediapool*. https://www.mediapool.bg/prouchvane-balgarite-sa-solidarni-s-rusiya-po-sluchaya-skripal-news277716.html. Accessed 15 Nov 2019.

Milo, D., Klingová, K., & Hajdu, D. (2017). *GLOBSEC Trend 2017: Mixed Messages and Signs of Hope from Central & Eastern Europe*. Bratislava: GLOBSEC Policy Institute. https://www.globsec.org/wp-content/uploads/2017/09/globsec_trends_2017.pdf. Accessed 15 Nov 2019.

Ministry of Foreign Affairs of Denmark. (2020). *Strengthened safeguards against foreign influence on Danish elections and democracy*. https://um.dk/en/news/newsdisplaypage/?newsid=1df5adbb-d1df-402b-b9ac-57fd4485ffa4.

Ministry of Information Policy of Ukraine. (2018). *Bila kniga specialnih informacijnih operacij proti Ukraïni 2014–2018*. https://mip.gov.ua/files/pdf/white_book_2018_mip.pdf. Accessed 15 Nov 2019.

Ministry of Interior of the Czech Republic. (2017). *Centre Against Terrorism and Hybrid Threats*. https://www.mvcr.cz/cthh/clanek/centre-against-terrorism-and-hybrid-threats.aspx. Accessed 15 Nov 2019.

Mohan, M. (2017, May 9). Macron Leaks: The Anatomy of a Hack. *BBC*. https://www.bbc.com/news/blogs-trending-39845105. Accessed 15 Nov 2019.

National Cyber and Information Security Agency. (2019a). Software i hardware společností Huawei a ZTE je bezpečnostní hrozbou [Huawei and ZTE Software and Hardware Are Security Threat]. https://www.govcert.cz/cs/informacni-servis/hrozby/2680-software-i-hardware-spolecnosti-huawei-a-zte-je-bezpecnostni-hrozbou/. Accessed 15 Nov 2019.

National Cyber and Information Security Agency. (2019b). *Report on the State of Cyber Security in the Czech Republic in 2018*. https://www.nukib.cz/cs/informacni-servis/publikace/. Accessed 15 Nov 2019.

NATO Strategic Communications Centre of Excellence. (2020a). *FAQ*. https://www.stratcomcoe.org/faq. Accessed 15 Nov 2019.

NATO Strategic Communications Centre of Excellence. (2020b). *About Us*. https://www.stratcomcoe.org/about-us. Accessed 15 Nov 2019.

ODS. (2018). Alexandra Udženija: Respekt k výsledku voleb přece neznamená, že mají lidé mlčet [Alexandra Udženija: Respect to the Election Results Does Not Mean That People Should Be Silent]. https://www.ods.cz/clanek/16828-respekt-k-vysledku-voleb-prece-neznamena-ze-maji-lide-mlcet. Accessed 15 Nov 2019.

Press TV. (2017, February 28). *Germany to Help Baltic States Establish Russian-Language Media*. https://www.presstv.com/Detail/2017/02/28/512397/Germany-Russianlanguage-media-Baltic-states. Accessed 15 Nov 2019.

Procházková, P. (2018, October 17). Výrok prezidenta Zemana o Novičoku se stal samostatnou kapitolou v Kapesním průvodci po ruské propagandě [Comments of President Zeman About Novichok Has Become New Chapter in Pocket Guide in Russian Propaganda]. *Nový deník*. https://denikn.cz/1864/prezident-zeman-se-stal-samostatnou-kapitolou-v-kapesnim-pruvodci-po-ruske-propagande/. Accessed 15 Nov 2019.

Řehka, K. (2017). *Informační válka* [Information War]. Praha: Academia.

Reuters. (2020, January 24). *Bulgaria Expels Two Russian Diplomats for Espionage*. https://www.reuters.com/article/us-bulgaria-russia/bulgaria-expels-two-russian-diplomats-for-espionage-idUSKBN1ZN10K. Accessed 17 Feb 2020.

Robinson, O., Coleman, A., & Sardarizadeh, S. (2019). *A Report of Anti-Disinformation Initiatives*. Oxford Technology and Election Commission. https://comprop.oii.ox.ac.uk/wp-content/uploads/sites/93/2019/08/A-Report-of-Anti-Disinformation-Initiatives. Accessed 15 Nov 2019.

Roden, L. (2017, March 13). Swedish Kids to Learn Computer Coding and How to Spot Fake News in Primary School. *The Local*. https://www.thelocal.se/20170313/swedish-kids-to-learn-computer-coding-and-how-to-spot-fake-news-in-primary-school. Accessed 15 Nov 2019.

Rozgonyi, K. (2018). *The Impact of the Information Disorder (Disinformation) on Election*. European Commission for Democracy Through Law. https://www.venice.coe.int/webforms/documents/default.aspx?pdffile=CDL-LA(2018)002-e. Accessed 15 Nov 2019.

SANS. (2016). *Annual Report 2016*. State Agency for National Security. http://www.dans.bg/images/stories/Information/Doklad_DANS_2016_en.pdf. Accessed 15 Nov 2019.

SANS. (2020). *Annual Reports*. State Agency for National Security. http://www.dans.bg/en/report-23012018-sec-en. Accessed 21 Feb 2020.

Scarsi, A. (2019, January 29). Denmark Calls on EU to Act Against Putin: Copenhagen FURY at Russia 'Aggressive Behaviour'. *Express*. https://bit.ly/2UbQqPF. Accessed 15 Nov 2019.

Scott, M. (2018, June 30). Cambridge Analytica Did Work for Brexit Groups, Says Ex-staffer. *Politico*. https://www.politico.eu/article/cambridge-analytica-leave-eu-ukip-brexit-facebook/. Accessed 15 Nov 2019.

Security Information Service. (2019). *Annual Report of the Security Information Service*. https://www.bis.cz/public/site/bis.cz/content/vyrocni-zpravy/en/ar2018en.pdf.pdf. Accessed 15 Nov 2019.

Sternstein, A. (2017). *Estonia's Lessons for Fighting Russian Disinformation*. https://www.csmonitor.com/World/Passcode/2017/0324/Estonia-s-lessons-for-fighting-Russian-disinformation. Accessed 15 Nov 2019.

Stone, J. (2019, May 20). Austrian Government Cannot Be Trusted with Intelligence Due to Far-Right Links, German Security Service Warns. *Independent*. https://www.independent.co.uk/news/world/europe/austria-germany-intelligence-security-services-russia-bfv-a8921966.html. Accessed 15 Nov 2019.

Swedish Civil Contingencies Agency. (2018). *If Crisis or War Comes*. http://www.documentcloud.org/documents/4481608-Om-Krisen-Eller-Kriget-Kommer-Engelska.html#document/p1. Accessed 15 Nov 2019.

Swedish Civil Contingencies Agency. (2019). *Countering Information Influence Activities: A Handbook for Communicators*. https://www.msb.se/RibData/Filer/pdf/28698.pdf. Accessed 15 Nov 2019.

The Danish Government. (2018). *Denmark Foreign and Security Policy Strategy 2019–2020*. https://www.dsn.gob.es/sites/dsn/files/2018_Denmark%20Foreign%20and%20security%20policy%20strategy%202019-2020.pdf. Accessed 15 Nov 2019.

The European Centre of Excellence for Countering Hybrid Threats. (2019). *Joining Dates of the Hybrid CoE Member States*. https://www.hybridcoe.fi/wp-content/uploads/2019/12/Joining-Dates-Alfabetic-Order-1.pdf. Accessed 3 Feb 2020.

The NATO Cooperative Cyber Defence Centre of Excellence. (2020). https://ccdcoe.org/about-us/. Accessed 15 Nov 2019.

Tsolova, T. (2016, November 11). Bulgarian Vote Shows Russia Winning Hearts on EU's Eastern Flank. *Reuters*. https://www.reuters.com/article/us-bulgaria-election-russia/bulgarian-vote-shows-russia-winning-hearts-on-eus-eastern-flank-idUSKBN13611H. Accessed 15 Nov 2019.

Ukrainian Independent Information Agency of News. (2019, February 12). *Ukraine's Ministry of Information Policy Presents "White Book" of Info-ops Against Ukraine*. https://www.unian.info/politics/10443192-ukraine-s-ministry-of-information-policy-presents-white-book-of-info-ops-against-ukraine.htm. Accessed 15 Nov 2019.

CHAPTER 8

Civil Society Initiatives Tackling Disinformation: Experiences of Central European Countries

Jonáš Syrovátka

8.1 Introduction

One of the most significant milestones of the disinformation debate and one which is referenced constantly was the situation following the June 2014 downing of Malaysian Airlines Flight MH17 in eastern Ukraine. Consequently, a mass of disinformation literally flooded the Internet and thus complicated the ability to judge what had actually happened. Despite that, the nature, causes, and culprits of the incident were disclosed quite swiftly, and a number of false stories were identified and debunked. The key role in this development was played by the organisation Bellingcat, composed of independent investigative journalists who put all the pieces

J. Syrovátka (✉)
Department of Political Science, Faculty of Social Studies, Masaryk University, Brno, Czechia
e-mail: syrovatka10@seznam.cz

M. Gregor and P. Mlejnková (eds.), *Challenging Online Propaganda and Disinformation in the 21st Century*, Political Campaigning and Communication,
https://doi.org/10.1007/978-3-030-58624-9_8

of this tragic story together and introduced it to the public (Bellingcat 2019).

However, the famous story of Bellingcat and the MH17 incident represents only one of many examples of civil society initiatives tackling disinformation. In recent years, a number of various entities from already established civil society organisations (CSOs) to passionate individuals all over Europe started to focus on this phenomenon. This wave of activity comprises varied initiatives like the Baltic Elves volunteers exposing trolls and fake profiles on social media, fact-checkers from the Ukrainian organisation StopFake, or activists from the Stop Funding Hate initiative trying to convince private companies not to advertise on websites spreading hate speech or conspiracy theories.

An attempt to provide an exhausting account of all civil society initiatives tackling disinformation within one chapter would be far too descriptive, far too long, and more too confusing than a phonebook. The author, however, does not intend to choose the opposite approach either, which would be to cherry-pick the most interesting cases. Especially since this narrow perspective brings with it the danger of taking a story out of its original context, not allowing its successes as well as the limitations of its application in other environments to be properly explained. Therefore, this chapter attempts to find a middle way between both mentioned approaches and to describe all the relevant initiatives tackling disinformation launched by civil society in central European countries. Specific attention will be dedicated to Czech Republic, Hungary, Poland, and Slovakia. This geographical limitation, which, as will be explained, is quite logical in relation to the given subject, will allow a (still relatively) precise description of the approaches applied to tackle disinformation by various civil society actors. However, the chapter has further ambitions and focuses also on the identity and dynamic of civil society activities in the analysed countries. By doing so, it might comment not only on civil society actors themselves but also on the context in which they are operating.

This perspective has proved to be relevant. The findings of the chapter show that the context matters as significant differences among civil society actors tackling disinformation in the analysed countries were identified. While, on the one hand, there is vivid debate involving a wide variety of actors producing innovative approaches to the issue in Czech Republic and Slovakia, in Hungary and Poland, on the other hand, the issue of disinformation attracts limited attention, resulting in a low number of activities dedicated to it as well as the choosing of rather conservative strategies to tackle this issue. This finding to a certain extent questions the possibility of transporting the experiences to different countries and recalls the importance of properly evaluating local contexts.

8.2 Civil Society and Disinformation in Current Understanding and Literature

A vibrant, active, and daring civil society is perceived as a key element of a democratic political system. Some theories even consider it to be one of the necessary conditions for the existence of democracy (Diamond and Morlino 2005). Despite the resonance of this term, its definition remains contested, which is not that surprising given not only the heterogeneity of various civil society actors but also the fact that this topic has attracted the attention of social scientists only relatively recently. However, among all definitions, the strongest emphases are put on the role of civil society as a balance to the power of state, its heterogeneity, and its voluntary nature. For the purposes of this text, civil society is understood as a 'sphere of institutions, organisations and individuals located between the family, the state and the market in which people associate voluntarily to advance common interest' (Anheier 2013, 22).

Among many areas in which civil society might advance *common interests*, the security domain is one of the most interesting, especially since this area used to be seen as reserved for state institutions, such as military, police, or intelligence services, in the past. This view has however been challenged, and some scholars in security studies today put more emphasis on a wider spectrum of threats, including the societal one (Collins 2010). In this view, obviously, the role of civil society in security is becoming equally as important as the role of state intuitions. This fact has been reflected by various authors who have evaluated the role civil society actors might play in the security domain. It has, for example, been argued that civil society is sensitive to the various changes occurring in society, and so it might serve as an early warning system against upcoming threats (Anheier 2013). Nevertheless, civil society actors are also seen as important players in formulating security policies because they provide feedback and recommendations to state institutions active in the security domain as well as to political decision-makers. At the same time, emphasis has been placed on their important role as watchdogs scrutinising state security policies, warning against them should they be considered a threat to the democratic system (Caparini et al. 2006). The underlining thesis of this chapter is that the reactions of civil society to the disinformation phenomenon represents an exemplary case study of its ability to advance common interests in the area security.

An illustrative example of this thesis is the Ukrainian case, in which state intuitions were ill-prepared for the confrontation with the Russian Federation starting in 2014. In addition to other areas, Ukrainian civil society was able to mobilise and defend itself in the information domain, which represented an important part of the conflict, from threats of propaganda and disinformation campaigns launched by the adversary (for a detailed account of these initiatives, see Gerasymchuk and Maksak 2018). Since the Ukrainian initiatives tackling disinformation were operating in the *laboratory of information warfare*, they are often used as models for civil society actors in other countries (for example, Pesenti and Pomerantsev 2016). In fact, civil society started to be perceived as an indispensable part of the effort to tackle disinformation (see Nimmo 2015; Fried and Polyakova 2018). Based on this assumption, in the years that followed, a number of civil society initiatives aiming to expose and tackle disinformation were launched all over the Europe; among many others, it is possible to name the Brussels-based EU DisinfoLab, the UK-based Bellingcat, the German Marshall Fund's Hamilton 68, and the Atlantic Council's Digital Forensic Research Lab. The relevance of these initiatives was acknowledged at the political level as manifested, for example, by their mention in the European Union's Action Plan against Disinformation (European Commission 2018).

The list of initiatives launched to tackle disinformation could continue for a long time. However, to list the countless civil society actors which have emerged over the past several years all over Europe (or even globally) and the strategies they have employed against disinformation would not be helpful in understanding the topic. On the contrary, not only could this list never be complete or up-to-date given the vibrant development in this area, moreover, it would not be able (especially with such limited space) to properly contextualise the presented initiatives either. This problem might be solved by cherry-picking the most well-known initiatives. However, the author is convinced that this approach would have added little value since their activities have already been described elsewhere.

Therefore, the author has tried to find a middle path and describe civil society initiatives which have emerged in a selected group of central

European countries: Czech Republic, Hungary, Poland, and Slovakia. This narrowing of the research scope can be defended by several arguments. First, it is an attempt to find a reasonable compromise between the range of presented examples and their proper description within the space provided by this chapter. The second rather pragmatic reason is the author's acquaintance with the development of Czech civil society in tackling disinformation[1] and the network of contacts with other researchers from the analysed countries. This background allowed the author to conduct a meticulous assessment of the situation in the region. The analyses in the chosen countries, thirdly, provide an interesting comparative perspective. Although they have national specifics, this perspective is possible to apply due to the fact that the analysed countries are to the certain extent similar: the same geographical position between western and eastern Europe, a similar history symbolised by democratisation after the fall of the Iron Curtain, integration into Western political structures (such as NATO and European Union), the emergence of populist and nationalists forces in recent years, and being perceived by the Russian Federation as within its wider area of influence. At the same time, however, as this chapter also shows, it is possible to witness a number of differences in the field this edited volume is dedicated to; for example, the respective civil societies have a different level of interest in the issue of disinformation, varying perceptions of this phenomenon, and they use different strategies to tackle it. Hence a narrowing of the research scope will not only allow for a description of the existing initiatives themselves but also their proper contextualisation.

This kind of contribution is highly necessary since the comparative perspective is missing in existing literature dedicated to civil society initiatives tackling disinformation, and not only in central Europe. Most publications dedicated to this issue were published by local CSOs, which brings with them certain deficiencies. The content of these studies is not in question, but it is appropriate to highlight certain limitations in their use as a foundation of academic research. Firstly, there is the lack of methodology as well as a non-transparent evaluation and editing procedure which does not allow, for example, one to understand why certain examples of practices were chosen for presentation and others not.

[1] The author works as programme manager of projects related to disinformation and strategic communications in the think-tank Prague Security Studies Institute based in Czech Republic.

This limitation is closely related to a second, which lies in the pragmatic reasoning of these publications. This results in (from perspective of CSOs completely legitimate) ambition not to provide in-depth analysis of civil society actors and their actions but rather a selection of the most interesting examples to follow. This tendency is strengthened even more by the multiple aims of these publication, which are usually dedicated exclusively to civic society actors as well as other subjects that hinder in-depth analysis and predefine the perspectives in which the actions of civil society are understood.

Examples of studies produced by CSOs which map civic society activities tackling disinformation are as follows: The Czech think-tank European Values Center for Security Policy described the activities of civil society in Western states in a study of countermeasures against the subversion operations of the Kremlin (Kremlin Watch 2018) as well as in *The Prague Manual*, presenting best practices in countering malign foreign influences (Janda and Víchová 2018). The pro-Kremlin propaganda in central and eastern Europe and various initiatives against it was mapped by Czech CSO Nesehnutí (Dufkova and Hofmeisterova 2018). Another study, also focused on the same region and its resilience against disinformation and which mentioned projects in the area of media literacy, was published by the Ukrainian think-tank Prism (Damarad and Yeliseyeu 2018). The Slovak think-tank GLOBSEC Policy Institute also published a study focused solely on youth and media literacy as well as projects trying to enhance it within central Europe and western Balkan countries (Hajdu and Klingová 2018).

The activities of civil society initiatives tackling disinformation have also already become the subject of rather critical scrutiny from academic researchers who have pointed out their influence over the public discourse about this issue. Their studies are focused on the identity and interactions of chosen civil society actors. Even though these investigations are less interested in practices, they still provide interesting accounts of actors in this area. Unfortunately, at the moment, they remain limited to Czech Republic and focused on a period between 2014 and 2016; therefore, they are not able to capture recent developments (Daniel and Eberle 2018; Kohút and Rychnovská 2018).

To summarise, there are important reasons why researchers should be focused more on the currently understudied issue of civil society actors tackling disinformation. Firstly, this example represents an interesting case study of civil society mobilisation in the area of security, which was until very recently seen as reserved to state institutions. Further research may produce interesting findings about the role of civil society in democratic societies in general. Secondly, this kind of research may prove extremely useful in preserving civil society initiatives. Since currently existing initiatives are not mapped properly, it is highly likely that, in the hectic environment of CSOs with very low-level institutional memory, the gathered expertise will be lost. Bringing more clarity to already-existing projects also contributes to efficiency in the planning of future activities by CSOs themselves and in the organising of networks that will allow effective labour sharing. Thirdly, it is necessary to bring more clarity to the role of civil society actors in decision-making. Since CSOs may have impact on public discourse about disinformation and (possibly also) how measures tackling this phenomenon are crafted by state institutions and policymakers, they should be subject to public scrutiny like any other actor involved in the decision-making process.

8.3 How to Research Civil Society Properly and Ethically?

As was already mentioned, the concept of civil society remains vague, and it is thus not easy to decide which initiatives can be considered a part of this category. This obstacle is even more problematic since civil society itself is heterogenous and comprises a number of various actors from individual activists focused on local communities up to large CSOs operating internationally. Another obstacle in mapping civil society is its dynamism, which results in changes to their topic of interest and, consequently, their activities. This fact was quite profound in the researched area of disinformation, which was in many cases not a primary but rather a supplementary field of interest among the described actors.

The author decided to overcome the challenge of the applied concept's unclear boundaries by creating a dataset of actors who declared themselves as active in the area of disinformation and are based in the analysed countries. Activity in this area does not mean only occasionally commenting on the issue but rather long-term and consistent interested in the topic. Even though the chapter tries to provide a complex account of initiatives in the analysed countries, the author cannot guarantee some of civil society initiatives were not omitted. However, given his personal experience and consultations with experts from the analysed countries, he dares to claim the chapter presents all actors whose activities are relevant and are having tangible results and influence on local debates and communities.

The chapter aims to analyse not only the activities and strategies of civil society actors but also the dynamic of the debate on the issue of disinformation in the analysed countries. This knowledge will provide further understanding of the context in which these actors operate. The dynamic of the debate will be assessed from the number of civil society actors who have started to be involved in activities tackling disinformation over time. The dynamic development of civil society actors complicates the assessment of which time they started to be interested in the particular issue. However, for our purposes, this category will be measured according to the year their first public output—publishing research, an article, or a book; conducting certain activity; or launching a website—was identified. Even more problematic is assessing whether they are still active in the area. Therefore, the focus is solely on the year a civil society actor became active in tackling disinformation; its eventual termination of activities in this filed will be mentioned only if is possible to prove.

In assessing the identity of a civil society actor, Anheier's (2013) methodology was utilised in identifying individuals, organisations, and institutions. This categorisation allowed inclusion into the dataset of two other types of actors whose affiliation with civil society might be questioned: journalists and academics. These actors were crucial for the debate on disinformation in the analysed countries, and so their exclusion from the dataset would obscure the research results. At the same, their specificity must be understood, and they are therefore treated as separate categories in the chapter. As for 'regular' civil society actors, their inclusion in the dataset is conditioned by long-term, consistent, and self-proclaimed interest in the area. Therefore, the dataset will, for example, include only those journalists who write about disinformation on a regular basis and have tried to move the debate on this issue further through their own (for example, investigative) projects. In summary, the categories described in the chapter are as follows:

- individuals—persons or smaller informal groups established to tackle disinformation via various means;
- organisations (CSOs)—organised and structuralised entities with a broad area of interest who have added the topic of disinformation to their agenda; and

- institutions—established institutions operating independently from the state, including
  - media (outlets or individual journalists who were or are active in the debate on disinformation) and
  - academia (universities, research institutions, or individual researchers affiliated with academic institutions who were or are active in the debate on disinformation).

Before presenting the research itself, it should be noted that this kind of area requires certain ethical consideration. Since disinformation might be a useful weapon to foreign or domestic non-democratic actors, one could argue that describing those who tackle this phenomenon puts them in danger, especially when organisations and individuals are named and their activities described. Despite that understanding of this argument, the author does not consider it to be a limitation in this research. Since the data presented in the chapter relies solely on open sources—in most cases published by researched civil society actors themselves—the chapter does not mention anything that the researched organisations would not be willing (and maybe even be eager) to communicate to the public. While the security concerns certainly should be seriously considered in context of authoritarian regimes, the situation in central European countries, despite a certain indisputable backlash against democratic principles in some of them, is still far from severe. As such, there is no need to anonymise the proponents of civil society (Freedom House 2019).

8.4 Civil Society Actors Tackling Disinformation in Central Europe

Even at first sight, it is obvious that debates in individual countries differ. Dissimilarity concerns all the observed category variables: the time at which most actors came to be involved in the tackling of this issue and the identity of civil society actors, as well as their activities (Fig. 8.1).

Generally, it is possible to distinguish two groups among the analysed countries. In the first, consisting of Czech Republic and Slovakia, it is possible to identify the involvement of a large number of civil society actors in tackling disinformation (30 in Czech Republic and 26 in Slovakia). The identities of the involved actors are very diverse and

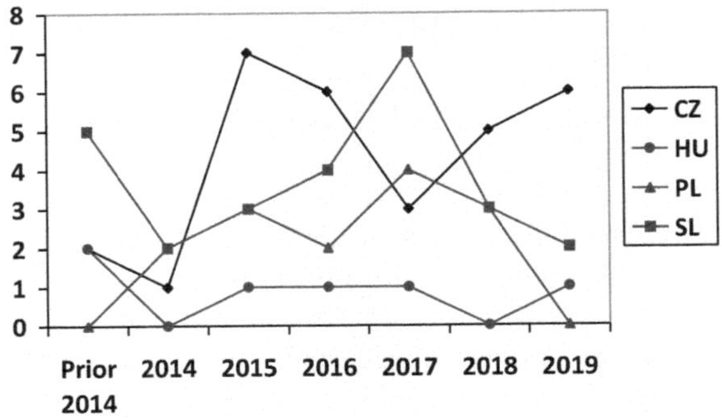

Fig. 8.1 Number of newly established civil society initiatives tackling disinformation by year (*Source* Author)

comprises almost all the categories covered in the chapter. In both countries, the debate also had similar dynamics: It peaked in Czech Republic in 2015–16, and the following year in Slovakia. Given the wide variety of civil society actors involved, it is possible to encounter various strategies and approaches in tackling disinformation. It is also worth mentioning that civil society in Czech Republic and Slovakia stimulates activities related to disinformation across the whole region since local CSOs initiate cross-border projects related to this issue, and initiatives from these countries are copied elsewhere.

The situation in the second group, consisting of Hungary and Poland, is very different. The number of civil society actors tackling disinformation is lower (6 in Hungary and 14 in Poland). Moreover, the issue of disinformation is not usually the primary interest of the presented civil society actors but rather a secondary activity (often caused only be involvement in projects conducted in cooperation with partners from Czech Republic or Slovakia). This situation has led to the application of a limited set of strategies to tackle disinformation which are often untraditional, do not going beyond the goal of a particular project, or are conditioned by the identity of the civil society actor. A slight difference between Hungary and Poland is the intensity of the debate as such. While in the case of Hungary, it is not possible to indicate any turning point from which civil society has started to be interested in this issue, for Poland this occurred in 2017 (Fig. 8.2).

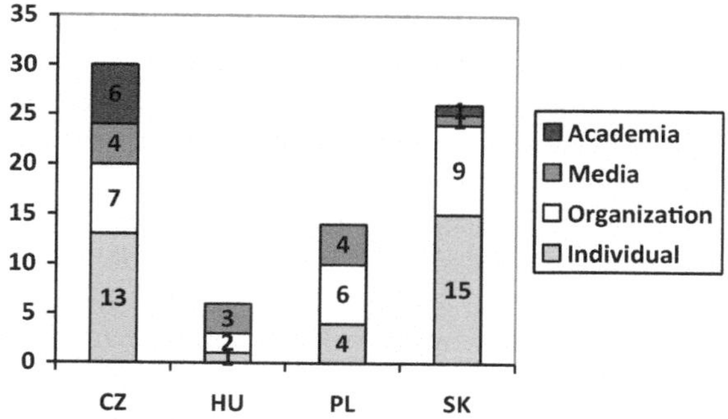

Fig. 8.2 Identity of civil society actors in individual countries (*Source* Author)

These differences clearly illustrate that even in such a coherent region, domestic factors clearly matter. Therefore, the rest the chapter will offer a closer look into the separate civil societies of the central European countries, describing individual actors and their most important activities and strategies.

8.4.1 Czech Republic

The number of civil society actors tackling disinformation in Czech Republic was the highest among the analysed countries—30 in total. As visible in Fig. 8.1, the number of civil society actors included in the dataset skyrocketed in 2015 when seven new individuals and organisations became active. This trend continued the following year when another six new actors got involved in tackling disinformation. Interest in the issues of disinformation remains high even now as illustrated by the fact that new initiatives are still emerging—five new civic society actors became active in 2018 and another six in 2019. The identity of civil society actors is the most heterogenous out of all the analysed countries. In the dataset, 13 individuals are present, seven CSOs, four actors from the media, and six actors from academia. The particularly high level of involvement of universities and research institutes in the initiatives tackling disinformation is unique in the context of the central European region. This variety of actors has resulted in different strategies, including research, fact-checking, educational activities, political advocacy, and investigative journalism. A significant effort was also made to create platforms where various civil society actors involved in this issue might interact. Moreover, the Czech debate on disinformation is unique due to the existence of civil society actors who present critical reflection upon the current discourse of this issue, and it has thus stimulated a debate about the legitimacy and effectivity of the applied initiatives.

Individuals and smaller, rather informal civil society initiatives started to be involved in the issue of disinformation even before this issue became an important part of public agenda. Prior to 2014, it is possible to identify two initiatives which might not necessarily have been perceived themselves as tackling disinformation at the time of their foundation but were already applying the strategies currently utilised to tackle this phenomenon later on: The website Hoax (established in 2000) aims to warn users against various hoaxes, chain mail, and other internet content which might endanger the user and is not in accordance with netiquette guidelines (Hoax, n.d.), and the project 'Demagog' (launched in 2012) focuses on the fact-checking of political debates (Demagog CZ, n.d.). A distinct feature were individuals (as well as other civil society actors) which started to tackle disinformation after 2015 with a strong emphasis on the security dimension of the phenomena, also seen as closely interlinked with Russian influence operations launched against Western states after the start of the conflict in Ukraine in 2014. The influence of these events on the Czech debate is illustrated by Roman Máca, an independent blogger who first started to write about the situation in Ukraine and then became interested in describing and exposing various platforms and groups spreading disinformation related to Ukraine in Czech Republic. At the time of this writing, in January 2020, he is still working on this issue as a programme manager at the think-tank Institute for Politic and Society (Institute for Politics and Society, n.d.), run by the Czech political party ANO. Another initiative, launched in 2015, is the website Manipulátoři (Manipulators), which raises awareness about the issue of disinformation as well as fact-checking and launching smaller investigative projects (Manipulátoři 2020). One of the founders of Manipulátoři Petr Nutil published the book *Média, lži a příliš rychlý mozek* (Media, lies, and a brain that's too fast) focused on issues of online manipulation, propaganda, and media literacy in 2018 (Nutil 2018). Before the release of Nutil's publication, three other books focused on disinformation were published. First was *Průmysl lži—Propaganda, konspirace a dezinformační válka* (Industry of lies—propaganda, conspiracy, and disinformation warfare) by PR expert Alexandra Alvarová, who also conducts public lectures dedicated to these issues (Rozsypal 2019). The second contribution to the debate was the book *Informační válka* (Information warfare) by a colonel of the Czech Army Karel Řehka, which focused on the issue of disinformation and propaganda in military operations (Řehka 2017). The third case, published in 2018, represents a popular book called *Nejlepší kniha o fake news, dezinformacích a manipulacích!!!* (The best book on fake news, disinformation, and manipulation!!!) written by scholars Miloš Gregor, Petra Vejvodová, and their students (Gregor et al. 2018). The same year, based on an example from the Baltics, a group of activists started the civic movement Čeští elfové (Czech elves) focused on mapping the spread of disinformation via chain mail and social network trolls. Monitoring dedicated to these issues is published on monthly basis (Romea 2018). At the same time, the issue of disinformation also attracted greater attention in the private sector. František Vrábel, CEO of the company Semantic Visions, which is involved in open source analysis, started to be more present in the media while presenting its research related to disinformation (Semantic Visions 2019). In 2019, a former member of the East Stratcom Task Force[2] Jakub Kalenský moved from Brussels back to Prague and, as a senior fellow of the Digital Forensic Research Lab of the Atlantic Council, started to contribute to the Czech debate as well. Another book focused on disinformation, *V síti (dez)informací* (In the net of (dis)information) by PR consultant Jiří Táborský, focused on manipulation techniques and the current situation in information space (Táborský 2019). Two further initiatives were launched as well: '#jsmetu' (#wearehere), aiming to decrease the polarisation of debate on social media inspired by an example from Sweden (#JsmeTu, n.d.), and 'Fair Advertising', raising awareness about online advertisements on platforms known to be spreading disinformation by publishing examples on its Twitter account similar to the US organisation Sleeping Giants (Cemper 2019).

Over time the issue of disinformation started to attract the attention of various established CSOs focused on issues of security, media, or human rights, and who included various projects related to this topic in their portfolio. The most prominent example of this approach is the CSO European Values Center for Security Policy (EVCSP), which, upon

[2] A department of the European External Action Service tasked with tackling disinformation.

entering the area of disinformation in 2015, significantly shifted the development of the whole organisation, especially by launching its programme 'Kremlin Watch' in 2016 focused on raising awareness about the issue of Russian influence operations. EVCSP put the issue of disinformation at the centre of its agenda. Due to this fact, EVCSP became not only a publicly acclaimed authority on the issue but also a counterpart for state institutions, for example, while drafting the 2016 *National Security Audit* (Ministry of the Interior of the Czech Republic 2016). Another CSO, which entered the scene in 2015, was the Prague Security Studies Institute, which over time switched its focus from the role of disinformation in Russian influence operations to researching the influence of disinformation on Czech elections and the area of strategic communications (Prague Security Studies Institute, n.d.). The well-established CSO Association for International Affairs, which focused on research and education in the area of international relations, started to be involved in tackling disinformation in 2016 through the launch of a Czech version of the Ukrainian initiative 'StopFake' (StopFake, n.d.a); it also became a research partner in international projects focused on this area. The rapid development in civic society also attracted the attention of CSOs facilitating funding and networking among various civil society actors.[3] The most noteworthy example is a project of the Open Society Foundation Prague (OSF), focused on Russian influence activities in Czech Republic and Slovakia and which launched in 2016. Aside from funding projects related to this topic, OSF also attempted to create a network among organisations active in this area, conducted its own research, and hold events. The programme was concluded in 2018, and OSF is no longer active in this area (Nadace OSF, n.d.). Another CSO, which is at the same time a financial donor, is the Endowment Fund for Independent Journalism, which has supported various projects focused on disinformation since its establishment in 2016 (NFNŽ, n.d.). One of the biggest Czech CSOs People in Need, which is focused primary on humanitarian aid and human rights, had already started to conduct projects tackling disinformation in 2015 when it included this topic in its educational activities

[3] The chapter takes into an account only CSOs with a presence in Czech Republic (and, respectively, other analysed countries) and were active in creating the network of domestic civil society actors. Therefore, donors from abroad (such as the US National Endowment for Democracy) are not mentioned despite the fact that they played an important role in shaping the debate on disinformation in central Europe.

(Jeden svět na školách, n.d.). However, it has also recently started being involved in events facilitating the network of civil society actors interested in this issue by, for example, organising the conference 'Cyber Dialogue' in 2019 (Cyber Dialogue 2019). In 2018, the CSO Transitions, focused mainly on the education of journalists, became involved in tackling disinformation by launching a series of lectures and workshops about media literacy for the elderly (Transitions 2018).

The dynamic activities of Czech civil society related to tackling disinformation did not go unnoticed by the media due, in part, to the fact that journalists themselves played an important role in the debate about this phenomenon. Investigative journalist Ondřej Kundra (working for the weekly *Respekt*) started to write about disinformation extensively in 2015 and conducted an in–depth investigation into the notorious conspiracy website Aeronet (Kundra 2015). Other actors involved in writing about disinformation were the news portal Hlídací Pes (Watch Dog), especially in its news section dedicated to Russian interests in Czech Republic, and the news portal Neovlivní (Uninfluenced), which published in 2016 one of the first lists of websites spreading disinformation (Neovlivní 2016). Another journalist who contributed to the debate about disinformation is Jakub Zelenka, who in 2018 received a young journalists award for the project 'Dezinformace: Co pro vás znamenají lži?' (Disinformation: What do lies mean to you?) (Poljakov et al. 2017).

As in other analysed countries, universities also played a role in tackling disinformation. It should be highlighted that this does not mean they 'only' conducted academic research on this topic, but rather they mainly sought to actively enter the public debate on this issue. Masaryk University started to be engaged in research on this issue in 2016. The environment at this university also allowed for the creation of two student initiatives focused on raising awareness about these issues and empowering critical thinking and media literacy among youth by introducing the educational activities 'Zvol si info' (Choose the information; established in 2016) and 'Fakescape' (established in 2018). These two projects were later separated from the university and now operate independently. Furthermore, it was at this university that the project 'Dezimatrix', aimed at conducting multidisciplinary research about disinformation, was launched in 2019 (Dezimatrix, n.d.). In the same year, Palacký University Olomouc launched the project 'Euforka' focused on informing about the European Union as well as debunking disinformation related to this issue. This initiative later involved other Czech universities (Palacky University Olomouc 2019). Researchers of the Institute of International Relations, a research institution supervised by the Ministry of Foreign Affairs, published a 2018 article on the Czech debate about hybrid threats (in which disinformation was one of the main topics) and reflected the argumentation and development of its actors (Daniel and Eberle 2018). An important role in the increasing awareness of the disinformation phenomena and the promotion of critical thinking was played by the wide net of libraries in Czech Republic. For example, in 2019, the Moravian Library in Brno launched the project 'Používej mozek' (Use your brain), comprised of a series of lectures dedicated to critical thinking and media literacy (Winkler and Pazdersky, n.d.).

8.4.2 Hungary

The number of Hungarian civil society actors tackling disinformation was the lowest of all the analysed countries (six in total). Given the low number of civil society actors, it is not possible to trace any dynamic in the debate on this issue (see Fig. 8.1). However, in looking at the time scale, it is possible to observe that research on the topic of disinformation had started already in 2010 when the CSO Political Capital launched research projects focused on anti-Semitic conspiracy theories. This example is quite illustrative since it shows that the roots and focus of the debate on disinformation in Hungary is different than that of Czech Republic. While Czech civil society perceived disinformation as an external phenomenon related to Russian influence operations in Europe after 2014, Hungarian actors were more interested in those originating from the domestic environment. This is especially true of media (representing three civil society actors in total), who usually started as independent news sites with an emphasis on investigative reporting related to domestic issues and later added the issue of disinformation to their agendas.

Similarly, as in the Czech case, the spread of hoaxes on the Internet had already attracted the attention of civil society at the beginning of millennium. The website Urbanlegends had already started to map these kinds of stories in 2004 (Urbanlegends, n.d.). However, disinformation as a security threat or, more broadly, as a phenomenon which could jeopardise democracy was introduced only later. As was mentioned, one of the key players in this debate was the CSO Political Capital, which focused on researching policy related topics and who had already started to focus on them in 2010. Since then, this CSO conducts research projects focused on foreign (namely Russian) and homegrown disinformation and propaganda campaigns (Political Capital 2019). The CSO Centre for Euro-Atlantic Integration and Democracy (n.d.) was a partner organisation in several projects focused solely on Russian information warfare between 2016 and 2018.

As was previously mentioned, the attention of media dedicated to the phenomenon of disinformation is mostly related to other malfunctions of the Hungarian government, such as corruption or the undermining of democratic institutions. An illustrative case is a group of investigative reports from the website Átlátszó (Transparent), which started to be active in 2011 and proclaims its mission as mainly investigative reporting, working with whistle-blowers and other watchdog practitioners. Nevertheless, in 2017, Átlátszó added a new government propaganda section to its website focused on media freedom and homegrown disinformation campaigns (Átlátszó, n.d.). A similar story might be told about other media outlets, such as Direkt36, established in 2015 (Direkt36, n.d.), or K-Monitor, which conducted workshops on disinformation in 2019 (K-Monitor 2019). These media publications were primarily focused on investigative reporting but later added the issue of disinformation and propaganda to their agendas as well.

8.4.3 Poland

As Fig. 8.1 shows, the dynamicity of Polish civil society initiatives tackling disinformation peaked in 2017 with fourteen in total during the covered period. The number of actors is low given that Poland is bigger than the other three countries combined. The proportional representation of CSOs among the categories of civil society actors is the highest of all analysed countries. However, for Polish CSOs, disinformation remains a rather secondary topic of interest in which they have become involved mainly due to participation in cross-border projects or the interest of individual researchers. These factors likely contributed to the fact that several initiatives described below are no longer active. Another remarkable feature of the Polish debate on disinformation is the differing perception of the phenomenon. While CSOs usually research it in the context of Russian influence operations, the majority of media have focused on those of domestic origin. These different understandings of the causes and context of disinformation has resulted in different strategies being applied in tackling this issue.

As in other countries, individuals and smaller civil society initiatives started to be involved in tackling disinformation first. In the Polish environment, 2014 saw the launch of the Slovak-inspired project 'Demagog' in order to fact-check political debates (Demagog PL, n.d.) as well as the Polish branch of the Ukrainian initiative 'StopFake' (StopFake, n.d.b). In 2015, the initiative 'Rosyjska V kolumna w Polsce' (Fifth Russian column in Poland) was launched with the aim of increasing awareness about Russian propaganda in Poland and debunking disinformation. However, the initiative stopped in 2019 after the project founder was sued for claims publicised on the project's Facebook site (WirtualneMedia 2019). In 2018, the initiative 'Wojownicy Klawiatury' (Keyboard fighters) was launched with the aim of debunking disinformation related to the European Union and to promote a positive image of it (Partycypacja Obywatelska 2019).

The involvement of Polish CSOs in tackling disinformation, as mentioned above, is unstable. The most telling story is that of the Cybersecurity Foundation, whose mission is to increase awareness about various threats related to cyberspace. Due to this specialisation, it launched two projects aiming to raise awareness about this issue: in 2015, the Twitter account 'Disinfo Digest', reporting and debunking disinformation in the information environment, and, in 2017, a project with a similar aim called 'Infoops Poland' (Warsaw Institute 2018). However, both of these projects were supervised by Kamil Basaj, who left the foundation in 2018, effectively halting their activities related to disinformation. Basaj later established his own organisation, INFO OPS Polska (Fundacja INFO OPS Polska, n.d.). As in Czech Republic, established Polish CSOs active in research on international relations and security did not adopt the issue of disinformation to their agenda. For example, the Centre for International Relations conducted several projects focused on the research of disinformation in relation to Russian influence operations starting in 2015, but most of them were dependent on the activity of one researcher, Antoni Wierzejskii (Centrum Stosunków Międzynarodowych, n.d.). Similarly, the Centre for Eastern Studies, whose focus on Russian politics and society might have led to broader interest in disinformation in relation to Russian influence operations, aside from several commentaries on this issue, did not become involved in the Polish debate on disinformation. The one exception is the Center for Propaganda and Disinformation

Analysis; established in 2017, it researches Russian propaganda (Centrum Analiz Propagandy i Dezinformacji, n.d.). It also cooperated with the Casimir Pulaski Foundation, which increased the awareness about the disinformation issue by putting it on the agenda of the Warsaw Security Forum in 2018 and 2019 (Casimir Pulaski Foundation 2019).

Like the majority of previously mentioned Polish initiatives, media interest was focused primarily on the dynamic of this phenomenon in the domestic political debate. The only exception from this trend is the news site CyberDefence24, launched in 2016. It is focused mainly on security-related issues and has played an active role in increasing awareness about Russian influence operations (CyberDefence 24, n.d.). Similar to Hungary, some media publications were started by investigative journalists with a focus on government malpractice and only later added the topic of disinformation to their portfolio. An illustrative example is the independent news portal OKO.press, established in 2017 with a focus on investigative journalism; it started to write regularly on disinformation in 2019 (OKO.press, n.d.). Similarly, the Reporters Foundation, which chiefly provided media training, started its own investigative work focused on various issues including disinformation in 2016 (Fundacja reporterow, n.d.). The private television channel TVN24 launched the project 'Kontakt24' in 2018 aiming to tackle homegrown disinformation by promoting quality journalism and fact-checking (Kontakt 24, n.d.).

8.4.4 Slovakia

Among the analysed countries Slovakia represent probably the most interesting example. The total number of civil society actors tackling disinformation is the second highest (26 in total). Even though the most dynamic year in the Slovak debate about disinformation was 2017, it should be noted that it was closely interlinked with other topics that civil society had already tackled—namely, right-wing extremism, which is on the rise in the country. The number of individuals and smaller initiatives tackling disinformation is the highest out of the four analysed countries (15 in total) and comprise a wide variety of actors from civil activists and independent bloggers to IT developers and PR experts. Due to this vibrancy, Slovakia might be considered a hub of civil society initiatives tackling disinformation from which ideas and strategies are spreading across the whole region. Given the similarity of the languages, the findings and results emanating from Slovak projects are utilised predominantly in

Czech Republic. At the same time, Slovakia possesses a vibrant community of CSOs focused on researching security-related issues which have incorporated the issue of disinformation into their agendas. The innovativeness of the Slovak approach to tackling disinformation lies not only in the use of digital technologies in its research of the phenomenon, but mainly in the ability to address disinformation as such and to tackle the roots of this phenomenon by promoting media literacy, deradicalising youth, or using humour.

One of the streams from which the Slovak debate about disinformation took its inspiration were activities focused on monitoring right-wing extremists. An interesting example of a civil society action is pensioner and former engineer Ján Benčík, who early on started to uncover various networks of conspirators, mainly related to extreme right-wing groups, on his blog in 2012. Benčík was later awarded by the Slovak president for his activates in 2016 (*Deutsche Welle* 2017). Another important actor was the independent investigative journalist Radovan Bránik, who maps right-wing extremist movements and other security-related issues (Bránik 2020). The role of conspiracy theories among Slovak right-wing extremists was also an issue of interest for political scientist Gregorij Mesežnikov (IVO, n.d.).[4] All the abovementioned individuals are still active in the Slovak debate on disinformation and played an important role not only in its beginnings but also in its further development. 'Demagog', an initiative which has focused on fact-checking political debates since its launch in 2010 (Demagog SK, n.d.), has served as an important inspiration for further projects in the region. A significant turning point in the Slovak debate on disinformation came when high school teacher Juraj Smatana compiled the first list of websites spreading pro-Russian propaganda and disinformation in 2015, thus framing the debate about this issue (Šnídl 2015). Consequently, in 2016, PR expert Ján Urbančík launched the website Konšpirátori.sk (Conspirators) aiming to undercut the gains made from online advertisements on websites spreading problematic content, including disinformation. This initiative also had an international footprint since the Czech online browser Seznam.cz included it in its interface

[4] According to the chosen categorisation, Radovan Bránik (as a journalist) and Gregorij Mesežnikov (as an academic) should be presented separately as individuals tackling disinformation. However, they are mentioned here together since it is logical from the chronological perspective and both individuals are only examples of civic society actors in their given category.

for commercial providers (Sblog 2018). The list of websites created by Konspirátori.sk was also used by the webhosting company WebSupport, which created the Google Chrome plug-in B.S. Detector (see Chapter 5) in 2017 warning against sites spreading problematic content (Bullshit Detector, n.d.). Advanced digital means were also used in the project 'Blbec.online' (Jerk.online), which scrapes content in real time from Facebook pages known to be spreading disinformation. In so doing, it has been able to warn against those going viral since 2017 (Blbec.online, n.d.). Another noteworthy project using digital technologies to tackle disinformation is 'Checkbot', a Facebook plug-in which helps users to debunk online disinformation; it was produced by a team led by Peter Jančárik from the PR company Seesame in 2019 (Insight 2019). Several civil society initiatives approached the topic more proactively and started to challenge the spread of disinformation directly. This is the case for the group #somtu (#Iamhere), which has, since its establishment in 2017, aimed to decrease polarisation in debates on social media (Mikušovič 2017). Slovenskí elfovia (Slovak elves) started to be active in 2018 and, inspired by their Baltic counterparts, have focused on exposing trolls on social networks (Brenier 2019). As was mentioned, several initiatives tried to approach the issue of disinformation more broadly by focusing on the reasons people are led to believe it. Similarly, as in other analysed countries, educational projects were launched which focused on media literacy—'Zmudri' (Get wise) in 2018 (Zmudri, n.d.)—and raising awareness about the issue—'Infosecurity' in 2019 (Infosecurity, n.d.). Given the close link between disinformation and right-wing extremism, several initiatives were also launched aiming to deradicalise youth and counter extremist and conspiracy narratives: In 2016, the project 'Mladi proti fašismu' (Youth against fascism) (Mladi proti fašismu, n.d.) and, a year later, the project 'Sebavedome Slovensko' (Self-confident Slovakia) (Sebavedome, n.d.) were launched. One strategy used by Slovak civil society differs from other covered countries in its use of humour and sarcasm to ridicule conspiracy theories and their disseminators. The two most popular initiatives of this kind are the Facebook pages 'Preco ludem hrabe' (Why people become loony), launched in 2014, and 'Zomri' (Die), launched in 2016.

The high number of civil society activities run by smaller, informal groups is mirrored in the equally active CSOs community. The first CSO which started to focus on the issue of disinformation was Memo98, which has been monitoring the information space before elections in various countries globally since 1998 (Memo98, n.d.). The Slovak branch of the Open Society Fund started projects focused on tackling hate speech in 2014 (Open Society Foundation 2015). After 2015, basically every Slovak CSO covering security-related issues conducted at least one project related to disinformation, mostly understood in the context of Russian influence operations. The Slovak Security Policy Institute launched the website Antipropaganda about this phenomenon in 2015 (Antipropaganda, n.d.). The GLOBSEC Policy Institute started to be involved in the debate on disinformation in 2015, and it became one of the beacons of research on this issue in central Europe. Its resources allowed this CSO to conduct several studies with an international scope, such as the opinion poll GLOBSEC Trends which maps public opinion of security and policy issues in Eastern European countries. It has become an important networker, with a cross-border network of contacts, and a promoter of the debate on disinformation—especially by putting it on the agenda of the GLOBSEC Tatra Summit (Globsec, n.d.). In 2016, the Strategic Policy Institute organised several public events about hybrid warfare on NATO's eastern flank and information warfare in Ukraine (Strategic Policy Institute, n.d.). Among the projects conducted by the Slovak Foreign Policy Association, the most significant was the informal Slovak Forum Against Propaganda platform, established in 2017 and which provides a space for various activists to meet and a hub for future cooperative projects (Slovak Forum against Propaganda, n.d.). The Centre for European and North Atlantic Affairs published an analysis on information warfare as a tool of Russian foreign policy in 2017 (Centre for European and North Atlantic Affairs 2019), and, in 2018, the Slovak branch of the CSO People in Need launched the project 'Nenávistný skutok' (Hatefull deed) involving lawyers prosecuting the cases of hate speech on the Internet (Človek v ohrozeni, n.d.).

8.5 Summary

The ongoing activities of civil society initiatives tackling disinformation represent an exemplary method of studying the possibilities and limitations of active citizen involvement in the area of security. There is broad consensus among experts, state servants, and politicians of the fact that individuals, organisations, and institutions from civil society are important players in overcoming challenges related to the current information disorder and (in some cases) take their findings into account while making policy decisions. Considering previous statements, it is surprising how little has been done in providing systematic accounts of civil society initiatives tackling disinformation.

Despite the number of similarities among analysed countries, the chapter presents two very different stories of the approach of civil society towards disinformation. There is a vibrant debate on this issue in Czech Republic and Slovakia, where local civil society actors not only research the topic—usually with a strong emphasis on Russian information operations—but they also are able to devise various innovative solutions; form coalitions and networks, including cross-border ones; achieve particular aims; and in some cases also influence the policymaking processes. In both countries, the issue of disinformation has become embedded in the agendas of already-existing CSOs focused on researching security-related issues, as well as in universities.

Contrariwise, for civil society in Hungary and Poland, the issue of disinformation has a rather secondary importance and does not attract much attention. For some civil society actors (mainly from media), disinformation is not perceived as an external threat but rather as product of domestic government malpractice. This may, of course, be connected to the domestic political situation in these countries. The small number of involved actors as well secondary importance of the topic complicates the building of stable coalitions among various actors, which results in a lower number of projects with less sustainability. Moreover, strategies chosen to tackle disinformation tend to be quite traditional and predetermined by the identity of the actors. The number of approaches and initiatives is instead the product of cross-border cooperation rather than genuine interest in the topic by domestic actors.

Stark differences among civil society actors in the analysed countries show that interest in the issue of disinformation and strategies to tackle this phenomenon are very much dependent on the local context. This fact should be considered when attempting to transplant these experiences with tackling disinformation to different sociopolitical contexts outside of central Europe. This chapter provides convincing evidence that a one-size-fits-all approach is not suitable even within a coherent region, and, therefore, a more nuanced approach supported by proper research is needed. Before finding common ways of tackling disinformation, it is necessary to understand national specifics and context and to be sure that all civil society actors perceive the problem in the same manner—which is not always the case, even in the rather similar countries of central Europe.

Acknowledgements The author would like to thank to Lóránt Győri, Marta Kowalska, Tomáš Kriššák, Jakub Tomášek, and Veronika Víchova for their valuable insights.

Bibliography

#JsmeTu. (#WeAreHere). (n.d.). https://www.jsmetu.org/. Accessed 3 Feb 2020.

Anheier, H. (2013). *Civil Society: "Measurement, Evaluation, Policy"*. London: Taylor and Francis.

Antipropaganda. (n.d.). *O nás* [About Us]. https://antipropaganda.sk/o-nas/. Accessed 3 Feb 2020.

Átlátszó. (n.d.). *About Us, Fundraising*. https://english.atlatszo.hu/about-us-fundraising/. Accessed 24 Nov 2019.

Bellingcat. (2019, June 19). *Identifying the Separatists Linked to the Downing of MH17*. UK&Europe. https://www.bellingcat.com/news/uk-and-europe/2019/06/19/identifying-the-separatists-linked-to-the-downing-of-mh17/. Accessed 24 Nov 2019.

Blbec.online. (n.d.). *Monitoring Extrémistov Na Sociálnych Sieťach* [Monitoring of Extremists on Social Networks]. https://blbec.online/preco. Accessed 3 Feb 2020.

Bránik, R. (2020). *Blog.sme.sk*. https://branik.blog.sme.sk/. Accessed 3 Feb 2020.

Brenier, V. (2019, August 13). Slovenskí elfovia sa prihlásili k odstráneniu propagandistického videa Kotlebovcov [Slovak Elves Announced That They Are Responsible for Removal of Propagandistic Video of Kotleba's Political Party]. *INFOSECURITY.SK*. https://infosecurity.sk/domace/livia-a-elfovia/. Accessed 3 Feb 2020.

Bullshit Detector. (n.d.). https://www.websupport.sk/en/bullshit-detector. Accessed 3 Feb 2020.

Caparini, M., Fluri, P., & Molnár, F. (2006). *Civil Society and the Security Sector: Concepts and Practices in New Democracies*. Münster: Lit.

Casimir Pulaski Foundation. (2019). *On Disinformation of the Margin of Warsaw Security Forum*. https://pulaski.pl/en/on-desinformation-of-the-margin-of-warsaw-security-forum-2/. Accessed 3 Feb 2020.

Cemper, J. (2019, November 15). Projekt Fair Advertising upozorňuje na nevhodnou inzerci na konspiračních webech. Společnosti už reagují [Project Fair Advertising Draws Attention to Advertising on Conspiracy Sites. Companies Are Already Responding]. *Manipulátoři*. https://manipulatori.cz/projekt-fair-advertising-upozornuje-na-nevhodnou-inzerci-na-konspiracnich-webech-spolecnosti-uz-reaguji/. Accessed 3 Feb 2020.

Centre for Euro-Atlantic Integration and Democracy. (n.d.). *Assessment of Kremlin's Soft Power Tools in Central Europe*. http://ceid.hu/assessment-of-kremlins-soft-power-tools-in-central-europe/. Accessed 24 Nov 2019.

Centre for European and North Atlantic Affairs. (2019). *Information Warfare*. http://www.cenaa.org/en/research/information-warfare/news. Accessed 3 Feb 2020.

Centrum Analiz Propagandy i Dezinformacji. (n.d.). *About Foundation*. https://capd.pl/en/mission-and-goals. Accessed 3 Feb 2020.

Centrum Stosunków Międzynarodowych. (n.d.). *Projects*. http://csm.org.pl/en/projects. Accessed 3 Feb 2020.

Človek v ohrozeni. (n.d.). *Na čo slúži táto stránka* [The Purpose of This Webpage]. https://nenavistnyskutok.sk/blog/co-je-ns. Accessed 3 Feb 2020.

Collins, A. (2010). *Contemporary Security Studies*. Oxford: Oxford University Press.

Cyber Dialogue. (2019). *Cyber Dialogue: Active Citizens Against Fakes and Hatred Online*. https://www.cyberdialogue.cz/. Accessed 24 Nov 2019.

CyberDefence24. (n.d.). *Bezpieczeństwo Informacyjne CyberDefence24.Pl*. https://www.cyberdefence24.pl/bezpieczenstwo-informacyjne/. Accessed 3 Feb 2020.

Damarad, V., & Yeliseyeu, A. (Eds.). (2018). *Disinformation Resilience Index*. Kyiv: Ukrainian Prism.

Daniel, J., & Eberle, J. (2018). Hybrid Warriors: Transforming Czech Security Through the 'Russian Hybrid Warfare' Assemblage. *Sociologicky Casopis, 54*(6), 907–931.

Demagog CZ. (n.d.). *O Nás* [About Us]. https://demagog.cz/stranka/o-nas. Accessed 3 Feb 2020.

Demagog PL. (n.d.). *Stowarzyszenie*. https://demagog.org.pl/stowarzyszenie-demagog-pierwsza-w-polsce-organizacja-factcheckingowa/. Accessed 3 Feb 2020.

Demagog SK. (n.d.). *O Nás* [About Us]. https://demagog.sk/o-nas/. Accessed 3 Feb 2020.

Deutsche Welle. (2017, June 13). Slovak pensioner blogs against neo-Nazis. https://www.dw.com/en/slovak-pensioner-blogs-against-neo-nazis/av-39626676. Accessed 3 Feb 2020.

Dezimatrix. (n.d.). *New Ways to Prevent Disinformation*. https://www.dezimatrix.org/. Accessed 3 Feb 2020.

Diamond, L. J., & Morlino, L. (2005). *Assessing the Quality of Democracy*. Baltimore: Johns Hopkins University Press.

Direkt36. (n.d.). *Russian Connection*. https://www.direkt36.hu/en/category/orosz-kapcsolatok/. Accessed 3 Feb 2020.

Dufkova, K., & Hofmeisterova, P. (Eds.). (2018). *Characteristics of Pro-Kremlin Propaganda in Central and Eastern Europe and Practical Examples How to Tackle It*. Brno: Nesehnutí.

European Commission. (2018). *Action Plan against Disinformation*. Brussels: High Representative of the Union for Foreign Affairs and Security Policy.

Freedom House. (2019). *Freedom in the World 2019*. https://freedomhouse.org/report/freedom-world/freedom-world-2019. Accessed 3 Feb 2020.

Fried, D., & Polyakova, A. (2018). *Democratic Defense Against Disinformation*. Washington: Atlantic Council.

Fundacja INFO OPS Polska. (n.d.). *Fundacja Info Ops Polska. Projekt Na Rzecz Zapewnienia Bezpieczeństwa Środowiska Informacyjnego*. http://infoops.pl/. Accessed 3 Feb 2020.

Fundacja reporterow. (n.d.). *About Us*. https://fundacjareporterow.org/en/about-us/. Accessed 3 Feb 2020.

Gerasymchuk, S., & Maksak, H. (2018). Ukraine: Disinformation Resilience Index. *Disinformation Resilience Index*. http://prismua.org/en/english-ukraine-disinformation-resilience-index/. Accessed 3 Feb 2020.

Globsec. (n.d.). *Projects*. https://www.globsec.org/projects/. Accessed 3 Feb 2020.

Gregor, M., Vejvodová, P., & Zvol si info. (2018). *Nejlepší kniha o fake news, dezinformacích a manipulacích!!!* Praha: CPRESS.

Hajdu, D., & Klingová, K. (2018). *From Online Battlefield to Loss of Trust? Perceptions and Habits of Youth in Eight European Countries*. Bratislava: GLOBSEC Policy Institute.

HOAX.CZ. (n.d.). https://hoax.cz/cze/. Accessed 3 Feb 2020.

Infosecurity. (n.d.). *O Stránke* [About the Webpage]. https://infosecurity.sk/o-stranke/. Accessed 3 Feb 2020.

Insight. (2019, March 27). *Checkbot je slovenský chatbot, který lidem pomáhá odhalovat fake news* [Checkbot Is Slovak Chatbot, Which Helps to Debunk Fake News]. https://www.insight.cz/2019/03/27/checkbot-je-slovensky-chatbot-ktery-lidem-pomaha-odhalovat-fake-news/. Accessed 3 Feb 2020.

Institute for Politics and Society. (n.d.). *Member—Roman Máca*. https://www.politikaspolecnost.cz/en/who-we-are/roman-maca-2/#main. Accessed 3 Feb 2020.

IVO. (n.d.). *Inštitút pre verejné otázky* [Institute for Public Affairs]. http://www.ivo.sk/165/sk/pracovnici/grigorij-meseznikov. Accessed 3 Feb 2020.

Janda, J., & Víchová, V. (Eds.). (2018). The Prague Manual. *Kremlin Watch*. https://www.kremlinwatch.eu/our-reports/. Accessed 3 Feb 2020.

Jeden svět na školách. (n.d.). *Publikace a metodické příručky k mediálnímu vzdělávání* [Publications and Methodical Materials for Media Literacy]. https://www.jsns.cz/projekty/medialni-vzdelavani/materialy/publikace. Accessed 3 February 2020.

K-Monitor. (2019). *Outriders Meetup in Budapest: Disinformation.* https://www.kmonitor.hu/article/20190316-outriders-meetup-in-budapest-disinformation. Accessed 3 Feb 2020.

Kohút, M., & Rychnovská, D. (2018). The Battle for Truth: Mapping the Network of Information War Experts in the Czech Republic. *New Perspectives, 26*(3), 1–37.

Kontakt 24. (n.d.). *O Serwisie.* https://kontakt24.tvn24.pl/o-serwisie.htm. Accessed 3 Feb 2020.

Kremlin Watch. (2018). 2018 Ranking of Countermeasures by the EU28 to the Kremlin's Subversion Operations. *European Values.* https://www.europeanvalues.net/vyzkum/2018-ranking-countermeasures-eu28-kremlins-subversion-operations/. Accessed 3 Feb 2020.

Kundra, O. (2015, February 28). Putinův hlas v Česku [Putin's Voice in Czechia]. *Respekt.* https://www.respekt.cz/z-noveho-cisla/putinuv-hlas-v-cesku. Accessed 3 Feb 2020.

Manipulátoři. (2020). *Manipulátoři.cz mají nový web a chystají rozšíření* [Manipulatori.cz Has New Website and Prepares Extension]. https://manipulatori.cz/manipulatori-cz-maji-novy-web-a-chystaji-rozsireni/. Accessed 3 Feb 2020.

Memo98. (n.d.). *About Us.* http://memo98.sk/p/o-nas. Accessed 13 Jan 2021.

Mikušovič, D. (2017, June 27). #Somtu: Ako Mladí Slováci Prinášajú Slušnosť a Fakty Do Nenávistných Diskusií [#IamHere: How Young Slovaks Bring Politeness and Facts in Hateful Discussions]. *Denník N.* https://dennikn.sk/792819/somtu-ako-mladi-slovaci-prinasaju-slusnost-a-fakty-do-nenavistnych-diskusii/. Accessed 3 Feb 2020.

Ministry of the Interior of the Czech Republic. (2016). National Security Audit.

Mladi proti fašismu. (n.d.). *O projekte* [About project]. https://mladiprotifasizmu.sk/o-projekte/. Accessed 13 Jan 2021.

Nadace OSF. (n.d.). *Podpořené Projekty* [Supported Projects]. https://osf.cz/podporene-projekty/. Accessed 3 Feb 2020.

Nadační fond nezávislé žurnalistiky. (n.d.). *Již ukončené projekty* [Completed Projects]. https://www.nfnz.cz/podporene-projekty/jiz-ukoncene-projekty/. Accessed 3 Feb 2020.

Neovlivní. (2016). *Databáze proruského obsahu od A-Z* [Database of Pro-Russian Content from A to Z]. https://neovlivni.cz/databaze-proruskeho-obsahu-od-a-z/. Accessed 3 Feb 2020.

Nimmo, B. (2015). The Case for Information Defence: A Pre-emptive Strategy for Dealing with the New Disinformation Wars. In Legatum Institute (Ed.), *Information at War: From China's Three Warfares to NATO's Narratives.*

Nutil, P. (2018). *Média, lži a příliš rychlý mozek: Průvodce postpravdivým světem* [Media, Lies and Too Fast Brain: Guideline Through Post-Factual World]. Praha: Grada.

OKO.press. (n.d.). *Propaganda*. https://oko.press/tag-rzeczowy/propaganda/. Accessed 3 Feb 2020.

Open Society Foundation. (2015). *SAY IT TO MY FACE Campaign*. https://osf.sk/en/aktuality/kampan-povedz-mi-to-do-oci/. Accessed 3 Feb 2020.

Palacky University Olomouc. (2019). *Euforka: UP a další vysoké školy chtějí lépe informovat o Evropě* [Euforka: UP and Other Universities Want to Better Communicate About Europe]. https://www.upol.cz/nc/zpravy/zprava/clanek/euforka-up-a-dalsi-vysoke-skoly-chteji-lepe-informovat-o-evrope/. Accessed 24 Nov 2019.

Partycypacja Obywatelska. (2019, February 14). Wojownicy Klawiatury – społeczność w walce z fake newsami [Wojownicy Klawiatury—Community Fighting with Fake News]. https://partycypacjaobywatelska.pl/wojownicy-klawiatury-spolecznosc-w-walce-z-fake-newsami/. Accessed 3 Feb 2020.

Pesenti, M., & Pomerantsev, P. (2016). *How to Stop Disinformation*. Legatum Institute. https://lif.blob.core.windows.net/lif/docs/default-source/publications/how-to-stop-disinformation-lessons-from-ukraine-for-the-wider-world.pdf?sfvrsn=0. Accessed 3 Feb 2020.

Prague Security Studies Institute. (n.d.). *Russia's Influence Activities in CEE*. http://www.pssi.cz/russia-s-influence-activities-in-cee. Accessed 3 February 2020.

Political Capital. (2019). *Conspiracy Theories and Fake News*. https://www.politicalcapital.hu/conspiracy_theories_and_fake_news.php. Accessed 3 Feb 2020.

Poljakov, N., Prchal, L., & Zelenka, J. (2017). *Dezinformace: co pro vás znamenají lži?* [Disinformation: What Do Lies Mean to You?]. https://zpravy.aktualne.cz/domaci/valka-dezinformace-fake-news/r~7bfb35b23bb311e7886d002590604f2e/. Accessed 3 Feb 2020.

Řehka, K. (2017). *Informační válka* [Information War]. Praha: Academia.

Romea. (2018, November 5). *Czech Internet Trolls Have Competition—"Elves" Are Combating Disinformation and Propaganda*. http://www.romea.cz/en/news/world/czech-internet-trolls-have-competition-elves-are-combating-disinformation-and-propaganda. Accessed 24 Nov 2019.

Rozsypal, M. (2019, October 9). *Alvarová: Lež je pro každého vždy něčím sexy a vždy je atraktivnější než pravda* [Lie Is Always Sexy for Everyone and Always More Attractive Than the Truth]. *iRozhlas*. https://www.irozhlas.cz/zivotni-styl/spolecnost/alexandra-alvarova-prpaganda-dezinformace-fake-news_1910091950_pj. Accessed 3 Feb 2020.

Sblog. (2018, February 2). *Sklik nabídne klientům možnost neinzerovat na webech označených iniciativou Konšpirátori.sk jako dezinformační* [Sklik Will Offer Clients the Option Not to Advertise on Websites Identified as a Disinformation by Konspirátori.sk]. https://blog.seznam.cz/2018/02/sklik-nabidne-klientum-moznost-neinzerovat-webech-oznacenych-iniciativou-konspiratori-sk-jako-dezinformacni/. Accessed 3 Feb 2020.

Sebavedome. (n.d.). *O Nás* [About us]. http://sebavedome.sk/o-nas/. Accessed 3 Feb 2020.

Semantic Visions. (2019). *Semantic Visions Wins $250,000 Tech Challenge to Combat Disinformation*. https://semantic-visions.com/semantic-visions-wins-250000-tech-challenge-to-combat-disinformation/. Accessed 3 Feb 2020.

Slovak Forum against Propaganda. (n.d.). http://www.sfpa.sk/projects/slovenske-forum-proti-propagande/. Accessed 3 Feb 2020.

StopFake. (n.d.a). *O nás* [About us]. https://www.stopfake.org/cz/o-nas-2/. Accessed 3 Feb 2020.

StopFake. (n.d.b). *Najnowsze informacje o nas*. https://www.stopfake.org/pl/category/najnowsze-informacje-o-nas/. Accessed 3 Feb 2020.

Strategic Policy Institute. (n.d.). *Projects*. https://stratpol.sk/projects/. Accessed 3 Feb 2020.

Šnídl, V. (2015, February 26). Proruskú propagandu o zhýralom Západe u nás šíri 42 webov [Pro-Russian Propaganda About the Decadent West Is Spreading Through 42 Websites]. *Denník N*. https://dennikn.sk/57740/proprusku-propagandu-o-zhyralom-zapade-u-nas-siri-42-webov/. Accessed 3 Feb 2020.

Táborský, J. (2019). *V síti (dez)informací* [In the Network of (Dis)Information)]. Praha: Grada.

Transitions. (2018). *Debunking Disinformation at Third Age Universities*. https://www.tol.org/client/project/27365-debunking-disinformation-at-third-age-universities.html. Accessed 24 Nov 2019.

Urbanlegends.hu. (n.d.). http://www.urbanlegends.hu/. Accessed 3 Feb 2020.

Warsaw Institute. (2018). *In the Age of Post-Truth: Best Practices in Fighting Disinformation*. https://warsawinstitute.org/age-post-truth-best-practices-fighting-disinformation/. Accessed 3 Feb 2020.

Winkler, M., & Pazdersky, M. (n.d.). Používej MoZeK [Use the Brain]. *Moravská zemská knihovna*. https://www.mzk.cz/pouzivej-mozek. Accessed 3 Feb 2020.

WirtualneMedia. (2019, October 11). *Fundacja otwarty dialog złożyła 20 pozwów. Chce 1,7 mln Zł od TVP, Polskiego Radia, Fratrii, Sakiewicza i Polityków PiS*. https://www.wirtualnemedia.pl/artykul/fundacja-otwarty-dialog-zlozyla-w-sumie-20-pozwow-m-in-tvp-polskie-radio-fratrie-i-tomasza-sakiewicza?fbclid=IwAR0omUMPalg-vkdEna8qZ9-8576fqBAiqhCkkUn-fJnEfu l5KygVP7-VkPk. Accessed 3 Feb 2020.

Zmudri. (n.d.). *Nauč Sa Veci Potrebné Pre Život* [Learn Things Important for Life]. https://zmudri.sk/#section-about-project. Accessed 3 Feb 2020.

CHAPTER 9

Conclusion

Miloš Gregor and Petra Mlejnková

The world is witnessing awesome and rapid technological development, including the development of virtual space believed, on the one hand, to be a tool of societal democratisation and, on the other, a tool of empowerment, allowing societies to be more informed and, therefore, more resilient towards lies and manipulation. Nevertheless, belief in such causality is false and naive. It is correct that technological development has brought amazing things into our lives, that it has created a window of opportunity for democratisation processes in many spaces around the world, and that it has empowered plenty of initiatives to make our lives better. But there is also a dark side to this process. Just as it has brought new opportunities to improve the quality of our existence and governance of our societies, so too has it also brought the same opportunities for

M. Gregor · P. Mlejnková (✉)
Department of Political Science, Faculty of Social Studies, Masaryk University, Brno, Czechia
e-mail: mlejnkova@fss.muni.cz

M. Gregor
e-mail: mgregor@fss.muni.cz

M. Gregor and P. Mlejnková (eds.), *Challenging Online Propaganda and Disinformation in the 21st Century*, Political Campaigning and Communication,
https://doi.org/10.1007/978-3-030-58624-9_9

those with villainous intentions motivated by profit. And it is here that we aimed our edited volume.

Based on the expertise and research of our team of authors, we have introduced in this book threats and challenges related to the ancient and well-known phenomena of disinformation and propaganda, enhanced, however, by the new aspect of *being online*. This book was not written with the aim of spreading fear and panic. Instead, the purpose of the volume was to discuss the current challenges and reflect on the new developments and possible threats we are being forced to face in a realistic manner. It is obvious that we have not covered all the areas relevant to the researched issue; nevertheless, we believe we have brought a multidisciplinary and relevant view. The importance of the discussed issues was unexpectedly confirmed when finishing this book. The world is now facing the COVID-19 pandemic (though we hope when reading this, the pandemic is reaching or has met its end), and we have again seen disinformation media spreading stories about the coronavirus being artificially cultivated in US laboratories and intentionally spread in China; using the epidemic for the purposes of spreading hate towards migrants in Europe, as well as in the USA; or circulating 'totally true' instructions in virtual space about how to prevent and heal COVID-19, such as drinking red wine or disinfectants (see Lilleker and Gregor 2021).

Current online disinformation and propaganda exploit vulnerabilities at multiple levels: at the level of (1) information itself, at the level of (2) the target audience, at the level of (3) networks and connections among users of virtual space, and finally, at the level of (4) systems as wholes, such as the social, legal, or political ones. At all of these levels, it is possible to manipulate and abuse weaknesses. The character of virtuality, however, also affects the offline world deeply. Online and offline sphere of our lives are intensively interconnected and influencing each other, which is necessary to keep in the mind when considering measures.

Due to the technical development and change in the information environment, those who manipulate through disinformation operations and propaganda have been able to upgrade their tactics and strategies—they can use the new tools while still keeping the good old, tried and true methods. New actors with new roles have entered into this modified information environment. The traditional role of gatekeepers assessing the quality of information has been eroded, and basically everybody who knows how to run a blog, vlog or social media account can become a source of information. Social media has changed the information environment a good deal, but not solely. Digital journalism has led to quick growth in the media landscape, including media providing fake news and selling them as so-called alternative fact or real truth.

Technical development also enables interference into social behaviour through the use of algorithms. Based on our virtual attitudes and the behaviour and networks we are active in, such algorithms can predict what individual users might like more and decide what they will be exposed to. We might not know it, but these algorithms and the echo chambers they stimulate contribute to the radicalisation of people's beliefs and attitudes. Algorithms can also be abused for the purpose of micro-targeting and, therefore, make the influence of disinformation and propaganda more efficient. Every single user might get more or less tailored content—and rather a lot more in the future. But this is also given by the fact that users help this algorithmic abuse by carelessly providing too much personal information. In this regard, we recall the Cambridge Analytica case as exemplary.

The next stage and near future of manipulation through technological instruments is in the use of artificial intelligence and tools based on deep machine-learning, such as the deepfake or fake virtual identities. They represent a technical challenge and a challenge for human cognitive abilities because, without technical support, it will not be possible to detect whether a piece of material has been doctored or is real. Given the amount of such material produced and consumed on a daily basis, it is not within human capacity to detect and distinguish them. Artificial intelligence is needed to recognise materials produced by artificial intelligence. However, despite the possibility of information credibility being assessed automatically based on the identification of text style (in the case of written material), information flow characteristics, source credibility, or exact fact-checking, the final safeguards thus far remain at the mercy of human psychological and cognitive vulnerabilities.

The described changes in the information environment motivate actors using disinformation and propaganda to use new tactics and strategies in order to reach their goals. We have written about relativisation and overwhelming the information space with different, often contradictory and false information. This can be called information fog or information noise. Under such conditions, it is much easier to erode trust in anything and anybody or push individuals to give up on efforts to be informed and active. Currently, the great challenge seems to be what is described as the post-truth era, which is typified by decreased trust in expert opinions, the belief in alternative facts, and the relativisation of just about everything. It is an era in which experts must enter into bizarre disputes not on what is true, but what is fact.

The adaptation of democratic systems and societies to the new information environment is the ultimate goal in such a context. Based on what has been researched, we stress the necessity of a *society-centric approach*. Such an approach underlines disinformation and propaganda as threats designed to influence the cognitive skills of humans as targets. In the online environment, state and non-state actors are engaged in a continual race to influence and protect from influence groups of online users (Kelton et al. 2019). It is humans affecting and acting against other humans.

Therefore, the protection of human beings seems crucial for the adaptation of democratic systems. However, protection might evoke passivity on the side of actors under potential influence—that is why it is better to speak about resilience. Resilience might take different forms and might be related to different aspects of the system, but, when seen through the lens of a society-centric approach, it refers to *human/societal resilience*. Human resilience goes to the micro-level, while societal resilience is the meso-level; nevertheless, in case of malicious information, human and societal resilience are intensely interconnected, and it does not make much sense to separate them. We identify four levels to which it is important to pay deep attention, four levels that turn human and societal resilience into a more tangible concept. Among them, this edited volume identified important challenges for contemporary democracies in (1) cognitive resilience, (2) institutional arrangement, (3) technological operation and (4) legal framework.

Cognitive resilience is probably the most challenging level and, concurrently, it is probably the most often reflected in psychology and educational literature. This is the only level directly connected with the individual and with one's ability to interpret social reality. Cognitive resilience serves to prevent disinformation and propaganda from taking root and being internalised by the target audience. It relates to world views and interpretative schemata, making sense of information and affecting the process of decision-making (Bjola and Papadakis 2020; Hansen 2017). The quality of cognitive resilience on the individual level directly influences the quality of societal resilience. The building of such resilience falls predominantly on the shoulders of the education and training of abilities in the cognitive domain (delivered by the education system and civic society).

The other three levels (institutional, technological and legal) refer to the more systematic and coordinated response of the state/regime/community to online disinformation and propaganda and their support of efforts to build cognitive resilience. At the institutional level, it is about the multi-agency and multidisciplinary setting of cooperation. As we demonstrated throughout the chapters, even though disinformation and propaganda represent a global issue, it is necessary to pay attention to local context—both from the perspectives of threats and measures. Different contexts have an impact on the form of response system and the measures taken in facing such a threat. Instead of looking for a universal winning formula against it, it is crucial to understand the complexities of the societies and regimes we intend to protect. This advice is of course not valid for institutional settings only, but for all areas where measures and countermeasures are planned to be implemented.

The legal and technological boundaries are here because cognitive resilience building has its natural limits. Technological development shaping online disinformation and propaganda has crossed our cognitive abilities in recognition of what is real and what is fake; the information environment might be too complicated and, therefore, too expensive (as regards time and resources) to orientate within it. Legal and technological measures have the potential to support our cognitive resilience and boost human and societal resilience. As for the technology, one of the challenges is learning to use opportunities and data existing in the virtual space. We specifically discuss cases of detection and analytical tools as well as digital evidence as an outcome of such tools in the European context. Computers have the ability to detect and analyse data in a much faster manner and at much bigger volumes; however, one of the barriers is the trust given to computers. Moreover, the tools operate with incomplete data and must unavoidably function with a non-negligible level of uncertainty and lack of explainability. Here we discuss the role of an expert witness, a digital forensic practitioner who fulfils the crucial role of transforming collected data into electronic evidence. Such human mediation and interpretation return us to the need for cognitive resilience among individuals. The argument of cognitive resilience is empowered even from the technological and legal level.

From the legal perspective, the issue of freedom of speech is a crucial part of the discussion. This then demands high standards of reliability from the measures and tools aimed at labelling speech as disinformation and propaganda. In the European context, we conclude that efforts against broadly or generically defined disinformation would most likely be impermissible under the European Convention on Human Rights, and a case-by-case assessment of expressions is due in this regard. It is mainly the risk of false positives which act as an obstacle. The regulatory activity is therefore shifting to the actions of hosting service providers, given that they share liability for the content due to their role in facilitating its dissemination.

And one more thing. There is another aspect related to human/societal resilience, one which is also derived from the society-centric approach: *the protection of networks*. Instead of a narrow understanding of networks as just telecommunication networks, wires and cables, we consider networks as connections between online users. It includes a virtual landscape of users and the virtual linkage through which they can interact with each other. Such a landscape is composed of technological solutions (ICTs, social media) as well as the social aspect of networking. ICTs are already considered critical in security policy, and it is a common knowledge that ICTs belong among the elements of critical infrastructure. These elements are so crucial for the system that their incapacitation or destruction would have a serious impact on state security, physical or economic security, and public health or safety.

The technological aspects and possibilities of virtual space have enabled propagandists and disinformers to go a step further, and online disinformation and propaganda do not concentrate exclusively on the dissemination of content anymore. Real strategical advantage does not lie in the creation of functional manipulative content. Instead, it is control over the network through which information is disseminated and which can then be used anytime by the actor controlling such a network. We are considering here infrastructural protection of connections between individuals and the networks in which they are organised—virtually and, consequently, physically as well. The risk is very high because social media's rise and wide acceptance make it the primary source of internet-enabled mass collection of social data, and it enables an ever-richer understanding of social behaviour. Social behaviour is now directly observable at low cost. It is easy to observe even small communities and test their reactions to different stimuli (Hwang 2019). It is possible to target the connections between groups and target the structure and intensity of connections. Controlling the networks means access to the possibility of connecting individuals and groups who would likely never find each other in the offline world. It provides opportunities to manipulate the landscape of connections and target social ties. Furthermore, it begs the question: is it not time social media and the integrity of data be recognised as a strategic asset and therefore an element of critical infrastructure?

Bibliography

Bjola, C., & Papadakis, K. (2020). Digital Propaganda, Couterpublics and the Disruption of the Public Sphere: The Finnish Approach to Building Digital Resilience. *Cambridge Review of International Affairs*, online first.

Hansen, F. S. (2017). *Russian Hybrid Warfare: A Study of Disinformation*. Copenhagen: Danish Institute for International Studies.

Hwang, T. (2019). *Maneuver and Manipulation: On the Military Strategy of Online Information Warfare*. Carlisle: Strategic Studies Institute and U.S. Army War College.

Kelton, M., Sullivan, M., Bienvenue, E., & Rogers, Z. (2019). Australia, the Utility of Force and the Society. *International Affairs, 95*(4), 859–876.

Lilleker, D., & Gregor, M. (2021). World Health Organisation: The Challenges of Global Leadership. In D. Lilleker, I. Coman, M. Gregor, & E. Novelli (Eds.), *Political Communication and COVID-19: Governance and Rhetoric in Times of Crisis*. London and New York: Routledge.

Index

M. Gregor and P. Mlejnková (eds.), *Challenging Online Propaganda and Disinformation in the 21st Century*, Political Campaigning and Communication,
https://doi.org/10.1007/978-3-030-58624-9

D

The manufacturer's authorised representative in the EU is Springer Nature Customer Service Centre GmbH, Europaplatz 3, 69115 Heidelberg, Germany. If you have any concerns regarding our products, please contact ProductSafety@springernature.com

Printed and bound by CPI Group (UK) Ltd, Croydon, CR0 4YY
22/09/2026
02221066-0006